D0140406

Introducing English Linguistics

Are you looking for a genuine introduction to the linguistics of English
that provides a broad overview of the subject, that sustains students'
interest and avoids excessive detail? *Introducing English Linguistics*
accomplishes this goal in two ways. First, unlike traditional texts, it takes
a top-down approach to language, beginning with the largest unit of
linguistic structure, the text, and working its way down through
successively smaller structures (sentences, words, and finally speech
sounds). The advantage of presenting language this way is that students
are first given the larger picture – they study language in context – and
then as the class progresses, they see how the smaller pieces of language
are really a consequence of the larger goals of linguistic communication.
Second, *Introducing English Linguistics* does not contain invented examples,
as is the case with most comparable texts, but instead takes its sample
materials from the major computerized databases of spoken and written
English, giving students a more realistic view of language.

CHARLES F. MEYER is Professor in the Department of Applied Linguistics at
the University of Massachusetts, Boston. His recent publications include
English Corpus Linguistics: An Introduction (Cambridge, 2002).

Cambridge Introductions to Language and Linguistics

This new textbook series provides students and their teachers with accessible introductions to the major subjects encountered within the study of language and linguistics. Assuming no prior knowledge of the subject, each book is written and designed for ease of use in the classroom or seminar, and is ideal for adoption on a modular course as the core recommended textbook. Each book offers the ideal introductory material for each subject, presenting students with an overview of the main topics encountered in their course, and features a glossary of useful terms, chapter previews and summaries, suggestions for further reading, and helpful exercises. Each book is accompanied by a supporting website.

Books published in the series:
Introducing Phonology David Odden
Introducing Speech and Language Processing John Coleman
Introducing Phonetic Science Michael Ashby and John Maidment
Introducing Second Language Acquisition Muriel Saville-Troike
Introducing English Linguistics Charles F. Meyer

Forthcoming:
Introducing Sociolinguistics Miriam Meyerhoff
Introducing Morphology Rochelle Lieber
Introducing Historical Linguistics Brian Joseph
Introducing Language Bert Vaux
Introducing Semantics Nick Riemer
Introducing Psycholinguistics Paul Warren

Introducing English Linguistics

CHARLES F. MEYER

CAMBRIDGE
UNIVERSITY PRESS

CAMBRIDGE UNIVERSITY PRESS
Cambridge, New York, Melbourne, Madrid, Cape Town, Singapore, São Paulo, Delhi

Cambridge University Press
The Edinburgh Building, Cambridge CB2 8RU, UK

Published in the United States of America by Cambridge University Press, New York

www.cambridge.org
Information on this title: www.cambridge.org/9780521541220

First published 2009

Printed in the United Kingdom at the University Press, Cambridge

A catalogue record for this publication is available from the British Library

Library of Congress Cataloguing in Publication data
Meyer, Charles F.
Introducing English linguistics / Charles F. Meyer.
    p.   cm. — (Cambridge introductions to language and linguistics)
Includes bibliographical references.
ISBN 978-0-521-83350-9
1. English language — History.   2. Linguistics.   I. Title.   II. Series.
PE1075.M5995   2009
420 — dc22

                                            2009009162

ISBN 978-0-521-83350-9 hardback
ISBN 978-0-521-54122-0 paperback

Contents

Preface

English is currently the most widely spoken language in the world. Mandarin Chinese may have more speakers, but no language is spoken in more parts of the world than the English language. The global reach of English is one reason the language has more non-native speakers than native speakers. The popularity of English, it must be emphasized, has little to do with the language itself, and more to do with geopolitical considerations: the initial spread of English worldwide as a consequence of British colonization, and the rise in the twentieth century of the United States as an economic and political power in the world.

Because of the importance of English as a world language, it has been widely studied and taught: English has been the focus of many linguistic descriptions, and it is taught worldwide in thousands of classrooms and language institutes. In fact, more people are learning English from non-native speakers of the language than native speakers. For this reason (and many others), it is important that teachers of English as well as others having an interest in the structure and use of the language have an adequate understanding of the language. This book attempts to provide such an understanding, but it does so in a manner that is different from many other introductions to the English language.

Because language involves not just individual sentences but sentences that are parts of texts, the book is organized on the principle that an adequate introduction to the study of the English language requires a top-down rather than a bottom-up discussion of the structure of English. That is, instead of beginning with the smallest unit of language (the phoneme) and working up to the largest unit (the text), this book begins at the level of the text and works its way down to progressively smaller units of language. The idea behind this organizational strategy is that the structure and use of smaller structures is in many cases dependent on larger linguistic considerations. For instance, in Boston, whether one pronounces the word *never* with a final /ɹ/ [nɛvɚ] or without one [nɛvə] depends not just upon whether the speaker's grammar contains a rule deleting /ɹ/ after vowels but upon other factors as well, such as the social context (e.g. formal vs. informal) in which the individual is speaking.

To provide a top-down description of English, the book is divided into two main sections: one dealing with more general characteristics of English – its development as a language and the pragmatic considerations governing its use – and a second focusing on the grammatical characteristics of the language, from the sentence down to the individual speech sound.

Chapter 1 ("The study of language") discusses how linguists study language, advancing but also critiquing the widely held view in linguistics that all languages are valid systems of communication and that it makes little sense to claim that one language is "better" than another. Chapter 2 ("The development of English") provides a historical perspective on English: where it has stood over time in relation to the other languages of the world, and how its development can be explained by general principles of language change. The next two chapters focus on the various pragmatic principles that affect how English is used. Chapter 3 ("The social context of English") examines the social factors influencing linguistic interaction, such as politeness considerations and speaker variables (e.g. age, gender, ethnicity, and level of education). Chapter 4 ("The structure of English texts") describes how English texts (both written and spoken) are structured, and why they have the structure that they do.

The second section of the book contains chapters concerned with examining the grammar of English. Chapter 5 ("English syntax") discusses the major syntactic categories in English, focusing on how the structure of English sentences can be described in terms of the particular constructions that they contain – clauses (main and subordinate) and phrases (e.g. noun phrase and verb phrase) – and the functions within clauses (e.g. subject and object) that these forms serve. Chapter 6 ("English words: Structure and meaning") is concerned with the structure and meaning of words. The chapter begins by discussing how morphemes, the smallest unit of meaning, are combined to create words, and continues with a description of how the meanings of words are described by lexicographers (those who produce dictionaries) and semanticists (linguists who theorize about meaning in language). Chapter 7 ("The sounds of English") discusses the sound system of English, beginning with a description of speech segments (phonemes) and concluding with an overview of word stress and intonation.

Much current work in linguistics has demonstrated that linguistic descriptions are most accurate and meaningful if they are based on actual examples of spoken and written English rather than on examples invented by the linguist him or herself. Therefore, most of the examples included in this book were taken from a number of different linguistic corpora: computerized databases containing various kinds of spoken and written English, such as transcriptions of actual conversations that

people had, or samples of articles appearing in newspapers. The appendix contains a list of the corpora that were used as well as a brief description of the kinds of texts that they contain.

There are many people to whom I owe a huge debt of gratitude for their help with this book. First of all, I want to thank Andrew Winnard of Cambridge University Press for his help and support throughout the process of writing this book. I also wish to thank three anonymous reviewers for Cambridge University Press for the many useful comments they provided that helped improve the book considerably; Malcolm Todd, whose expert copy-editing skills greatly improved the clarity of the book; Bill Kretzschmar for his feedback on sections of Chapter 3; Stephen Fay, who did the artwork for Figures 6.3 and 7.1; my colleagues in the Applied Linguistics Department at the University of Massachusetts, Boston; the many students whom I have taught over the years who have helped me refine and improve the way that I teach linguistics; and, most importantly, my wife, Libby, and son, Freddie, who offered their constant love and support while I spent many hours away from them writing this book.

Copyright acknowledgment

My thanks to Mouton de Gruyter for giving me permission to include material in chapter 6 taken from my forthcoming paper 'Pre-electronic corpora' to be published in *Corpus Linguistics: An International Handbook,* ed. Anke Lüdeling and Merja Kytö (Berlin: Mouton de Gruyter).

1 The study of language

CHAPTER PREVIEW

This chapter provides an overview of how linguists approach the study of language. It describes language as one of many different systems of communication, a system that is unique to human beings and different from, for instance, the systems of communication that animals employ. Language exists in three modes: speech, writing, and signs (which are used by people who are deaf). Although all languages (with the exception of sign languages) exist in spoken form, only some have written forms. To study language, linguists focus on two levels of description: **pragmatics**, the study of how context (both social and linguistic) affects language use, and **grammar**, the description of how humans form linguistic structures, from the level of sound up to the sentence.

Introduction

Unless a human being has a physical or mental disability, he or she will be born with the capacity for language: the innate ability to speak a language, or in the case of someone who is deaf, to sign a language (i.e. use gestures to communicate). This capacity does not involve any kind of learning – a young child, for instance, does not need to be taught to speak or sign – and occurs in predictable stages, beginning with the babbling cries of an infant and culminating in the full speaking abilities of an adult.

The study of language is conducted within the field of linguistics. Contrary to popular belief, linguists are not necessarily polyglots – individuals fluent in many languages. Instead, their primary interest is the scientific study of language. Like a biologist studying the structure of cells, a linguist studies the structure of language: how speakers create meaning through combinations of sounds, words, and sentences that ultimately result in texts – extended stretches of language (e.g. a conversation between friends, a speech, an article in a newspaper). Like other scientists, linguists examine their subject matter – language – objectively. They are not interested in evaluating "good" versus "bad" uses of language, in much the same manner that a biologist does not examine cells with the goal of determining which are "pretty" and which are "ugly." This is an important point because much of what is written and said about language is highly evaluative: many teachers tell their students not to use a word like *ain't* because it is "ignorant" or the product of "lazy" speech patterns; similar sentiments are expressed in popular books and articles on English usage. Linguists do have their biases, a point that will be covered later in this chapter in the section on the ideological basis of language, but it is important to distinguish the goal of the linguist – describing language – from the goal of the teacher or writer: prescribing English usage, telling people how they should or should not speak or write.

Because linguistics is multidisciplinary, specialists in many disciplines bring their own expertise to the study of language. Psychologists, for instance, are interested in studying language as a property of the human mind; they have contributed many insights into such topics as how people acquire language. Anthropologists, on the other hand, have been more interested in the relationship between language and culture, and early work by anthropologists provided extremely valuable information about, for instance, the structure of the indigenous languages of the Americas. Prior to the study of these languages in the early twentieth century, most of what was known about human language was based upon the investigation of western languages, such as Greek, Latin, and German: languages that are structurally quite different from the indigenous languages of the Americas. This new knowledge forced linguists to reconceptualize the notion of human language, and to greatly expand the number of languages subjected to linguistic analysis. Other disciplines – sociology, computer science, mathematics, philosophy, to name but a few – have likewise brought their interests to the study of language.

Despite the many influences on the study of language, it is possible to isolate some basic principles that have guided all studies of language, and it is these principles that will serve as the focus of this chapter. The chapter opens with a discussion of language as one part of a larger semiotic system. Semiotic systems are systems of communication and include not just human language but, for instance, gesture, music, art, and dress as well. Like any system, language has structure, and the succeeding sections provide an overview of this structure: the modes (speech, writing, signs) in which language is transmitted, and the conventions (both linguistic and social) for how sounds, words, sentences, and texts are structured. Speakers of English know that the phrase *day beautiful* is not English because as speakers of English they have an unconscious knowledge of a rule of English sentence structure: that adjectives come before nouns (e.g. *beautiful day*), not after them. In addition, speakers of English know not to ask directions from a stranger by saying *Tell me where the museum is* because, according to conventions of politeness in English usage, such an utterance is impolite and would be better phrased more indirectly as *Could you tell me where the museum is?*

Because linguists are engaged in the scientific study of language, they approach language, as was noted earlier, "dispassionately," preferring to describe it in an unbiased and objective manner. However, linguists have their biases too, and the next section explores the ideological basis of language: the idea that all views of language are grounded in beliefs about how language should be valued. The final section describes two competing theories of language – Noam Chomsky's theory of generative grammar and Michael A. K. Halliday's theory of functional grammar – and how these theories have influenced the view of language presented in this book.

Language as part of a semiotic system

Because language is a system of communication, it is useful to compare it with other systems of communication. For instance, humans communicate not just through language but through such means as gesture, art, dress, and music. Although some argue that higher primates such as chimpanzees possess the equivalent of human language, most animals have their own systems of communication: dogs exhibit submission by lowering their heads and tails; bees, in contrast, dance. The study of communication systems has its origins in semiotics, a field of inquiry that originated in the work of Ferdinand de Saussure in a series of lectures published in *A Course in General Linguistics* (1916).

According to Saussure, meaning in semiotic systems is expressed by **signs**, which have a particular form, called a signifier, and some meaning that the signifier conveys, called the signified. Thus, in English, the word *table* would have two different signifiers. In speech, it would take the form of a series of **phonemes** pronounced in midwestern American English as [teɪbəl]; in writing, it would be spelled with a series of **graphemes**, or letters: t-a-b-l-e. Signifiers, in turn, are associated with the signified. Upon hearing or reading the word *table*, a speaker of English will associate the word with the meaning that it has (its signified). Other semiotic systems employ different systems of signs. For instance, in many cultures, moving the head up and down means 'yes'; moving the head left to right means 'no.'

Although semiotic systems are discrete, they often reinforce one another. In the 1960s it was common for males with long hear, beards, torn blue jeans, and necklaces with the peace sign on them to utter expressions such as "Far out" or "Groovy." All of these systems – dress, personal appearance, language – worked together to define this person as being a "hippie": someone who during this period lived an unconventional lifestyle in rebellion against the lifestyles of mainstream society. If a delivery person shows up at someone's house with a large box, and asks the person where the box should be placed, the person might respond "Put it there" while simultaneously pointing to a location in his or her living room. In this case, the particular linguistic form that is uttered is directly related to the gesture that is used.

The fact that language and gestures work so closely together might lead one to conclude that they are part of the same semiotic system. But there are many cases where gestures work quite independently of language and therefore are sometimes described as paralinguistic in nature. In the middle of one of the 1992 presidential debates in the United States, the first President Bush was caught on camera looking at his watch while one of the other candidates was answering a question. This gesture was interpreted by many as an expression of impatience and boredom on President Bush's part, and since the gesture had no connection with any linguistic form, in this instance it was clearly part of its own semiotic system.

One of the hallmarks of the linguistic sign, as Saussure argued, is its arbitrary nature. The word *window* has no direct connection to the meaning that it expresses: speakers of English could very well have chosen a signifier such as *krod* or *fremp*. An examination of words for *window* in other languages reveals a range of different signifiers to express the meaning of this word: *fenêtre* in French; *ventana* in Spanish; *Fenster* in German; *ikkuna* in Finnish. Although most linguistic signs are arbitrary, there are instances where signs bear an iconic relationship to the meanings that they express. If in describing a recently viewed movie an individual utters *It was so loooong*, extending the length of the vowel in *long*, the lengthening of the vowel reinforces the excessive length of the movie. In the sentence *The cow mooed for hours*, the verb *mooed* mimics the sound that a cow makes. Likewise, in *The bee buzzed by my ear*, *buzzed* imitates the sound of a bee. English also has phonesthemes: sounds associated with particular meanings. The consonant [ʃ] at the end of a word is suggestive of rapid motion: *crash*, *bash*, *slash*, *smash*, *gash*.

However, not all words ending in this consonant have this meaning (e.g. *fish*, *dish*). Moreover, if there were true iconicity in language, we would find it more consistently cross-linguistically. Sometimes so-called onomatopoeic words occur across languages. For instance, the equivalent of

English *beep* and *click* can be found in French: *un bip* and *un click*. However, *whisper*, which is iconic in English, has equivalents in French and Spanish – *le chuchotement* and *el susurro* – that are different in form but iconic within French and Spanish. Thus, while it is clear that signs can be iconic, for the most part they are, following Saussure, arbitrary in nature.

The modes of language

Signifiers are transmitted in human language most frequently through two primary modes: speech and writing. A third mode, signing, is a system of communication used by individuals who are deaf. Contrary to popular belief, sign languages are not merely gestured equivalents of spoken languages. American Sign Language (ASL), for instance, has its own grammar, and those who use it go through the same stages of language acquisition as speakers of oral languages do. In fact, it is not uncommon for children of deaf parents who are not deaf themselves to learn a sign language as their first language, and a spoken language as a second language.

In linguistics, it is commonly noted that speech is primary and writing secondary. Linguists take this position because all languages are spoken (with the exception of dead languages such as Latin, which now exist only in written form), and only a subset of these languages are written. All children will naturally acquire the spoken version of a language if they are exposed to it during the formative period of language acquisition. However, to become literate, a child will need some kind of formal schooling in reading and writing. In many respects, though, calling speech "primary" and writing "secondary" unfortunately implies that writing has a second-class status when compared with speech. It is more accurate to view the two modes as having different but complementary roles. For instance, in most legal systems, while an oral contract is legally binding, a written contract is preferred because writing, unlike speech, provides a permanent record of the contract. Thus, if the terms of the contract are disputed, the written record of the contract can be consulted and interpreted. Disputes over an oral contract will involve one person's recollection of the contract versus another person's.

While writing may be the preferred mode for a contract, in many other contexts, speech will be more appropriate. Because the most common type of speech – face-to-face conversations – is highly interactive, this mode is well suited to many contexts: casual conversations over lunch, business transactions in a grocery store, discussions between students and teachers in a classroom. And in these contexts, interactive dialogues have many advantages over writing. For instance, individuals engaged in conversation can ask for immediate clarification if there is a question about something said; in a letter to a friend, in contrast, such immediacy is lacking. When speaking to one another, conversants are face to face and can therefore see how individuals react to what is said; writing creates distance between writer and reader, preventing the writer from getting any reaction from the reader. Speech is oral, thus making it possible to use intonation to emphasize words or phrases and express emotion; writing has punctuation, but it can express only a small proportion of the features that intonation has. Because speech is created "on-line," it is produced quickly and easily. This may result in many "ungrammatical" constructions, but rarely do they cause miscommunication, and if there is a misunderstanding, it can be easily corrected. Writing is much more deliberate, requiring planning and editing and thus taking much more time to produce.

Because of all of these characteristics of writing, if an individual desires a casual, intimate encounter with a friend, he or she is more likely to meet personally than write a letter. Of course, technology has made such encounters possible with "instant messaging" over a computer. And if someone wishes to have such an encounter with a friend living many miles away, then this kind of on-line written "chat" can mimic a face-to-face conversation. But because such conversations are a hybrid of speech and writing, they still lack the intimacy and immediacy of a face-to-face conversation.

While speech and writing are often viewed as discrete modes, it is important to note, as Biber (1988) has demonstrated, that there is a continuum between speech and writing. While speech is in general more interactive than writing, various kinds of spoken and written English display various degrees of interactivity. For instance, Biber (1988: 102, 128) found that various linguistic markers of interactive discourse (or "involved" discourse, to use his term), such as first and second person pronouns, contractions, and private verbs such as *think* and *feel*, occurred very frequently in telephone and face-to-face conversations but less frequently in spontaneous speeches, interviews, and broadcasts. In addition, while various kinds of writing, such as academic prose and official documents, exhibited few markers of interactive discourse, other kinds of written texts, particularly personal letters, ranked higher on the scale of interactivity than many of the spoken texts that were analyzed.

What Biber's findings demonstrate is that how language is structured depends less on whether it is spoken or written and more on how it is being used. A personal letter, even though it is written, will contain linguistic features marking interactivity because the writer of a letter wishes to interact with the individual(s) to whom the letter is written. On the other hand, in an interview, the goal is not to interact necessarily but to get information from the person (or persons) being interviewed. Therefore, interviews, despite being spoken, will have fewer markers of interactivity and contain more features typically associated with written texts.

Studying linguistic structure

Whether it is spoken, written, or signed, every language has structure, which can be described, as Leech (1983: 21–4) notes, by postulating:

(1) **rules** governing the pronunciation of sounds; the ways that words are put together; the manner in which phrases, clauses, and sentences are structured; and, ultimately, the ways that meaning is created;

(2) **principles** stipulating how the structures that rules create should be used (e.g. which forms will be polite in which contexts, which forms will not).

Rules are studied under the rubric of grammar, principles within the province of pragmatics. To understand what is meant by rules and principles, and why they are studied within grammar and pragmatics, consider why a three-year-old child would utter a sentence such as *I broked it* [ai bruʊkt ɪt] to his father, who just entered a room that the child was playing in to discover that the child had broken a wheel off a truck that he had been playing with.

To account for why the child uttered *I broked it* rather than, say, *Breaked it I*, it is necessary to investigate the linguistic rules the child is using to create the structure that he did. Linguistic rules are different from the rules that people learn in school: "Don't end sentences with prepositions"; "Don't begin a sentence with *but*"; "Don't split infinitives." These are **prescriptive rules** (discussed in greater detail in the next section) and are intended to provide guidance to students as they learn to speak and write so-called Standard English. Linguistic rules, in contrast, serve to describe what people know about language: the unconscious knowledge of language they possess that is part of what Noam Chomsky describes as our linguistic competence. Even though the sentence the child uttered does not conform to the rules of Standard English – the past tense form of the verb *break* is *broke*, not *broked* – it provides evidence that the child is aware of the rules of English grammar. He has applied a past tense ending for the verb, spelled *-ed* in writing, but has not reached a stage of acquisition where he is able to recognize the difference between regular and irregular verb forms.

Rules of grammar operate at various levels:

Phonetics/Phonology: This level focuses on the smallest unit of structure in language, the phoneme. Linguistic rules at this level describe how sounds are pronounced in various contexts. For instance, there is a rule of **voicing assimilation** in English that stipulates that when a past tense marker is added to the stem of a verb, the last sound in the stem determines whether the marker is **voiced** or **unvoiced** (i.e. whether or not the vocal cords vibrate when the consonant is pronounced). Thus, even though the child uses the wrong past tense form, the past tense marker is pronounced as /t/ because the last sound in the stem, /k/, is unvoiced. Had the stem been *kill*, which ends in voiced /l/, the past tense marker would have been voiced /d/. The sound system of English and the rules that govern it are discussed in detail in Chapter 7.

Morphology: The next level of structure is the morpheme, the smallest unit of meaning in language. Rules of morphology focus on how words (and parts of words) are structured. At the beginning of the sentence, the child uses the pronoun *I* rather than *me* because English has rules of case assignment – pronouns functioning as subject of a sentence take the **subjective form** (sometimes referred to as the nominative case) rather than the **objective form** (or accusative case). And because the number of the subject is singular, *I* is used rather than the plural form *we*. Rules of morphology describe all facets of word formation, such as how prefixes and suffixes are added, and are described in Chapter 6.

Syntax: The largest level of structure is the clause, which can be analyzed into what are called **clause functions**: subject, predicator, object, complement, and adverbial. The child's utterance, *I broked it*, is a **main clause** – it can stand alone as a sentence, as opposed to a subordinate clause, which has to be part of an independent clause – and can be analyzed as containing a subject (*I*), a predicator (*broked*), and a direct object (*it*). At the level of syntax, there are many rules stipulating how constituents within a clause are grouped. For instance, all languages have constraints on how constituents should be ordered. Because English is an SVO (subject–verb–object) language, the utterance is *I broked it* rather than *I it broked* (an SOV word order, found in languages such as Japanese). Chapter 5 contains an extensive discussion of the syntax of English, specifically how words, phrases, clauses, and sentences are structured.

Semantics: Because meaning is at the core of human communication, the study of semantics cuts across all of the other levels thus far discussed. At the level of sound, in the words *kick* /kɪk/ and *sick* /sɪk/, the choice of /k/ vs. /s/ results in words with two entirely different meanings. At the level of morphology, placing the prefix *un-* before the word *happy* results in a word with an opposite meaning: *unhappy*. At the level of syntax, the sentence *Jose wrote to Carla* means something entirely different than *Carla wrote to Jose* because in English, word order is a crucial key to meaning. But even though meaning is present at all levels of linguistic structure, the study of semantics is typically focused on such topics as the meaning of individual words (**lexical semantics**) and the ability of words to refer to points in time or individuals in the external world (**deixis**). For instance, the verb *broked* in the child's utterance has a specific meaning (e.g. the *Merriam-Webster Online Dictionary* defines *break* as "to separate into parts with suddenness or violence"), and is marked as occurring during a specific time (the past, as indicated by the past tense verb ending *-ed*). The utterance also contains the first person pronoun *I*, which refers to the speaker (in this case the child), and the pronoun *it*, which refers to something not in the text but in the context (the wheel on the child's car). Lexical semantics, deixis, and other topics related directly to the study of semantics are discussed in Chapter 6.

The various rules that were described above are part of the study of grammar. Grammar is a word with many meanings. To some, it involves mainly syntax: a study of the parts of speech (nouns, verbs, prepositions, etc.) or syntax in general ("I studied grammar in High School"). To others, it covers usage: correct and incorrect uses of language ("My grammar isn't very good"). For many linguists, however, grammar involves the study of

linguistic rules that are part of our linguistic competence: the unconscious knowledge of the rules of a language that any fluent speaker possesses. Writing a grammar of a language therefore involves codifying the
rules that are part of any speaker's linguistic competence: making explicit that in English, for instance, the voicing of a past tense marker depends
upon whether the sound preceding it is voiced or unvoiced, or that when
a pronoun is used as subject of a sentence the subject form of the pronoun
will be used rather than the objective form.

When studying rules of grammar, one really does not leave the speaker's brain, since the focus of discussion is the abstract properties of language that any human (barring disability) is naturally endowed with. But
understanding language involves more than describing the psychological
properties of the brain. How language is structured also depends heavily
on context: the **social context** in which language is used as well as the **linguistic context** – the larger body of sentences – in which a particular linguistic structure occurs. The study of this facet of language is conducted
within the domain of **pragmatics**, which is concerned less with *how* grammatical constructions are structured and more with *why* they have the
structure that they do.

Thus, to fully understand the meaning of *I broked it*, it is useful to see
the larger context in which this construction occurred, specifically the
father's response to it:

Child: I broked it.
Father: That's ok. Let's see if we can fix it.

When individuals communicate, they arrive at interpretations of utterances by doing more than simply analyzing their structure; their interpretations are also based on a variety of purely social considerations: the
age of communicants as well as their social class, level of education, occupation, and their relative positions on the power hierarchy (i.e. whether
they are **equals, disparates,** or **intimates**). In the excerpt above, the form
of each utterance is very much determined by the ages of the father and
son and the power relationship existing between them. Because the child
is young and has not fully mastered the grammar of English, he uses a
non-standard verb form, *broked*, rather than the standard form *broke*. And
because of the child's age, the father does not respond with an utterance
like *Did you mean to say "broke"?* because he understands the child is young
and that it would be inappropriate to correct him.

If the child were older (say, in high school), the father may very well
have corrected his speech, since in his role as parent, he and his son are
disparates: he is a **superordinate** (i.e. is higher on the power hierarchy),
his son a **subordinate** (i.e. lower on the power hierarchy). And given this
imbalance in power, the father could feel entitled to correct his son's
grammar. But other factors, such as education and social class, would also
affect language usage in this situation. If both the son and father spoke a
non-standard variety of English in which *broked* was commonly used, then
a correction of the type described above might never occur. The role that
the social context plays in language usage is discussed in Chapter 3.

In addition to describing the effect of the social context on language usage, it is important to also study the linguistic context and its effect on how language is structured. This involves studying language at the level of text. Texts are typically extended stretches of language. They have an overall structure (e.g. a beginning, a middle, and an end) and markers of **cohesion**: linguistic devices that tie sections of a text together, ultimately achieving **coherence** (i.e. a text that is meaningful). The exchange between the son and father above occurs at the start of a text. Many texts have standard beginnings. For instance, a conversation between friends may begin with a greeting: *Hi, how are you? – I'm fine, how are you?* Other texts, like the one between son and father, just start. The son utters *I broked it* simply because this is what he needs to say when his father enters the room. Many texts are highly structured: press reportage begins with a headline, followed by a byline and lead (a sentence or two summing up the main point of the article). Other texts are more loosely structured: while a conversation between friends might have an opening (greeting) and an ending (a salutation), the middle part may consist of little more than speaker **turns**: alternations of people speaking with few restrictions on topics discussed.

But a text will not ultimately achieve coherence unless there are linguistic markers that tie individual parts of the text together. The father responds to the son's utterance by saying *That's ok*. The word *That* is a pronoun that refers back to what the child said in the first utterance. Typically pronouns refer to a single noun phrase (e.g. *it* in the child's utterance refers to the broken wheel on his truck). But in casual conversation it is common to find pronouns with very broad **reference**, in this case a pronoun, *That*, referring to the entire sentence the child utters. This is one type of cohesion, what Halliday and Hasan (1976) refer to as reference: an expression that typically refers back to something said in a previous part of the text, and that serves to provide linkages in texts. The structure of texts is discussed in Chapter 4.

One major difference between the study of grammar and pragmatics is that grammar deals with "structure," pragmatics with "use." The rule of grammar for forming imperative sentences such as *Tell me how to get to the Kennedy Library* is fairly straightforward: the base (or infinitive) form of the verb is used, *Tell*, and the implied subject of the sentence, *you* (*You tell me how to get to the Kennedy Library*), is omitted. Every imperative sentence in English is formed this way (with the exception of first person imperatives like *Let's dance*). Thus, rules of grammar can be posited in fairly absolute terms. This is not to suggest that rules do not have exceptions. The rule of passive formation in English stipulates that a sentence in the **active voice** such as *The mechanic fixed the car* can be converted into a sentence in the **passive voice**, *The car was fixed by the mechanic*, by:

(1) making the direct object of the sentence (*the car*) the subject of the passive,

(2) adding a form of *be* (*was*) that agrees in number with the subject of the passive and retains the same tense as the verb in the active,

(3) converting the verb in the active into a participle (*fixed*),

(4) moving the subject of the active to the end of the sentence and making it object of the preposition *by* (*by the mechanic*).

However, not every sentence meeting this structural description can be converted into a passive. The verb *have*, for instance, cannot generally be passivized (e.g. *The woman has a new car* but not **A new car was had by the woman*), except in idiomatic constructions such as *A good time was had by all*.

Describing the use of imperative sentences, in contrast, is a much more complicated undertaking, particularly because imperative sentences in English are so closely tied to conventions of politeness. This is one reason why Leech (1983) posits "principles" of politeness rather than "rules" of politeness. It would be highly impolite to walk up to a complete stranger at the JFK/UMASS subway station in Dorchester, Massachusetts, and say *Tell me how to get to the Kennedy Library*. The sentence is certainly grammatical, but too direct to utter to a complete stranger. It would be more appropriate in this context to have said *Could you please tell me how to get to the Kennedy Library*, a form more conventionally associated in English with politeness.

It would be wrong, however, to simply posit a rule that states that imperatives should not be used with strangers. The same sentence, with slight modification, would be highly appropriate if placed farther into a conversation with the same stranger:

Speaker A (to stranger
on subway platform):   I'm lost. I'm trying to get to the Kennedy Library.
Speaker B: Oh, it's quite easy to get there. Would you like
                        directions?
Speaker A: Yes, please tell me how to get there.

Because it is not possible to precisely specify which forms are polite and which are impolite, principles of politeness deal more with tendencies than absolutes: this form "tends" to be polite in this context but not in that context.

Rules and principles also raise issues of **grammaticality** and **acceptability**. A sentence is grammatical if its structure conforms to a rule of grammar. Thus, of the four sentences below, (a)–(c) are grammatical; only (d) is ungrammatical:

(a) I don't have any money
(b) I have no money.
(c) I ain't got no money.
(d) *Have I don't money any.

Sentences (a) and (b) conform to rules governing the placement of negatives in sentences: the negative can be placed either after the auxiliary (*do* in a) and optionally contracted with it, or before a noun phrase if the noun phrase contains a word such as *any* (as in b). Although sentences such as (c) containing *ain't* and double negation are often characterized as ungrammatical, they are actually grammatical: *ain't* now serves as a general marker of negation in English, and copying the negative (rather than simply moving it), creating an instance of multiple negation, is a grammatical process dating back to Old English. Objections to sentences such as (c) are more a matter of acceptability, not grammaticality. Only (d) is truly ungrammatical because the placement of words in this sentence violates rules of English word order (e.g. words such as *any* always come before nouns, not after them).

Acceptability judgments will vary from speaker to speaker and reflect the fact that we all have opinions about what we see as good and bad uses of language. Because *ain't* is a highly stigmatized word, many people will react very negatively to its usage, judging it as highly unacceptable in any context. Despite this attitude, *ain't* is still widely used, and those using it obviously find it acceptable, at least in some contexts. For instance, *ain't* occurs quite commonly in song lyrics: "You ain't nothin' but a hound dog," "Ain't that a shame," "There ain't no mountain high enough, Ain't no valley low enough, Ain't no river wide enough." One could hardly imagine these lyrics being changed: "You aren't anything but a hound dog." The distinction between grammaticality and acceptability is important because these notions describe what is possible in language versus what we prefer or do not prefer.

Language and ideology

The popular tendency to confuse grammaticality and acceptability illustrates a significant difference between what the general public feels about language and what the average linguist does. This ideological divide is the product of two very different belief systems, with linguists firmly committed to the scientific study of language and non-linguists typically preferring a much more subjective approach. The differences between these two very different ideologies are illustrated in the quotes below, both of which deal with the subject of language change.

The first quote is from an interview with John Simon, author of a book on English usage entitled *Paradigms Lost* and a former theater critic for *New York Magazine*. Simon was asked to give his views on language change and the current state of the language:

Well it [the violation of rules of syntax and grammar] has gotten worse. It's been my experience that there is no bottom, one can always sink lower, and that the language can always disintegrate further ... [The current state of the language is] Unhealthy, poor, sad, depressing, um, and probably fairly hopeless ... the descriptive linguists are a curse upon their race, uh who uh of course think that what the people say is the law. And by that they mean the majority, they mean the uneducated. I think a society which the uneducated lead the educated by the nose is not a good society ... I mean maybe [language] change is inevitable, maybe, maybe dying from cancer is also inevitable but I don't think we should help it along.

Excerpted from "Do You Speak American," which was narrated by Robert McNeil and originally broadcast on PBS, January 6, 2005

The second quote is from a book written by a linguist; it focuses on the relationship between language change and language decay:

In brief, the puristic attitude towards language – the idea that there is an absolute standard of correctness that should be maintained – has its origin in a natural nostalgic tendency, supplemented and intensified by social pressures. It is illogical, and impossible to pin down to any firm base. Purists behave as if there was a vintage year when language achieved a measure of excellence which we should all strive to maintain. In fact, there never was such a year. The language of Chaucer's or Shakespeare's time was no better or no worse than that of our own – just different.

Jean Aitchison, Language Change: Progress or Decay (1991)

Traditionally within linguistics, people like Simon have been labeled as **prescriptivists** because their goal is to prescribe usage: identify so-called correct and incorrect instances of language usage, and in essence tell people how they should speak and write. Aitchison, in contrast, is a **descriptivist**, an individual interested in describing how language is used, not in placing value judgments on particular instances of language usage.

As the two quotes illustrate, prescriptivists and descriptivists are often very antagonistic towards one another. In highly emotional language, Simon characterizes "descriptive linguists" as "a curse upon their race." Aitchison uses less emotionally charged language but is quite blunt in her assessment of critics of language like Simon, calling them "puristic," "nostalgic" for the past, and ultimately "illogical." Although Simon and Aitchison have very different views about language, both are engaging in what Deborah Cameron describes as verbal hygiene, the practice of discussing what is good and bad about language:

neither the folk nor the expert [view of language] is neutral with respect to what is "good" linguistically speaking, and both views distinguish between language (perfect/natural) and speakers (corrupters of perfection/ naturalness). Linguists and non-linguists each defend what they consider to be the natural order of things.

(Cameron 1995: 4)

For Simon, speakers of English are "corrupting" the language, causing it to change from its natural state of "perfection." For Aitchison, speakers of English are participants in a very normal and "natural" process: language change. And there is no point in intervening in this process, since it will happen regardless of any external intervention.

It is important to acknowledge that all views of language are ideologically based because in discussions of prescriptivism and descriptivism, many linguists simply dismiss prescriptivists as wrong. But in discussing prescriptivism, it is worthwhile to distinguish reactionary prescriptivists from informed prescriptivists. Simon is a classic example of a reactionary prescriptivist. He has little positive to add to any discussions of language. Instead, he merely reacts to what he perceives as the deplorable state of the language. Aitchison is correct in criticizing his views as being "impossible to pin down to any firm base." How exactly does Simon want people to speak and write? What state of linguistic perfection should we strive towards? Simon's views of language are also highly elitist, especially his idea that there is a great linguistic divide between the "educated" and "uneducated" masses. People like Simon should be ignored; they have nothing constructive to offer to discussions about language.

But while reactionary prescriptivism has little to offer to discussions of language, informed prescriptivism can play a more useful role, particularly in discussions of language and its relationship to public policy and teaching practices. Whether linguists like it or not, all language is subject to linguistic norms, and how these norms are set is often a matter of public discussion. It is better that linguists participate in such discussions than delegate participation to the reactionary prescriptivists of the world. Consider how a descriptive linguistic perspective can contribute to discussions of gender equality in language – whether, for instance, a word such as *mailman* should be replaced with *mail carrier*, which because it lacks the masculine word *man* is gender neutral.

Historically, English has changed from a language that exhibited **grammatical gender** to one exhibiting **natural gender**. In Old English, gender was marked on nouns, adjectives, demonstratives, and pronouns. However, the gender given to a noun, for instance, was rather arbitrarily assigned, resulting in a system of grammatical gender, a system in which there is no systematic connection between biological gender and the gender marking that a linguistic item receives. Thus, the Old English word for *hand* (whose stem form was *hond*) was marked for masculine gender, *pride* (Old English *wlencu*) for feminine gender, and *body* (Old English *līc*) for neuter gender. As English changed over time, gender no longer was marked on nouns, with some notable exceptions, such as the use of *man* and *-ess* in words referring to certain professions (e.g. *mailman, fireman* for males and females; feminine *actress, waitress* in opposition with masculine *actor, waiter*). Gender is still marked on pronouns (e.g. *he, him,* and *it*) but the gender assigned to a pronoun matches the actual gender of the noun to which the pronoun refers, resulting in a system of natural gender. This is why so-called generic uses of *he* (e.g. *A student must try his hardest to obtain good grades*) have come under criticism, since in a system of natural gender a pronoun such as *he* can refer only to males – it excludes reference to females. A truly generic pronoun refers to all members of a class, both males and females.

Public discussions of the shift to gender-neutral language have typically ignored the linguistic motivation for this change. Instead, the shift is often framed within the context of discussions of "politically correct" language usage, a discussion with purely political motivations. Certainly there is a political dimension to advocating the use of *mail carrier* instead of *mailman*, or *flight attendant* instead of *stewardess*: gender-neutral vocabulary not only acknowledges that both males and females can be found in many professions but reflects the feelings of many that language should not privilege one gender (males) over another (females). But the kind of informed linguistic prescriptivism that can be brought to such linguistic debates can helpfully augment the purely political underpinnings of such discussions.

Informed prescriptivism can also be useful in teaching contexts, since English teachers, for instance, often have to teach non-native speakers of English, or individuals speaking non-standard dialects of English (such as African American Vernacular English, or AAVE). Having knowledge of the linguistic backgrounds of such students can give teachers a greater appreciation of the difficulties that these students face learning English and a linguistic awareness of the linguistic systems underlying the languages/dialects that the students speak. On one level, a teacher can observe a commonly used construction in AAVE such as *He late*, and tell a student using this construction that he or she is speaking incorrectly and should instead say *He is late* or *He's late*. But this same teacher will better understand students uttering *He late* by knowing that AAVE has a grammatical rule of copula deletion not found in Standard English: whenever in Standard English a form of the verb *be* can be contracted with the subject (e.g. *He is late* → *He's late*), in AAVE the process can be taken one step further and the entire verb deleted. A teacher with knowledge of this rule can view sentences exhibiting copula deletion as not simply random errors but as the result of the application of a linguistic rule. And with this knowledge the teacher can better help the student learn the conventions of Standard English.

Linguists are often criticized for having an "anything goes" attitude towards language: the belief that because a linguistic construction is the product of a linguistic rule, its use in any context is allowable. But by bringing a linguistic perspective to prescriptivism, linguists can better help the general public understand how language works, and assist them in making more informed decisions about language usage.

Theorizing about language

Linguists differ ideologically not only with the general public but among themselves too. As a result, linguists have developed a variety of different theories about language, each having a different emphasis. Since the advent of generative grammar in the 1950s, many linguists have been primarily concerned with developing theories that are competence-based, i.e. centered on the belief that language is mainly a property of the mind. Other linguists have developed theories that are more performance-based, that is, focused on language use in social contexts. Still others have attempted to develop theories that combine these two interests: that are grounded in the assumption that language is a product of both the mind and the social contexts in which it is used.

Noam Chomsky is the principal proponent of competence-based theories of language. Chomsky revolutionized linguistics (as well as philosophy and psychology) in the 1950s by publishing a book, *Syntactic Structures* (1957), outlining his theory of generative grammar, and by writing a highly influential critique of B. F. Skinner's *Verbal Learning and Verbal Behavior* (1959). Chomsky developed his theory of language during a period when behaviorist psychology dominated thinking about language. Because behaviorists viewed language as a product of experience, they believed that children entered life with a *tabula rasa* (blank slate), and learned language only after being exposed to it.

Chomsky countered that this view had to be wrong because children were able to produce linguistic structures that they could not possibly have encountered through everyday experience (the notion of poverty of stimulus). Chomsky therefore concluded that all human beings were born with an innate capacity for language, and that it was therefore more important to study what languages had in common rather than how they differed. To reflect this emphasis, he postulated the notion of **universal grammar**: the idea that every individual, regardless of the language they ultimately spoke, had within their linguistic competence a language acquisition device containing a set of universal principles.

These universal principles formed the basis of Chomsky's theory of generative grammar. In this theory, which has undergone numerous modifications since its inception in the 1950s, Chomsky developed a formal notation, grounded in mathematics, that explicitly described the knowledge of language that is part of any speaker's linguistic competence. A key tenet of this theory is the notion of creativity: the idea that from a finite set of rules within a speaker's competence, an infinite set of sentences could be generated. The notion of creativity became a defining characteristic of human language – something that distinguished it from all other systems of communication. Chomsky's notions about human language were so revolutionary and influential that they completely changed the field of linguistics, and ushered in what is now referred to as the modern era of linguistics.

Because generative grammar is competence-based, it is concerned only with linguistic rules creating structures up to but not beyond the level of the sentence. In addition, performance (i.e. language use) is completely ignored and is often viewed as consisting of "errors": slips of the tongue, mispronunciations, and so forth. Many linguists, however, disagree with this view of performance and feel that a complete understanding of language cannot be obtained unless one considers the wider contexts – social and linguistic – in which language is used as well as the rules responsible for structures from the sentence down to the individual speech sound. Although many different linguists have pursued this more expansive view of language, Michael A. K. Halliday's theory of systemic/functional grammar (see Halliday and Matthiessen 2004) is one of the more comprehensive theories of both competence and performance.

As a functionalist, Halliday believes that language exists to satisfy the communicative needs of its users; that is, that language is a communicative tool. To reflect this view, Halliday proposes that language has three general "metafunctions": an ideational function, an interpersonal function, and a textual function. Halliday's ideational function is concerned with specifying how language serves as a means of structuring the internal and external realities of the speaker. When the child utters *I broke it*, he encodes in linguistic form an experience he has just had. He is engaging in what Halliday describes as a "material process," specifically a process of "doing ... some entity 'does' something – which may be done 'to' some other entity" (Halliday 1994: 110). In this case, the child – the "actor" in Halliday's terms – engages in a process ("breaking") affecting the wheel – the goal – on the truck with which he has been playing. Material processes – "processes of the external world" – are one of the three primary kinds of processes within Halliday's system of transitivity. The two other primary processes are mental processes, consisting of processes of "inner experience" and "consciousness," and relational processes, allowing speakers "to relate one fragment of experience to another" and to engage in the process of "classifying and identifying" (ibid.: 107).

Language has two additional functions – the interpersonal and the textual – that reflect the fact that language is influenced by the social and linguistic contexts in which it is used. On one level, language plays a key role in our social interactions, functioning either as a means by which "the speaker is giving something to the listener (a piece of information, for example) or he is demanding something from him" (ibid.: 68). As was noted earlier in this chapter, how we "demand" something from another individual is very much determined by our social roles: our age, gender, level of education, and so forth. On another level, language is very dependent on the linguistic context. Texts are functional, Halliday and Hasan (1985: 10) argue, because they consist of "language that is doing something in some context, as opposed to isolated words or sentences." All texts exhibit two types of unity: unity of structure and unity of texture (ibid.: 52). Press reportage, as discussed earlier, has a prearranged structure: a headline, a byline, a lead. Texts also have texture, linguistic markers of cohesion that insure that all parts of the text fit together: the word *therefore*, for instance, signals that one clause is a logical consequence of a preceding clause or clauses.

Summary

While linguists may share a number of assumptions about language, they approach the study of language from different theoretical perspectives. Because linguists influenced by Noam Chomsky's views on language believe that language is primarily a product of the mind, they are more concerned with studying linguistic competence: the unconscious knowledge of rules that every human possesses. Other linguists take a more expansive view of language, believing that it is just as valuable to study language in social contexts and to consider the structure of texts as well as the structure of sentences occurring in texts. This book takes this second approach to the study of the English language. After a discussion in the next chapter of the history of English and the basic concepts that explain language change, the subsequent chapters focus on the social basis of the English language, the various principles affecting the structure of texts, and grammatical rules describing the form of the smaller components of language found in texts, from the sentence down to the individual speech sound.

Self-study activities

1. Match the structures in the left-hand column with the area of linguistics in which they are studied in the right-hand column.

   (1) the structure of words   a. phonetics/phonology
   (2) word order/structure of clauses b. morphology
   (3) the meaning of words   c. syntax
   (4) individual sounds   d. semantics

2. If you are studying rules of syntax, are you studying linguistic competence or linguistic performance?

3. What is the difference between prescriptivist and descriptivist approaches to language study?

4. If you claim that the sentence *He don't know nothin'* is "incorrect," are you making a judgment about the grammaticality of the sentence or its acceptability?

5. American Sign Language (ASL) is gestured, not spoken, yet it is still considered a language. Explain how ASL is a language in the same sense that English or Spanish is?

6. While a language such as German has a system of "grammatical" gender, English has "natural gender." What's the difference between the two systems, and, in particular, why is it the case that Modern English employs a system of "natural" gender?

7. The Linguistic Society of America is a professional organization of linguists that periodically publishes statements dealing with linguistics and language policy. One of its statements, "Language Rights" (www.lsadc.org/info/lsa-res-rights.cfm, accessed June 22, 2008), describes the linguistic rights that speakers of languages other than English should have in the United States. The statement notes that "The vast majority of the world's nations are at least bilingual, and most are multilingual, even if one ignores the impact of modern migrations" and that "Multilingualism by itself is rarely an important cause of civil discord." The statement also lists specific rights that multilingual speakers should be accorded, such as being "allowed to express themselves, publicly or privately, in the language of their choice" and "to maintain their native language and, should they so desire, to pass it on to their children." Do the quotes provide examples of what Deborah Cameron describes as verbal hygiene?

Further reading

For an overview of the basic tenets of semiotics, see D. Chandler, *Semiotics: the Basics* (London: Routledge, 2002). A good introduction to Noam Chomsky's theory of generative grammar can be found in S. Pinker, *The Language Instinct: How the Mind Creates Language* (New York: Harper Perennial Modern Classics, 2007). For a critique of Chomsky's views on language, see G. Sampson, *The Language Instinct Debate* (London: Continuum International Publishing Group, 2005). Functional grammar is described in detail in M. A. K. Halliday and C. M. I. M. Matthiessen, *An Introduction to Functional Grammar*, 3rd edn. (London: Hodder Arnold, 2004).

The development of English

CHAPTER PREVIEW

This chapter focuses on the development of the English language as well as some general principles of language change. It not only describes how English has changed but offers explanations for the changes. The first section contains an overview of the current state of the language: how many people speak English vs. the other major languages of the world, and how calculating the number of speakers of a language is complicated by the many difficulties one encounters in distinguishing a language from a dialect. The next section describes the two principal ways of classifying languages: the **genetic system** of classification, which groups languages into family trees and traces their historical development through the process of linguistic reconstruction, and the **typological system** of classification, which focuses more on language similarities than differences and classifies languages in a manner that is aligned with the notion of language universals. The chapter concludes with a discussion of language "change" vs. language "evolution," i.e. whether it is justified to claim that evolutionary changes in biology parallel those in language, and with a consideration of other hypotheses that have been advanced to explain how and why languages change.

KEY TERMS

Cognate vocabulary

Comparative method

Dialect

Genetic classification

Internal/external influences on language change

Language

Language death

Linguistic reconstruction

Synchronic/diachronic change

Typological classification

Introduction

In the lectures published in *A Course in General Linguistics*, Saussure made the distinction between synchronic and diachronic studies of language. Synchronic studies involve investigating a language in its present form as it is currently spoken and written. A synchronic study of English would focus on Contemporary English: the current version of English spoken around the world. Diachronic studies, in contrast, examine the historical development of a language, taking into consideration changes it has undergone over time. The changes that English experienced have led to the positing of five distinct forms of English: Old English, Middle English, Early Modern English, Modern English, and Contemporary English. Various historical and linguistic events led to changes in English over time. For instance, the Norman Conquest of England in 1066 ushered in the French influence on the English language, an influence that was so significant, particularly in the area of vocabulary, that linguists saw the need to distinguish Old English from Middle English.

Even though it is useful to distinguish between synchronic and diachronic studies of language, the distinction is somewhat misleading, since languages are always changing, and how English is spoken today, for instance, will differ from how it is spoken next year. Of course, the difference will be small – much smaller than the difference between Old English and Modern English. But it is important to realize that languages are dynamic, not static, entities. They are always changing – in response to external forces (e.g. the desire in many English-speaking cultures for gender-neutral vocabulary), or as a consequence of internal changes within the language (e.g. irregular verbs becoming regular, such as *strived* replacing *strove* in the past tense).

Because of external and internal influences, English has changed quite significantly from the Old English period to the present. But perhaps one of the more striking changes concerns the rise of English as an international language. During the Old English period, English was a language spoken exclusively in England. But over time, it has become a language spoken across the globe, a change in the status of English that serves as the focus of discussion in the next section.

The current state of the English language

According to the *Ethnologue: Languages of the World*, English is one of approximately 6,900 living languages in the world (Gordon 2005: 16; see also www.ethnologue.com). Many of these languages have relatively few speakers; a small subset of them are widely spoken. Table 2.1 lists some of the most commonly spoken languages, and the number of individuals who speak them as a first or second language. Figures in this table are given in millions and are based on information in Gordon (2005), the *World Almanac*, and *Wikipedia's* "List of Languages by Number of Native Speakers" (en.wikipedia.org/wiki/List_of_languages_by_number_of_native_speakers, accessed June 6, 2008).

Table 2.1. Most widely spoken languages			
Language	# of First Language Speakers*	# of Second Language Speakers	Total
Chinese (Mandarin)	873 (83%)	178 (17%)	1,051
English	340 (25–40%)	500–1,000 (60–75%)	840–1,340
Hindi	370 (76%)	120 (24%)	490
Spanish	360 (86%)	60 (14%)	420
Russian	167 (60%)	110 (40%)	277
Arabic (standard)	206 (90%)	24 (10%)	230
Portuguese	203 (95%)	10 (5%)	213
Bengali	207 (98%)	4 (2%)	211
Indonesian	23 (14%)	140 (86%)	163
Japanese	126 (99%)	1 (1%)	127
German	95 (77%)	28 (23%)	123
French	65 (57%)	50 (43%)	115

*Numbers are in millions

As Table 2.1 illustrates, the most commonly spoken language is Mandarin Chinese, one of the so-called dialects of Chinese. However, including Mandarin in Table 2.1 but not the other dialects of Chinese (e.g. Cantonese) reflects a difference in how the terms language and dialect are defined in theory and in practice.

In theory, what distinguishes a language from a dialect is the notion of mutual intelligibility. If I speak Northern American English and you speak Southern American English, we will be able to understand each other. Therefore, we speak dialects of the same language. On the other hand, if I speak French and you speak Vietnamese, we will not be able to understand each other, meaning that we speak different languages. However, in practice this distinction is not consistently maintained. China is a unified political entity. As a result, many people refer to all of the languages spoken in China as dialects, even though the spoken forms of the dialects are mutually unintelligible. Speakers of Cantonese and Mandarin, for instance, may use the same writing system, but if they were to have a conversation, they would be unable to understand one another. The opposite situation exists with other groups of languages. Danish, Swedish, and Norwegian are referred to as separate languages, even though they are relatively mutually intelligible. These languages are not referred to as dialects of, say, Scandinavian, again because the countries of Denmark, Sweden, and Norway are autonomous political entities.

The issue of what is considered a dialect of a language also affects how one counts the number of speakers of a language. In tabulating the number of native speakers of English, Crystal (2003: 65) includes not just speakers of English in countries such as the United States or Canada who speak English from birth but speakers of English pidgins and creoles. As a result, he counts over 430 million speakers of English as a native language. A **pidgin** is a contact language. When slaves were brought to Jamaica, for instance, many spoke different West African languages, and none spoke English – the language of their slave masters. This resulted in the creation of a pidgin, a second language that was based on the dominant language spoken in Jamaica, English, and that enabled minimal communication among slaves and their owners. When the children of the slaves learned the pidgin as a first language, the pidgin became a **creole** that is now referred to as Jamaican Creole. Creoles are typically quite variable, with some forms close to the dominant language (English in Jamaica) and others farther away from the dominant language and unintelligible with it. This situation obviously complicates the task of accurately counting the number of speakers of a language.

Crystal (2003: 68) also notes that there are many countries in which English is spoken for which we have no information of numbers of speakers, and in which English is spoken as a second or foreign language. For instance, in Nigeria, a country with over 500 indigenous languages, English is a **second language**. It is not spoken as a native language but has been legislated as an official language: the language of government, law, education, and business. In Germany, in contrast, English is a **foreign language**: it is commonly taught in schools, but it has no official status. If the number of speakers of English includes speakers of pidgins and creoles as well as speakers of English as a foreign language, Crystal (2003: 69) estimates that roughly 1.5 billion people speak English.

But even if estimates of English speakers are made rather conservatively (as is the case in Table 2.1), English is the most widely spoken language not just in the world but in the history of civilization. English is widely used around the world – not just in countries in which it is a **native language** (Australia, Canada, Ireland, Great Britain, New Zealand, and the United States) but in many other countries in which it is either a second language (e.g. Hong Kong, India, Kenya, Tanzania, and Singapore) or a foreign language (e.g. most of Western Europe). In addition, anyone wishing to fly a commercial airliner must be fluent in English, since English is the lingua franca of the airline industry; in all major tourist areas of the world, shopkeepers, hotel clerks, and others involved in the tourist industry will commonly have some knowledge of English.

It is important to remember, however, that the widespread use of English has little to do with the language itself but more with the fact that British colonization spread English around the world, a phenomenon that was followed by the emergence of the United States (which has the highest percentage of native speakers) as a political and economic force. Had world events been different, English might still be a language spoken only in Great Britain, where it had its origins over 1,500 years ago.

Genetic classifications of languages

Languages have been traditionally classified in terms of the genetic relationships that they exhibit. The term "genetic" is being used metaphorically to describe relationships among languages, because only humans possess genes. However, it has proven useful to group languages into **language families**. Within a given family, languages can be "parents" of other languages, "siblings" of one another, and so forth. These relationships are expressed through successive branchings of a family tree.

Figure 2.1 provides an abbreviated depiction of the language family, Indo-European, of which English is a member. The Indo-European language family, according to the *Ethnologue* (Gordon 2005: 16–17), is one of 94 "top-level" language families in the world and comprises 430 actively spoken languages. While not the largest language family – with 1,495 languages, this honor goes to Niger-Congo – it contains eight of the twelve languages listed in Table 2.1: English, Hindi, Spanish, Russian, Bengali, Portuguese, French, and German. The remaining four languages in the table belong to different language families: Mandarin to Sino-Tibetan, Arabic to Afro-Asiatic, and Indonesian to Austronesian. Japanese is an isolate, a language whose classification into an existent language family has proven difficult and is the subject of much dispute among linguists.

*Indicates a dead, or extinct, language; two additional branches not represented above, Anatolian and Tocharian, are also dead.

FIGURE 2.1
The Indo-European
language family.

English is a member of a language family, Germanic, that is a direct descendant of Indo-European and that consists of fifty-three languages (www.ethnologue.com/show_family.asp?subid-90017). Figure 2.2 lists some of the more commonly spoken Germanic languages and the three branches – West, North, and East – in which Germanic languages can be classified.

While the one East Germanic language listed in Figure 2.2, Gothic, is now dead, North Germanic contains languages commonly spoken in Scandinavia, and West Germanic languages spoken throughout the world (English and Yiddish) as well as in Europe (German, Dutch, and Frisian) and South Africa (Afrikaans).

Figure 2.2 provides a further breakdown of the five stages of development that English has gone through: Old English, Middle English, Early

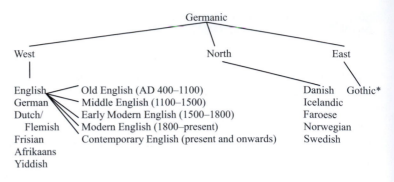

FIGURE 2.2
The Germanic branch.

*Indicates a dead, or extinct, language.

Modern English, Modern English, and Contemporary English. Not every-one divides English into five distinct phases. Contemporary English is included in the list because, as mentioned earlier in this chapter, languages are dynamic, not static, entities, and the designation of Contemporary English is used to reflect the fact that the English language is constantly changing. It is also important to note that all languages can be divided into stages similar to those for English. For instance, the two varieties of German spoken in Germany – High German (Hochdeutsch) and Low German (Niederdeutsch) – each went through two earlier stages of development: Old and Middle High/Low German.

The comparative method

The family-tree model of language development provides a temporal view of how languages change over time. Indo-European, for instance, is thought to date back to approximately 4000 BC (perhaps earlier); Germanic to 500 BC; and East, West, and North Germanic to 350 BC. To develop family trees and establish genetic relationships between languages, various kinds of historical, archeological, and linguistic evidence are examined. In the case of English, this evidence can be directly obtained, since we have written records of settlement patterns in England and surviving manuscripts written in Old English. For Indo-European and Germanic, however, no such records exist. These languages are therefore **proto-languages** – languages whose existence has been established through the process of linguistic reconstruction. Reconstruction involves examining languages for which we have surviving records and which we know are related and then inferring what an ancestral language for these languages might have looked like. The assumption underlying linguistic reconstruction is that if so-called "sibling" languages within a language family all possess a specific group of words, then the parent language from which these languages are descended must have also had these words.

The process of examining languages, grouping them into language families, and reconstructing ancestral languages is known as the comparative method. To illustrate how this method works, the following sections examine the three kinds of evidence used to establish the members of the

Indo-European language family – cognate vocabulary, grammatical similarities, and historical/archeological information.

Cognate vocabulary. The comparison of cognate vocabulary is the hallmark of the comparative method. Cognates are words that are passed down the family tree as languages change and develop and have proven extremely important for determining not just which languages are siblings within a language family but what the parent language of the sibling languages might have looked like. The comparative method works best when vocabulary representing common human experiences is compared. Watkins (2000) lists many semantic categories containing words that were instrumental in developing the Indo-European family (examples from Modern English are used for purposes of illustration): for instance, verbs of existence (e.g. English *be*); qualitative adjectives (*old, new, thin*); numerals (*one, two, three,* etc.); pronouns (*I, me, you,* etc.); seasons (*winter, spring, summer, autumn*); body parts (*hands, nose, feet,* etc.); and so forth. The advantage of comparing vocabulary such as this is that one can be assured that it will occur in almost any language. Vocabulary that is very culture-specific will have a highly restricted occurrence, making it ill-suited to the comparative method.

As an illustration of how the comparative method works, consider how cross-linguistic comparisons of words for Modern English *foot* can be used to determine which languages belong in the Indo-European language family, how the Germanic branch can be established as an independent sub-family of Indo-European, and what form and pronunciation *foot* had in Proto-Germanic and Indo-European. Figure 2.3 contains cognate words for *foot* in a variety of modern and older Indo-European languages.

Old English *fót*	Modern French *pied*
Modern English *foot*	Modern Italian *piede*
Modern German *Fuß*	Modern Portuguese *pé*
Modern Dutch *voet*	Modern Spanish *pie*
Modern Norwegian *fot*	Sanskrit *pāt*
Modern Danish *fod*	Latin *pēs*
Modern Swedish *fot*	Greek *peza*

FIGURE 2.3
Words in modern and older Indo-European languages equivalent to Modern English *foot.*

The left-hand column contains words from Germanic languages; the right-hand column words from other Indo-European languages. At first glance, the words for *foot* in the Germanic languages seem different from the other languages: the words of Germanic origin begin with orthographic *f* (the Dutch example, *voet*, begins with orthographic *v*, a written symbol that in speech would be pronounced as /f/). The other languages, in contrast, begin with orthographic *p* (a symbol that would be pronounced as /p/).

But rather than use this difference to put the Germanic languages in a language family other than Indo-European, the nineteenth-century philologist Jacob Grimm (who along with his brother Wilhelm wrote *Grimm's Fairy Tales*) postulated a principle of sound change known as Grimm's Law. This principle provided evidence for establishing the branch of Germanic and distinguishing it from the other branches of Indo-European. Although Grimm's Law has three parts, of most relevance is the part that noted that Indo-European /p/ became /f/ in Germanic. This sound change accounts for many additional words too. For instance, Modern English *father* is *Vater* in German (with *V* again pronounced as /f/) and *väder* in Dutch but *pater* in Latin, *padre* in Spanish, and *pére* in French. Of course, in doing comparisons of this nature, one has to be careful not to confuse **borrowings** with cognates. English has words such as *pedal* and *pedestrian* – each containing the root *ped* or *pod* and having something to do with the notion of 'foot' (e.g. a pedal is operated by foot). At first glance, words such as these might lead one to conclude that English is more like French or Latin than German or Dutch. But these words did not arrive in English via proto-Germanic. Instead, they were borrowed – they came across the language tree, in this case from Latin as a result of contact with speakers of Latin.

Cognate vocabulary can also be used to reconstruct ancestral languages. For instance, the *American Heritage Dictionary of Indo-European Roots* lists the stem **ped-* as the Indo-European word for Modern English *foot* but **fót* as the Germanic word. (The asterisk before these words indicates that they are hypothetical, or reconstructed, word forms.) Since all of the Germanic languages have words beginning with /f/, it is logical to assume that proto-Germanic had a word with /f/ as well. However, since all other Indo-European languages have /p/, proto-Indo-European must have had a word for *foot* beginning with /p/ too: pronunciation with /f/ was obviously unique to the Germanic languages.

Grammatical similarities.   While the comparison of cognate vocabulary is crucial to the comparative method, other linguistic similarities and differences among languages can provide additional evidence that languages should be classified in similar or different language families. One among many grammatical features of many Indo-European languages is that they contain inflections marking **case**, **number**, and **gender** on nouns, adjectives, and (sometimes) articles. Although this system can be traced back to Proto-Indo-European (PIE), some Indo-European languages have greatly simplified the system:

Case: PIE had eight cases: nominative, vocative, accusative, genitive, ablative, dative, locative, and instrumental (Baldi 1990: 54). Each of these cases marked the role that a noun and associated article and adjective played in a sentence. For instance, the nominative case is typically associated with the **subject** of a sentence, the accusative case with the **object**. Indo-European languages with fewer cases than PIE will usually have at least the nominative, accusative, genitive, and dative cases (e.g. Modern German and Dutch). Latin has six cases: the aforementioned cases, plus the ablative and vocative. Russian also has six cases, but instead of the ablative and vocative, it has the instrumental and locative. Modern English marks one case on nouns – the genitive – but three cases on pronouns: nominative (or "subjective" in some English grammars; e.g. *I*, *he*, *she*), accusative (or "objective"; e.g. *me*, *him*, *her*), and genitive (or "possessive"; e.g. *my*, *his*, *her*). Modern Spanish also marks case only on pronouns, but unlike English, has no case markings for nouns.

Number: PIE distinguished three classes of number: singular ('one'), dual ('two'), and plural ('more than two'). While many older Indo-European languages, such as Sanskrit (a language within the Indo-Aryan branch of Indo-European), preserve this three-way system, most mark only singular ('one') and plural ('more than one').

Gender: PIE had three genders: masculine, feminine, and neuter. Although languages such as German, Polish, Russian, and Czech exhibit all three genders, other Indo-European languages distinguish only masculine and feminine, a binary system evident in such Italic languages as French, Spanish, Portuguese, and Italian. English is like Spanish or French, except that gender is only indicated on pronouns: masculine (*he/him*) and feminine (*she/her*). The pronoun *it* is arguably neuter, but its plural counterpart, *they*, is really gender-neutral, since it can refer to any plural noun, regardless of its gender.

The variation in how Indo-European languages mark case, number, and gender is not indicative of a more general morphological trend. As Baldi (1990: 51) notes, many Indo-European languages exhibit highly "complex morphology," others "much less morphological complexity, with fewer formal categories and distinctions." To illustrate this contrast, Table 2.2 compares markings for case, number, and gender in Latin, a heavily inflected language, with Modern English, a language which has lost many of its inflections.

Table 2.2. The marking of case, number, and gender in Latin and Modern English for the word *girl*

Case	Latin		English	
	Singular	Plural	Singular	Plural
Nominative	puella	puellae	girl	girls
Genitive	puellae	puellarum	girl's	girls'
Dative	puellae	puellis	girl	girls
Accusative	puellam	puellas	girl	girls
Ablative	puella	puellis	girl	girls
Vocative	puella	puellae	girl	girls

Latin is a language in which nouns are marked for one of three genders: masculine, feminine, and neuter. In Table 2.2, the Latin word for Modern English *girl*, which contains the base form *puell-*, is marked for the feminine gender and would, accordingly, receive specific endings depending on its case – nominative, genitive, dative, accusative, ablative, and vocative – and its number (i.e. whether *girl* is singular or plural). Markings of this nature are what Comrie (1990: 337–8) terms as "fusional"; that is, there are not separate inflections for case and for number. Instead, case and number work together, producing a single combined inflection. This is a common system for many Indo-European languages.

As mentioned earlier, case forms correspond, roughly, to the function of a word in a given sentence or clause. Thus, in Latin, *puell-* will receive different markers if it is subject (nominative), possessive (genitive), indirect object (dative), direct object (accusative), vocative (a term of address, as *Mary* is in the English sentence *Hello, Mary*), or ablative (a mixed case corresponding, for instance, to the instrumental use of *with* in *I cut the bread with a knife*). For instance, in (1a) and (b), *puell-* is subject of each sentence; therefore, the nominative form *puella* is used in the singular and *puellae* in the plural.

(1) a. Puella est tarda.
    '[The] girl is late'
  b. Puellae sunt tardae.
    '[The] girls are late'

In (2a) and (b), *puell-* is a direct object, resulting in the accusative form *puellam* for the singular and *puellas* for the plural.

(2) a. Ego amo puellam.
    'I like [the] girl'
  b. Ego amo puellas.
    'I like [the] girls'

Adjectives in Latin also contain inflections that agree in case, number, and gender with the nouns that they follow. Thus, when the adjective *parvus* 'small' occurs before *puella* in the nominative case, it would be marked as nominative, singular, and feminine in a sentence such as *Puella parva est tarda*. Latin lacks articles, but in languages with inflectional systems similar to Latin that contain articles, definite articles too will have to agree with the nouns they precede. In Modern German, for instance, (3a) contains a noun, *Mann*, that is masculine, singular, and nominative; the article and adjective before it agree in case, number, and gender. Example (3b) contains the same noun phrase, but this time in the accusative case.

(3) a. Der müde Mann arbeitete spät.
    'The tired man worked late'
  b. Wir berieten den müden Mann.
    'We consulted the tired man'

Modern English has a relatively simplified system for marking case, number, and gender. The definite article *the* and all adjectives preceding nouns have no markings for case, number, or gender, though number is marked on demonstrative pronouns, which like articles are members of the more general class of **determinatives**: *this/that* in the singular (e.g. *this book*), *these/those* in the plural (*these books*). As Table 2.2 shows, on nouns, number and one case, the genitive, are marked: orthographic *s* marks both possessives (e.g. *the girl's book*) and plurals (e.g. singular *girl* → plural *girls*), except in cases of irregular plurals, such as *man's* and *men's*. Since *s* marks both plural and genitive nouns, a noun that is both plural and genitive will contain only a single inflection. In writing, an apostrophe is used before *s* to mark singular nouns (e.g. *mother's*) but after *s* (e.g. *mothers'*) to mark plural nouns. However, in speech, the pronunciation of both the singular and plural genitives is identical, since apostrophes have no spoken analogue: they are mainly a written form and have no distinct pronunciation in speech. Except when it is marked for the genitive case, the form of a noun such as *girl* will remain constant, regardless of its function; that is, there is no change in form for *girl[s]* whether it is functioning as subject (*The girl[s] bought some books*), for instance, or object (*We called the girl[s]*).

The tendency for older languages such as Latin to have considerable morphological complexity and newer ones such as English to have less complexity should not necessarily be viewed as a developmental trend. Although many modern Indo-European languages (e.g. English and Spanish) have indeed become morphologically less complex than their ancestral languages (Old English and Latin, respectively), many modern Indo-European languages (e.g. German, Greek, and Russian) remain morphologically quite complex.

Historical/archeological information.   As the previous two sections have demonstrated, the comparative method relies quite heavily on linguistic evidence to establish genetic relationships among languages. However, non-linguistic evidence, such as historical information and archeological evidence, can supplement linguistic evidence to help in the classification of languages, especially to help date the origins of proto-languages for which no linguistic evidence exists.

The farther back in time one goes, the more sketchy historical information about languages and their speakers becomes. This explains why we know so little about either Proto-Indo-European or Proto-Germanic. In the case of Proto-Indo-European, while the reconstruction of this language has, as Olson (2003: 142) comments, provided considerable information concerning how speakers of PIE lived, we currently have no hard evidence about "when and where these people lived." For this reason, we can only guess when this language might have initially been spoken, who spoke it, and how migrations of PIE speakers led to the development of sub-families of PIE (e.g. Proto-Germanic). Dixon (1997: 48) states that although the common consensus is that PIE began around 6,000 years ago, he notes that others have provided evidence that the language could have originated up to 10,500 years ago.

We can also only speculate about where PIE was initially spoken. The most widely accepted view of the origins of PIE is the Kurgan Hypothesis, which was originally proposed by the archeologist Marija Gimbutas (1956). This hypothesis places the original speakers of PIE just north of the Black Sea *c.* 6,000 years ago. Through a series of migrations, these speakers spread their language all the way to Europe, spawning over time the various sibling languages of PIE, including Proto-Germanic. Archeological and linguistic evidence suggests that original speakers of PIE were warriors who rode horses as they made their way to Europe. An alternative but much less widely accepted hypothesis is Renfrew's (1987) farming-dispersal hypothesis. Contrary to Gimbutas, Renfrew argued that the original speakers of PIE were not warriors but farmers, and that the spread of farming from Anatolia (Turkey) to Greece and eventually Europe was responsible for the spread of PIE. This hypothesis leads to a much earlier dating of the origins of PIE to *c.* 10,500 years ago. One of the problems with this hypothesis for historical linguists, Renfrew (2000: 14) acknowledges, is that "they assume some specific chronological threshold beyond which the techniques of the comparative method cannot penetrate." In other words, Renfrew's dates for the origins of PIE extend beyond those for which linguistic reconstruction can be reliably conducted and point to the limitations of the comparative method.

The comparative method has clearly yielded valuable information about languages and the extent to which they are related or unrelated. However, this method has limitations, particularly with respect to how far one can go back in time in the process of reconstructing languages and language families. We have clear evidence that the Germanic branch of Indo-European existed, and by examining languages grouped within the language family, we can infer the existence of Proto-Indo-European. But some linguists have attempted to go back further in time in the search for ancestral languages to find, for instance, a larger super-family that would include Proto-Indo-European. This process involves reconstructing a proto-language on the basis of other proto-languages that in turn may themselves have been reconstructed from proto-languages. While some linguists have argued that such a process is reliable, others have claimed that vocabulary, for instance, changes so quickly that this endless process of reconstruction is fraught with problems.

Greenberg (2000) has proposed a language family called Eurasiatic, which includes language families such as Indo-European, Uralic, and Altaic as well as other languages, such as Japanese and Korean, which have defied easy classification into the major existent language families. Eurasiatic dates back to *c.* 15,000 years ago and was reconstructed using a method called mass lexical comparison. This method involves comparing sound similarities between a set of common words in hundreds of languages. Statistical tests are then conducted to determine the statistical probability that the languages being compared are related. Another earlier language family that has been proposed is called Nostratic. Some view this family as an alternative to Eurasiatic, others as a family that would include Eurasiatic. Still others believe in the notion of monogenesis: the idea, as Trask (1996: 391) observes, "that human language evolved only once, and that all languages that have ever been spoken are descended from that single ancestor." This original language has been called Proto-World.

The problem with positing language families such as Eurasiatic and Nostratic is that the reliability of one's reconstruction diminishes considerably if a hypothetical language family is reconstructed from other language families. Moreover, if such reconstructions are based on comparisons of vocabulary, it is crucial that these comparisons be based on cognate words, not borrowings. And in many cases it is difficult to determine whether a given word in a language is a cognate or a borrowing. For these reasons, many linguists remain skeptical of reconstructed language families such as Eurasiatic and Nostratic.

While it may be difficult to precisely date the origins of PIE and Proto-Germanic, we can be much more confident about the external history of English. And knowledge of this history can be combined with surviving linguistic evidence to provide a fairly precise description of the history of the English language, and its various stages of development.

The development of English

Although it is difficult to date the precise beginning of any language, English is thought to have had its origins around AD 400, when the Romans ended their occupation of England. After the Romans departed, England was populated by Romans who had stayed behind, Celts, and various Germanic tribes who had begun coming to England during the Roman occupation. In the years that followed, additional Germanic tribes from Western Europe and Scandinavia (Angles, Saxons, and Jutes) continued to come to England through a series of invasions, pushing the Celts north and west to places such as Wales and Scotland and firmly establishing English as a Germanic language that in its earliest incarnation is known now as Old English (or Anglo-Saxon).

Old English. While Modern English, as noted earlier, has lost most of its inflections for case, number, and gender, many of these distinctions can be found in Old English. These grammatical features are evident in the Old English version of "The Lord's Prayer":

> "The Lord's Prayer" Matthew 6:9–13.
> 1 Fæder ure þu þe eart on heofonum;
>   Father our thou that art in heavens
> 2 Si þin nama gehalgod
>   be thy name hallowed
> 3 to becume þin rice
>   come thy kingdom
> 4 gewurþe ðin willa
>   be-done thy will
> 5 on eorðan swa swa on heofonum
>   on earth as in heavens
> 6 urne gedæghwamlican hlaf syle us todæg
>   our daily bread give us today
> 7 and forgyf us ure gyltas
>   and forgive us our sins
> 8 swa swa we forgyfað urum gyltendum
>   as we forgive those-who-have-sinned-against-us
> 9 and ne gelæd þu us on costnunge
>   and not lead thou us into temptation
> 10 ac alys us of yfele soþlice
>   but deliver us from evil. truly.

(Adapted from Dan Kies, "Cuneiform and Distance Learning": papyr.com/hypertextbooks/cuneifrm.htm, accessed June 5, 2008)

The prayer illustrates some notable differences between Old English and subsequent periods of English. For instance, many of the nouns contain inflections marking case, number and gender. In line (1), the *-um* on *heofonum* marks this noun as masculine, dative, and plural; in line (5), the *-an* on *eorðan* marks this noun as feminine, accusative, and singular. Lines (1) and (2) contain two forms of the verb *be*. In Modern English, of all the **irregular verbs**, *be* has the most different forms (e.g. *is*, *are*, *was*, etc.). In Old English, it had even more different forms. In line (2), *Si* is a subjunctive verb form. In Modern English, subjunctive forms of *be* can be found in hypothetical clauses such as *if I were you* to mark contrary-to-fact assertions. In Old English, *Si* is a subjunctive form expressing a desire or wish. Finally, the verb *gehalgod* in line (2) contains a prefix, *ge-*, commonly found on **participles** (i.e. verbs in English following the auxiliary *have*, as in *have driven* or *had walked*). Of course, there are many other grammatical features of Old English evident in the prayer, but the examples described here point to how truly different Old English is from Modern English.

It is important to note that during this period, English was purely a spoken language: the only literate people of the era were monks in monasteries, a consequence of St. Augustine's conversion of England to Christianity in the sixth century AD. One of the more famous pieces of English literature of this period, *Beowulf*, was part of the oral-formulaic style of this period and was written down by some unknown scribe or scribes who heard someone tell the story.

Middle English.   Old English continued being spoken in England until approximately 1100. What precipitated the change from Old English to Middle English was a significant historical event: the Norman conquest of England in 1066. The Normans came from the Normandy region of France and ruled England for approximately 300 years; they spoke a variety of French called Anglo-Norman. There were two significant changes to English during this period that have led to debates about the extent to which the Norman Conquest affected the English language: the addition of many words of French origin to the English lexicon, and the continuing decline in the number of inflections found in Old English.

To see these trends, it is worthwhile to view the opening stanzas of the *General Prologue* to Chaucer's *Canterbury Tales*:

> PROLOGUE
> Here bygynneth the Book of the tales of Caunterbury.
> Whan that Aprille, with hise shoures soote,
> The droghte of March hath perced to the roote
> And bathed every veyne in swich licour,
> Of which vertu engendred is the flour;
> Whan Zephirus eek with his swete breeth
> Inspired hath in every holt and heeth
> The tendre croppes, and the yonge sonne
> Hath in the Ram his halfe cours yronne,
> And smale foweles maken melodye,
> That slepen al the nyght with open eye

Words such as *perced* ('pierced'), *veyne* ('vein'), *licour* ('liquor'), and *vertu* ('virtue') are of French origin and entered the English language during the Middle English period. Only remnants of the inflectional system from the Old English period survive in the Middle English period. Plural *-(e)s* can be found on words such as *shoures*; adjectives such as *swete* ('sweet') do not contain the elaborate system of declension found in Old English but merely the ending *-e*. In fact, Middle English has more in common with Modern English than its immediate ancestor Old English.

The influx of French vocabulary into English as well as the simplification of its inflectional system have led some to claim that English underwent creolization during this period as a result of contact with French. However, as Thomason and Kaufman (1988: 308) argue, this is a rather extreme position: "There were never many speakers of French in England" during the Middle English period, the borrowing of words and affixes into English was "no more extreme than the kinds found in many other normal cases in history," and ancestral Normans became bilingual in English "within no more than 250 years of the Conquest." Thus, the linguistic changes to English during this period followed the natural course of linguistic change. Of course, other Germanic languages of this period, such as German, did not change to the extent that English did. But this merely illustrates that the paths that languages take are often unpredictable.

Early Modern English.   The transition from Middle to Modern English is not marked by any specific cultural event but rather by a linguistic event: the Great Vowel Shift. This shift resulted in vowels either being raised on the vowel chart (see Table 7.2 in Chapter 7) or becoming **diphthongs**. One way that vowels can be classified is according to how high the tongue is placed in the mouth when the vowel is articulated. What happened between Middle and Early Modern English is that in certain words, vowels began to be replaced by vowels pronounced higher in the mouth. For instance, in Middle English the first vowel in word *swete* would have been pronounced /eɪ/ (similar to the first vowel in Modern English *race*). However, in Modern English, /eɪ/ was raised to /i/. Thus, we get the Modern English pronunciation of *sweet*. In Middle English, the first vowel in *droghte* /u/ would have rhymed with Modern English *boot*. Because this is already a high vowel, it could not be raised in Early Modern English. Instead, it became the diphthong /aʊ/, two vowels pronounced simultaneously in a syllable and the vowel still present in the Modern English pronunciation of *drought*.

But while this sound change marks a formal change between Middle and Modern English, there were a number of other historical events that clearly contributed to English becoming the language that it currently is:

The Shift from an Oral to a Print Culture: During the Old and Middle English periods, English was largely a vernacular language: literacy rates were low, and for most people, the language existed only in its spoken form. After Caxton introduced the printing press in England in 1476, literacy rates increased. Some of the more significant early publications in English include William Tyndale's translation of the *New Testament* (1525) (an event that led to his being burned at the stake, since it was considered sacrilegious for the bible to exist in any language other than Greek or Latin); the King James Version of the bible (1611) (the first "legal" translation of the bible); Shakespeare's *First Folio* (1623); and the first English-language newspaper, *The Daily Courant* (1702).

The Publication of Dictionaries and Grammars, and the Subsequent Codification of English: As a language grows in stature, it begins being codified: dictionaries are written to provide a record of words, their meanings, and their pronunciations; grammars describe the structure of a language and often prescribe usage. In the Modern English period, a number of dictionaries and grammars of English begin appearing: Samuel Johnson's dictionary (1755) (the first major dictionary of English); Noah Webster's dictionary (1806) (the first major dictionary of American English); and numerous grammars of English, which begin appearing in the eighteenth century (e.g. Robert Lowth's 1762 *A Short Introduction to English Grammar*). There were also attempts in the eighteenth century to establish an "English Academy": a legislative body similar to the Académie française (French Academy) that issues proclamations on good and bad usage. However, attempts to establish an English Academy have never been successful.

The Colonization of America, its Independence from England, and its Rise as a Superpower: The colonization of the New World in the seventeenth century marked the first time that the English language was transplanted from England into a new geographical and social context. Even though the United States eventually gained independence from England, its colonization marked the beginning of British colonization, a process that led, as an earlier section of this chapter demonstrated, to the transplantation of English all over the world and the development of many new "Englishes." More people now speak American English than British English, and because of its size, power, and influence, the United States and, consequently, American English have wielded great power in the world.

Typological classifications of languages

While the comparative method involves classifying languages on the basis of linguistic and non-linguistic evidence, the typological method relies exclusively on linguistic information and uses this information to classify languages according to the linguistic characteristics that they share or do not share. For instance, languages can be classified as having subject–verb–object word order (SVO), as having subject–object–verb (SOV), and so forth. Although languages are classified typologically on the basis of phonological, morphological, and syntactic characteristics that they share or do not share, much of the research in this area has been centered on morphology and syntax, and this section explores two ways that languages can be typologically classified along morphological and syntactic lines.

Typological classifications based on morphology

Morphologically, languages have traditionally been classified as being **agglutinative**, **isolating**, or **fusional**. Turkish is a very agglutinative language because words have a very complex internal structure, and all of the morphemes in them can be easily identified. For instance, Kornfilt (1990: 630) analyzes the Turkish sentence *eve gitmek istiyorum* as having the following structure:

(4) ev + e   git + mek   isti   + yor   + um
    home + dat.   go + infin want + pres. prog. + 1 sg.
    'I want (*am wanting) to go home'

The sentence begins with *ev* ('home'), which is marked for the dative case (*e*). The verbal element comes next, with the verb *git* ('go') followed by an infinitive marker, *mek* (equivalent to English *to* before verbs, as in *to go*). The last part of the sentence contains the verb *isti* ('want'), a suffix, *yor*, which indicates that the sentence is in the present progressive aspect, and the first person singular pronoun *um* ('I').

At the other end of the spectrum are languages such as Chinese that are highly isolating. Languages that are isolating contain independent units that express various kinds of meaning. For instance, in Mandarin, the phrase *rè de tiānqì* ('hot weather') has the following analysis:

(5) rè   de   tiānqì
    hot   adjective particle   weather

In English, *hot* would be interpreted as an adjective largely because it is positioned before the noun *weather*, a position in English where adjectives are commonly placed. Chinese, in contrast, has a separate morpheme, *de*, that signals that the first word in the noun phrase is an adjective modifying the noun.

Fusional languages can be classified somewhere between agglutinative and isolating languages. Two languages discussed in the previous section, Latin and German, are fusional languages because unlike Turkish, they do not have separate morphemes marking, for instance, case and number. Instead, the categories of case, number, and gender work in combination to determine the particular morpheme to be used. In Russian, another fusional language, the stem DYEVUSHKA ('girl'), which takes feminine gender, would be marked as DYEVUSHKU in the accusative singular but DYEVUSHOK in the accusative plural.

Although the three morphology types constitute separate classes, some languages exhibit characteristics of more than one type. For instance, while Old English was a typically fusional language, Modern English has become increasingly isolating. In Modern English, to give one example, orthographic *s* is used to mark possessive nouns in both the singular and plural (e.g. *boy's* and *boys'*), a system of marking associated with a fusional language. However, -s usually occurs only with animate nouns; inanimate nouns tend to show possession with a separate word: the preposition of. Thus, it is more common to find *the roof of the house* than *the house's roof*. Marking possession with a separate word, *of*, is indicative of an isolating system of morphology. In general, English has seen a decline in inflections and an increase in prepositions as it has developed from Old English to Modern English.

Typological classifications based on syntax

At the level of syntax, languages can be typologically classified along many dimensions. One common way they are classified is to group them according to the dominant (i.e. most common) word orders that they exhibit.

Table 2.3 lists the six possible word orders that can potentially occur in human language, and the frequency with which they occurred in 402 languages that Tomlin (1986) studied.

Table 2.3. Word order types and frequencies		
Word order	Frequency	Example languages
SOV	180 languages (44.78%)	Bengali, Gothic, Hindi, Japanese, Kurdish, Latin, Persian, Turkish
SVO	168 (41.79%)	Arabic (colloquial), English, French, Malay, Mandarin, Portuguese, Russian, Spanish, Vietnamese
VSO	37 (9.20%)	Arabic (literary), Aramaic, Hebrew, Irish
VOS	12 (2.99%)	Aneityan, Baure
OVS	5 (1.24%)	Apalai, Arecua, Hixkaryana
OSV	0	
Total:	**402**	

Frequency information and example languages are taken from Tomlin (1986: 22, 155–259)

Of the 402 languages he surveyed, Tomlin (1986: 22) found that only five of these orders actually occurred (an OSV language could not be found). And of these five possibilities, SOV and SVO orders were overwhelmingly preferred (in 45% and 42% of the languages examined, respectively); the other orders were quite uncommon.

English and Japanese provide good examples of SVO and SOV languages, respectively, because these orders are the most common word orders in each of these languages. The sentence below is the norm in English because in a typical English sentence, the subject will come first, followed by the verb, and then the object:

(6) The child broke the toy.
         S   V   O

However, in Japanese, the same sentence would have a different order, namely the subject first, followed by the object, and then the verb:

(7) Kodomo   wa   omocha   o   kowashi-ta.
    Child   Top   toy   Acc   break-Past
    'The child the toy broke.'

Japanese would additionally contain other markers, such as *wa*, indicating that the subject, *Kodomo*, is the topic (what is being discussed) and an accusative marker, *o*, following the object *omocha*.

The most common criterion for determining word order in a language is the notion of **markedness**. Constructions within a language that are considered common and ordinary are unmarked; those that are rare and unusual are regarded as marked and typically occur in a specific context. As an illustration of how markedness applies to word order in English, consider the two boldfaced clauses at the conclusion of the transcribed interview below with the musician Bryan Ferry:

Interviewer: Have you ever met Bob Dylan?
Ferry: Never have, no. Probably never shall.
Interviewer: What if you did a duet with him?
Ferry: Wouldn't that be nice? That would be a very good idea. He's a friend of Dave Stewart's, who I know.
Interviewer: Dave played on your album ...
Ferry: Yeah, Dave and Jools work with lots of different people. Dave is quite a butterfly and he's terrific ... very positive energy ... funny, quite funny, so he gets on with a lot of people. **Dylan, he likes**, and I imagine **Dylan likes him**.

("An Interview with Bryan Ferry," www.nyrock.com/interviews/
2002/ferry_int.asp, accessed, June 5, 2008)

In the last sentence, there are two clauses – one illustrating SVO word order (*Dylan likes him*), the other OSV word order (*Dylan, he likes*). The clause with SVO order is unmarked because it represents the most frequently occurring word order in English and would not necessarily require any context to be considered acceptable. The clause with OSV order, on the other hand, is marked and definitely needs some kind of context to be fully acceptable. Specifically, clauses with OSV word order in English are often used to promote **topicalization** – the positioning of the discourse topic in the first position of a clause.

As the interview opens, the discourse topic – who or what is being discussed – is Bob Dylan. As the interview proceeds, the topic shifts to Dave Stewart, who is described as a friend of Bob Dylan. Dave Stewart continues as topic until the interviewee reintroduces Bob Dylan as topic by mentioning him at the start of the clause in the last sentence (*Dylan, he likes*). Notice that once Dylan is reintroduced as topic, he remains the topic in a subsequent clause (*Dylan likes him*) with SVO word order.

In other cases, determining a dominant word order can be more difficult, particularly in languages that mark case on nouns. Because English has lost so many case markers, word order is rather fixed. Thus, in English, a sentence such as *The boy called the girl* is completely different in meaning than *The girl called the boy*. However, in languages that mark case on nouns, it is relatively easy to move constituents around without a change in meaning. In Russian, for instance, all of the sentences below are synonymous because the subject of the sentence is marked for the nominative case and the object for the accusative case.

(8) a. Mal'čiki   čitaujut   knigi   SVO
         boys-NOM   read   books-ACC
     b. Mal'čiki   knigi   čitaujut   SOV
     c. Knigi   mal'čiki   čitaujut   OSV
     d. Knigi   čitaujut   mal'čiki   OVS
     e. čitaujut   mal'čiki   knigi   VSO
     f. čitaujut   knigi   mal'čiki   VOS

(Examples taken from Bailyn 2003: 157)

Because Russian permits so many different word orders, many have argued that it is a free word order language (i.e. that it has no dominant order). However, others, such as Bailyn (2003), claim that Russian is an SVO language, and variations from this order are motivated by contextual factors, such as topicalization.

   In German, grammatical rather than contextual factors cause variable word orders, making it difficult to determine whether German is an SVO language or an SOV language. In main clauses, while variations similar to Russian occur, the predominant word order is SVO and deviations from this order are contextually motivated. In subordinate clauses, in contrast, there is a grammatical rule in German that stipulates that all parts of the verb phrase have to occur at the end of a clause. Thus, in the example below, the word order is SVO in the main clause but SOV in the subordinate clause beginning with *because*:

(9) Die Frau mag Käse, weil ihr Kind Käse mag.
     Literal Translation: 'The woman likes cheese because her child cheese likes'

Because the variant word orders illustrated above are grammatically rather than contextually motivated, Comrie (1989: 89) comments that "controversy continues to rage over which, if any, of these word orders should be considered basic."

Language typology and language universals

The study of language typology is closely connected to the study of language universals. However, as Comrie (1989: 1–12) observes, linguists differ in how they use typological information to study universals.

   Linguists of the generative school of linguistics limit the number of languages they study, placing greater emphasis on the positing of "abstract structures" (Comrie 1989: 2) to explain language universals. For instance, languages can be classified according to whether they permit pro-drop: the omission of pronouns in subject position. While English mandates that the subject pronoun occur in a sentence like *I called my mother*, in Spanish the pronoun can be omitted: *Llamé a mi madre* (literally 'called my mother'). The abstract categories that generativists posit are an outgrowth of Chomsky's theory of principles and parameters: the belief that when all children are born, their linguistic competence contains both a set of universal principles that do not vary from language to language and parameters specifying a permissible range of variation within which languages may vary. Therefore, a child born in an environment in which he or she is exposed to Spanish will set the pro-drop parameter to "on." In contrast, a child exposed to English will set the parameter to "off." Linguists within the generative school study language typology as a means of revealing universal properties of human language in line with the generative notions of language universals and language acquisition.

Other typologists, most notably Greenberg (2000), are much more interested in surveying a wide range of languages, and then from these surveys postulating various linguistic universals. For instance, Tomlin's (1986) work on word order is based on an investigation of 402 different languages. Instead of postulating abstract principles specifying permissible vs. impermissible word orders, Tomlin's conclusion that SOV and SVO are the dominant word orders is based on statistical evidence: the fact that 87 percent of the languages he investigated had these orders. A generativist would never base his/her claims on statistics but on parameters, such as pro-drop, that make reference to universal grammar.

Why languages change

In addition to describing how languages have changed, many linguists have been interested in the factors that cause languages to change. Why, for instance, did German maintain a system of inflections for case, number, and gender over time, but English, a language in the same language family (Germanic), did not? Many hypotheses have been proposed to explain facts such as this, and this section surveys some of them, beginning with a discussion of whether language change is an evolutionary process and concluding with a description of the most extreme form of language change – language death: the actual extinction of a living language.

Change or evolution?

In their discussions of how languages develop over time, many linguists have used the terms "change" and "evolution" interchangeably. This reflects the fact that in common usage, these two words have become roughly synonymous. When an ad proclaims that "Microsoft Office has evolved," the implication is not that earlier versions of this software program had undergone "natural selection," the notion in Darwinian theories of evolution that over time a species will pass on traits that will insure its survival. Instead, the idea is that as this software has changed, it has been improved in a kind of step-by-step progression. In this context, "evolution" has become a metaphor and its meaning has been extended to cover not just the development of a species but development in general.

In linguistics, there is considerable confusion over the use of the term "evolution" to describe language change. Some linguists use this term metaphorically, never implying a direct relationship between language and evolutionary theories of biology but instead using the term to describe the gradual changes that any language experiences over time. Other linguists, in contrast, actually maintain that there are direct parallels between how species and languages evolve. Croft (2000) proposes a "Theory of utterance selection" that has its basis in Hull's (1988) "generalized theory of selection," a theory that extends the traditional idea of natural selection to "all evolutionary phenomena," including, Croft (2000: 6) argues, language change.

Croft's notion of utterance selection is heavily grounded in linguistic convention, the idea presented in Chapter 1 that an utterance such as the imperative sentence *Leave* is based on convention: a linguistic rule that stipulates how this construction is formed as well as a pragmatic principle governing its use. As speakers of a language communicate, they engage in what Croft (2000: 7) terms "normal replication" and "altered replication." The gradual replacement of *whom* by *who*, a process that is ongoing in English, provides a useful illustration of the two types of replication. Before *whom* started disappearing, speakers would have communicated with one another with an utterance such as *Whom do you trust?* Normal replication would have involved speaker after speaker using this form, passing it down generation after generation to children in the process of language acquisition. At some stage, however, some speakers started saying *Who do you trust?* – an example of altered replication, a deviation from the so-called "normal" way of structuring this utterance. Because this change is currently underway, both forms co-exist, the difference between them being primarily stylistic: *whom* is more formal than *who*. And because both forms are being passed on simultaneously, we even see instances of what Croft (2000: 121) terms **hyperanalysis** (or **hypercorrection**): an attempt to achieve formality even in constructions in which *whom* is used as subject. For instance, many might be tempted to use *whom* in *She's the person whom I believe is in charge*, even though technically *whom* is replacing a subject form, not an object form: *I believe that **she** [not **her**] is in charge*. Over time, however, the choice between *who* and *whom* will stop being an issue altogether: *whom* will die out of English, resulting in the passing on of *Who do you trust?* as a type of normal rather than altered replication. This process, Croft argues, parallels the transmission of human genomes from individual to individual.

Metaphorically, the term language evolution has some explanatory value, since languages do change slowly in a step-by-step manner. But to claim that the processes by which species and languages evolve are the same creates an equivalence that not all linguists accept, particularly because many examples of linguistic change, such as the replacement of *whom* by *who*, have other explanations, such as internal and external influences on languages that cause them to change. Croft (2000: 6) does not necessarily exclude such influences from his theory, claiming that they are part of a "comprehensive framework for understanding language change." At the same time, the influences can be discussed on their own without recourse to an evolutionary-based theory of language change, and the inevitable controversy and confusion that use of the term 'evolution' raises in discussions of language change.

Internal and external influences on language change

Traditionally, it has been claimed that languages change in response to internal and external influences. Internally influenced changes result from natural processes that all languages undergo: if it were possible to protect a language from any external influences (e.g. contact with other languages) by putting it in a hermetically sealed bottle, the language would still change, since there are systematic mechanisms of change that are purely internal to language. Externally influenced changes, as suggested above, result more from the social and cultural contexts in which languages are used. Although internal and external influences are often regarded as distinct motivations for language change, they are not necessarily mutually exclusive. For instance, the loss of *whom* in English is, on the one hand, a consequence of a more general process that all languages can potentially undergo: the gradual movement from a fusional to an isolating language. On the other hand, the loss could also be attributed to contact with other languages, such as French, that lack an elaborate morphology for case.

There are many examples of internal processes that languages undergo as they change. To explain why English has lost so many inflections over time and changed from a fusional language to an isolating language, Whaley (1997: 138) describes a cyclic process that all languages undergo. English is in one stage of the cycle, experiencing "morphological loss" as it very gradually transitions from a fusional to an isolating language. Other languages are at other stages, moving from isolating to agglutinative or agglutinative to fusional. Labov (1994) classifies the Great Vowel Shift in English as a type of chain shift, a sound change that involves vowels in a language changing places, with some vowels replacing others. As noted earlier, vowels were either raised or became diphthongs. This shift is not isolated to the Great Vowel Shift, but part of a more general pattern of sound change found in many languages.

External changes result from some kind of **language contact**: speakers of different languages coming into contact, resulting in changes to the languages that they speak. The effects of contact can vary. For this reason, Thomason and Kaufman (1988: 74–6) propose a "borrowing scale," a five-point scale ranging from the relatively minor effects on a language that result from "casual" contact to the more extensive effects that can result from "very strong cultural pressure." Throughout its history, English has had contact with many languages, resulting in varying degrees of change in the language. Latin, for instance, has heavily influenced English. During the Old English period, as a result of the introduction of Christianity into England, English borrowed from Latin words such as *mass*, *abbot*, and *candle*. These borrowings are fairly low on Thomason and Kaufman's (1988: 74) borrowing scale, since they entered English for "cultural and functional" reasons: to provide words not currently in English necessary for describing new concepts. Higher up on the borrowing scale (level 3 of 5) are Latin prepositions borrowed into English and converted into suffixes, and Greek and Latin words borrowed into English that have maintained their native inflections. For instance, the Latin preposition *sub* (meaning 'under') is now an English prefix found in words such as *subzero* or *subhuman*. Over time these prefixes can be found on words not derived from Latin. The word *postgame* (as in *The athlete gave a postgame interview*) is derived from the Latin preposition *post* (meaning 'after') and the Germanic word *game*. Latin words such as *medium/media* and *datum/data* contain Latin inflections (*-um* and *-a*) marking these nouns as neuter and, respectively, singular and plural. Of course, over time these words have become reanalyzed so that now one hears sentences such as *The media has too much power*, where *media* is not analyzed as a plural but instead as a singular collective noun, a noun designating a single entity composed of individuals. Because these borrowings involve changes in structure (rather than mere additions to English vocabulary), they represent a fairly significant influence on the structure of the English language.

Because English has experienced mainly "casual to intense contact" (Thomason and Kaufman 1988: 76) from other languages, it has undergone changes that have not fundamentally altered the language. However, other languages have been affected more dramatically by language contact to the point that some of them have undergone language death.

Language death

Language death is a type of language shift. However, unlike bilingualism, which involves speakers shifting from one language to another in different contexts, language death occurs when, over time, a language loses all its speakers. The process of language death is typically slow, and involves successive generations of speakers abandoning a language until only relatively few people remain as fluent speakers. Once these people die, the language dies too.

Latin is sometimes referred to as a dead language because it no longer has any native speakers and exists only in written texts surviving from earlier periods. But while Latin may have died, its legacy survives in its direct descendants, such as Spanish, Italian, French, and Portuguese. In this respect, Latin is similar to other languages in the Indo-European language family that are no longer spoken (e.g. Old English, Sanskrit). In other contexts, however, some languages simply die, leaving no direct descendants. For instance, as a result of the colonization of the Americas, numerous indigenous languages have died or are endangered. Of the forty-four languages in the Algic language family (a family of languages spoken in the United States and Canada), thirteen have died (www.ethnologue.com/show_family.asp?subid=91079, accessed June 2008). The remaining living languages have a mere 194,980 speakers (Gordon 2005: 18), and a number of these languages are "nearly extinct," a situation arising "when the speaker population is fewer than 50 or when the number of speakers is a very small fraction of the ethnic group" (Gordon 2005: 8). According to the latest figures in the *Ethnologue*, 516 of 6,912 languages in the world are nearly extinct (www.ethnologue.com/nearly_extinct.asp, accessed June 20, 2008).

In the Americas, language death is a direct consequence of colonization, which was accompanied by genocide, disease, and the overwhelming influence of the languages of the colonialists (e.g. English, Spanish, and Portuguese). Even a relatively healthy language like Navajo, which in the 1990 census had 148,530 speakers, is seeing a decline in the number of younger speakers: among ethnically Navajo first-graders in 1968, 90 percent spoke it as a native language; now only 30 percent do (Gordon 2005: 305). Attempts to revive endangered languages have yielded mixed results. While Welsh was successfully revived, with 19 percent of the population of Wales now able to speak it (Gordon 205: 566), most other attempts have been unsuccessful. Linguists have been actively involved in the movement to save endangered languages. The Linguistic Society of America (LSA) has a special committee, the Committee on Endangered Languages and their Preservation (CELP), whose mission is to promote linguistic research on endangered languages and to help speakers of endangered languages preserve their languages. Crystal (2000: 27f.) discusses why linguists feel so passionately about the preservation of endangered languages. He emphasizes the importance of linguistic diversity, and notes that because a speaker's identity is so closely associated with the language that he or she speaks, with the death of a language comes the loss of personal identity. Languages also contain records of human history, provide "a unique encapsulation and interpretation of human existence" (Crystal 2000: 44), and are inherently interesting in and of themselves, offering important insights into the human mind.

The issue of language death is relevant to any discussion of the English language, since it is sometimes argued that the globalization of English has led to the death or displacement of many of the languages of the world. Schneider (2003: 233) remarks that while many view English as "the world's leading language ... [an] indispensable tool for international economy, diplomacy, sciences, the media, and also individual interactions across language boundaries," others regard it as "a 'killer language,' responsible for the extinction of innumerable indigenous languages, dialects, and cultures around the globe." Just which perspective one takes is largely a political decision. Nevertheless, language change is not simply a phenomenon affecting individual languages in isolation from one another. Change in one language can potentially have implications for many other languages, as is the case with the rise of English as a world language.

The nature of language change

Language change is natural, normal, and (ultimately) inevitable. While many describe changes in the language as "corruptions" or markers of "decay," in reality so-called "errors" of usage can often be precursors of change. For instance, the word *flaunt* is often used by many in place of *flout*. A former president of the United States, Jimmy Carter, made this usage famous when in 1979, during the Iran hostage crisis, he said "the government of Iran must realize that it cannot flaunt with impunity the express will and law of the world community." Strictly speaking, he should have used *flout* here because *flout* means 'to violate,' while *flaunt* means 'to show off' (e.g. *The child flaunted his new fire truck*). However, the two words are quite close in pronunciation. In addition, while *flaunt* is a fairly common word, *flout* is not. The result is that many people confuse the words, and over time they have become interchangeable – perhaps *flout* will even become archaic and replaced by *flaunt*. And this confusion is not isolated. Because both *disinterested* and *uninterested* contain negative prefixes (*dis-* and *un-*, respectively), many people now view these words as synonyms, even though many insist that the two words have distinct meanings: *disinterested* can mean only 'impartial or unbiased' and *uninterested* only 'lacking interest.' Thus, in a court of law, a defendant would want a judge who is "disinterested," not "uninterested."

Some object to the use of *their* in a sentence like *Everybody is trying their hardest* on the grounds that the verb agreeing with *Everybody* is singular, while the pronoun referring to *everybody*, *their*, is plural. However, the alternatives to *their* (generic *his* or *his or her*) either exhibit gender bias or result in a stylistically awkward construction. The pronoun *their* does neither and, additionally, fills a gap in the language: it gives speakers of English a singular third person gender-neutral pronoun without having to resort to the creation of an entirely new pronoun. Some have proposed the word *ter* as a singular third person generic possessive pronoun. But adding a new pronoun to a language is difficult because pronouns are a closed class, a class that unlike nouns or verbs does not easily admit new members. Therefore, singular *they*, which is already in the language, provides a simple solution to what has proven a difficult problem.

All of the so-called mistakes in this section illustrate the capability of human languages to adapt and change in response to the needs of their users in a manner that is consistent with the mechanisms of change inherent in all languages. English may need, as described above, a new gender-neutral pronoun, but because this need cannot be easily accommodated, speakers have been forced to use an existent form – *they/their* – in a new way. And while this change is disruptive too, over time it is likely to succeed, since language change and subsequent acceptance of new forms is a slow, gradual process, proceeding in fits and starts and, more often than not, ultimately succeeding. But if a change does not succeed, the entire process simply starts all over again.

Summary

In studying languages such as English and Mandarin, linguists have developed two different ways of classifying languages and studying their linguistic development over time. The traditional method, the genetic system of classification, involves grouping languages into language families and constructing family trees. English, for instance, is a member of the Germanic branch of the Indo-European language family. As a Germanic language, English originated around AD 400 and went through five successive stages, beginning with Old English and culminating in Contemporary English, the language of the moment.

Linguists are also interested in studying not just *how* languages change but *why* they change. While linguists disagree about whether language change has an evolutionary basis, there is wider agreement on other motivations for language change.

Self-study activities

1. Match the country in the left-hand column with the primary status of English in that country listed in the right-hand column.

    (1) Germany   a. native language
    (2) Australia   b. second language
    (3) Ireland   c. foreign language
    (4) Singapore
    (5) Japan
    (6) United States
    (7) England
    (8) Finland

2. Go to the entry for the English language in the *Ethnologue* (www.ethno-logue.com(show_language.asp?code=eng) (accessed June 3, 2008) and find a country in which English is a second or foreign language. Click the link for the country and (1) explain why English is a second or a foreign language in the country; (2) make a note of how many people in the country speak English vs. native languages other than English; and (3) record any other information you find that seems relevant to the status of English in the country.

3. One way to study the historical and cultural influences on a language is to research place names, or toponyms, which often provide interesting information not just on the people who settled a region and the languages they spoke but on the history or the area, even features of its geography (e.g. whether it has mountains or rivers). A number of dictionaries and reference guides provide information on place names, including J. Everett-Heath's *The Concise Dictionary of World Place Names* (Oxford University Press, 2005) or V. Watts *et al.*'s *The Cambridge Dictionary of English Place-Names* (Cambridge University Press, 2004). In addition, you can go to the main page of *Wikipedia* (en.wikipedia.org/wiki/Main_Page) and type in the place name to find information as well. Select a place name in any English-speaking country and record (1) the etymology of the place name (the language on which it is based and its date of origin, however approximate), (2) whether any other place names preceded the place name you chose, and (3) what the name literally means. Does it describe a particular group of people who originally populated the area? Does it provide any geographical information about the area? Note any additional information you find too.

4. What role does cognate vocabulary play in grouping languages into language families?

5. Explain how English and Mandarin Chinese are typologically similar but genetically different?

6. In what respects does English have characteristics of both a fusional and isolating language?

7. Are borrowings into a language a consequence of an internal or external influence on a language?

8. In many of his writings, John Simon laments that English is in decline. Does this mean that English is undergoing the process of language death?

Further reading

For a discussion of English as a world language, see D. Crystal, *English as a Global Language*, 2nd edn. (Cambridge: Cambridge University Press, 2003). A description of the comparative method as it applies to the Indo-European language family can be found in O. J. L. Szemerényi, *Introduction to Indo-European Linguistics* (Oxford: Oxford University Press, 1996). An overview of the typological approach to language classification is presented in W. Croft, *Typology and Universals* (Cambridge: Cambridge University Press, 1990). There are many introductions to the history of the English language, including A. Baugh and T. Cable, *A History of the English Language*, 5th edn. (Upper Saddle River, NJ: Prentice Hall, 2001) and T. Pyles and J. Algeo, *The Origins and Development of the English Language*, 5th edn. (Belmont, CA: Wadsworth Publishing, 2004). The factors influencing language change can be found in two books by W. Labov: *Principles of Linguistic Change,* vol. I: *Internal Factors*, and vol. II: *Social Factors* (Oxford and Malden, MA: Blackwell, 1994 and 2001).

The social context of English

CHAPTER PREVIEW

KEY TERMS

Conversational implicature

Cooperative principle, the

Grammatical and pragmatic meaning

Honorifics

Politeness

Power relationships

Sentences and utterances

Social distance

Speaker intentions

Speaker variables

Speech acts

Tact

This chapter explores how the social context in which language is used affects human communication. It begins with a discussion of the need to distinguish **grammatical meaning** from **pragmatic meaning**, i.e. meaning as a part of our linguistic competence vs. meaning derived from our interactions in specific social contexts. Because the discussion in this chapter will be centered on pragmatic meaning, it is also necessary to distinguish a **sentence** from an **utterance**, the primary unit upon which the study of pragmatic meaning is based. The next sections describe how utterances are used and structured in human communication, starting with **speech act theory**, a theory that formalizes the notion that what people actually intend their utterances to mean is often not clearly spelled out in the words that they speak or write.

Introduction

In July of 2005, John Roberts was nominated to be a justice on the Supreme Court of the United States. Newspaper accounts of the nomination described Roberts as being a "strict constructionist": someone who applies a literal interpretation to the language of the United States Constitution. Commenting on this description of Roberts, the noted literary and legal theorist Stanley Fish (2005) argued that Roberts was not really a proponent of "strict constructionism" but of "textualism," the belief that interpretation involves "sticking to the meanings that are encoded in the texts and not going beyond them." To illustrate the limitation of this view of interpretation, Fish notes that if a wife asks her husband *Why don't we go to the movies tonight?*

The answer to that question depends on the history of the marriage, the kind of relationship they have, the kind of person the husband thinks the wife is. **The words themselves will not produce a fixed account of their meaning** [emphasis added].

What Fish is arguing in this statement is that communication does not exist in a vacuum: to engage in a conversation, for instance, we do not simply decode the meanings of the words that people speak but draw upon the larger social context in which the conversation takes place. To understand the larger point that Fish is making, it is first of all necessary to distinguish grammatical meaning from pragmatic meaning.

Grammatical vs. pragmatic meaning

In his description of the sentence *Why don't we go to the movies?* Stanley Fish is distinguishing meaning at two levels. On one level, how we interpret the sentence is determined by the meaning of the individual words that it contains. To make sense of this sentence, we need to know, for instance, what words such as *go* and *movies* mean; that *we* refers outside the text to the speaker and addressee; that *the* indicates that a specific movie is being referred to; and so forth. At this level, we are within grammar studying what is known as **semantics**: how words have individual meaning (**lexical semantics**) and can be used to refer to entities in the external world (**reference**). Semantics is one component of grammar, and is therefore part of our linguistic competence (a full treatment of semantics is given in Chapter 6). As Fish correctly observes, however, interpretation of a sentence goes beyond understanding its meaning at the level of grammar. We need to understand the entire social context in which a sentence was uttered, a different level of interpretation that is studied within **pragmatics**, which explores the role that context plays in the interpretation of what people say.

Although many linguists agree with this view of the relationship between grammar and pragmatics, others believe that the boundary between grammar and pragmatics is not this discrete. For instance, Fillmore (1996: 54) notes that "this view yields a *subtractive* view of pragmatics, according to which it is possible to factor out of the full description of linguistic activities those purely symbolic aspects which concern linguistic knowledge independently of notions of use or purpose." The problem with making a clear divide between grammar and pragmatics, Fillmore argues, is that this view ignores the role that conventionality plays in language, i.e. that our interpretation of a sentence such as *Could you please pass the salt?* as a polite request is as much a matter of the social context in which this sentence is uttered as the fact that in English, yes/no questions with verbs such as *can* or *could* have been conventionalized as markers of polite requests (e.g. *Can you spare a dime? Could you help me with my homework?*).

Even though the boundary between grammar and pragmatics may be "fuzzy," most linguists do accept that certain elements of language are best studied under the rubric of grammar, others within the realm of pragmatics. Some linguists, such as Noam Chomsky, do not study pragmatics, mainly because they see the study of grammar as the primary focus of linguistic analysis and the investigation of pragmatics as a source of irregularities not amenable to systematic linguistic description. Others see the study of pragmatics as crucial to understanding human language, since the study of linguistic competence is no more important than the study of communicative competence: Dell Hyme's (1971) notion that human communication involves not just knowledge of how to form linguistic structures but knowledge of how to use these structures in specific communicative contexts. To appreciate this perspective, an individual need only have the experience of studying a foreign language in a classroom and then traveling to a country in which the language is spoken and discovering how little he or she truly knows about the language: that its use among speakers in differing social contexts involves more than simply "knowing the rules."

Sentence vs. utterance

Because this chapter will focus on both spoken and written language, it is important to define the basic unit of structure – the utterance – that will serve as the basis of discussion.

Many people mistakenly think that complete sentences are the norm in both speech and writing. However, as Carter and Cornbleet (2001: 3) correctly observe, "We do *not* set out to speak in sentences – in fact, in informal speech we rarely do that – rather, we set out to achieve a purpose which may or may not require full, accurate sentences." To illustrate this point, consider the short excerpt below taken from an actual conversation:

Speaker A: Lots of people are roller skating lots of people do rollerblade
Speaker B: Just running around the city
Speaker A: Uh mainly in Golden Gate Park

(ICE-USA)

Speaker A's first turn contains two grammatical sentences: constructions consisting of a subject (*lots of people* in both sentences) and a **finite verb** (*are* and *do*, respectively). In contrast, Speaker B's turn and Speaker

A's second turn do not contain sentences: B's turn contains a construction centered around the verbal element *running*; A's turn is a prepositional phrase. But while these turns do not contain complete sentences, they are nevertheless meaningful. Implied in B's turn, for instance, is that those who are roller skating are "running around the city" and in A's turn that they are skating "mainly in Golden Gate Park." Therefore, when discussing pragmatics, linguists tend to avoid labels such as sentence, instead preferring to describe the constructions under discussion as utterances, a category that includes not just sentences but any construction that is meaningful in the context in which it occurs.

Speech act theory

According to J. L. Austin (1962), when speaking (or writing, for that matter), we perform various "acts": locutionary acts, illocutionary acts, and perlocutionary acts. The difference between locutionary and illocutionary acts is sometimes referred to as, respectively, the difference between "saying" and "doing." Thus, if I utter *Leave*, I am on one level producing an imperative sentence having a specific form (the **base form** of the verb with an implied *you*) and meaning (e.g. 'depart'). This is the locutionary force of this utterance, what has thus far in this chapter been referred to as being a component of grammar. Additionally, I have intentions when uttering this sentence, specifically I am using what is known as a directive to get someone to do something. This is the illocutionary force of the utterance. But utterances also have effects on the individuals to whom they are directed: uttering *Leave* may have the effect of actually causing an individual or individuals to leave, it may upset them, it may have no effect, etc. This is considered the perlocutionary force of the utterance.

Although speech act theorists have proposed these three general types of speech acts, they are primarily interested in speaker intentions: the illocutionary force of utterances. To study this facet of human communication, various types of speech acts have been proposed. Below are five described in Searle's (1979) seminal book on speech acts:

Assertives/Representatives: Utterances reporting statements of fact verifiable as true or false (e.g. *I am old enough to vote*; *Columbus discovered America in 1492*; *Water freezes at zero degrees centigrade*)

Directives: Utterances intended to get someone to do something (e.g. *Stop shouting*; *Take out the garbage*)

Commissives: Utterances committing one to doing something (e.g. *I promise to call you later*; *I'll write your letter of recommendation tomorrow*)

Declarations: Utterances bringing about a change in the state of affairs (e.g. *I now pronounce you husband and wife*; *I hereby sentence you to ten years in jail*)

Expressives: Utterances expressing speaker attitudes (e.g. *That's a beautiful dress*; *I'm sorry for being so late*)

A speech act can be **explicit** or **implicit**, **direct** or **indirect**, and **literal** or **non-literal**. If a speech act is explicit, it will contain a **performative verb**, a verb that names the speech act and has a very specific structure. For instance, even though both of the examples below are apologies (a type of expressive), only the first example contains a performative verb:

I was abominably ill-mannered, and I apologize.

(BNC AN8 1949)

You guys I'm sorry that I was late

(MICASE SGR200JU125)

Apologize is a performative verb because it literally names the speech act that the sentence represents. In addition, it is in the present tense and occurs with a first person pronoun. Note that if the subject and verb tense are changed, a very different sentence results, one in which no real apology is being made by the speaker but instead an apology given by somebody else at some other time is described:

He apologized for all the harm he'd done.

While *You guys I'm sorry that I was late* is also an apology, here the apology is implicit because the verb *am* (contracted in *I'm*) does not fit the structural definition of a performative verb: the naming of the speech act is conveyed by the adjective *sorry*, not the verb *am*.

Additional examples of performative verbs are given below for each of the five types of speech acts:

Assertives/Representatives
Mr Deputy Speaker that strong sympathy expressed at the time of the last debate on these matters was approved overwhelmingly by the Labour party conference last October and I **state** that for the record less [sic] there be any misunderstanding about our position on the issue of voting systems.

(BNC JSF 262)

We **affirm** the importance of this principle.

(BNC CLY 473)

I hereby **declare** that I am the sole author of this thesis.
(Egidio Terra, "Lexical Affinities and Language Applications," unpublished doctoral dissertation. etd.uwaterloo.ca/etd/elterra2004.pdf
accessed June 18, 2008)

Directives
Pursuant to Proclamation No. 1081, dated September 21, 1972, and in my capacity as Commander-in-Chief of all the Armed Forces of the Philippines, I hereby **order** you as Secretary of National Defense to forthwith arrest or cause the arrest and take into your custody the individuals named in the attached lists ...
(www.lawphil.net/executive/genor/
go1972/genor_2-a_1972.html, accessed July 27, 2006)

I **direct** the witness to answer the question.

(BNC ACS 1187)

If you go and see this film I *recommend* that you don't eat first.

(BNC A4S 153)

Commissives
okay um, now I *promise* to, give out the uh, the the uh, take home essay, final, assignment, today

(MICASE LES315SU129)

I *pledge* to recycle as much waste as possible at home and/or I pledge to help organise recycling at work or at school/college.

(BNC G2V 2448)

Declarations
I *declare* the meeting closed.

(BNC GUD 618)

The friar raised his hand. "Absolvo te," he intoned. "I *absolve* you."

(BNC F9W 791)

Expressives
I *thank* you all again for the very hard work and real effort put into our business at all levels through 1992 without which we would not be able to have the confidence to face the coming year.

(BNC HP4 1215)

We *congratulate* Mr. Hay on this well deserved honour.

(BNC GXG 624)

While performative verbs such as *apologize* and *promise* are common in everyday usage (the 100-million-word British National Corpus contains thirty-two examples of *I apologize* in conversation), many performative verbs, as the examples above illustrate, are restricted in usage and sometimes occur in conjunction with the highly formal and legal-sounding expression *hereby* (only 3 of 258 examples of *hereby* in the BNC occur in conversation). For this reason, most performatives would be quite inappropriate in other contexts, as the rather tongue-in-cheek example below illustrates:

As titular Chief o' the Clan McTaylor, I hereby order you to remove that mauve and puce tea-towel from your web site.

(downunderandbeyond.blogspot.com/2006/03/tartan-tastic.html, accessed June 6, 2008)

Speech acts can also be either direct or indirect. A speech act is direct if its intent is clearly conveyed by the words and structure of the utterance. For instance, each of the three examples below is a directive.

That's enough go away

(SBCSAE)

Will you go away

(SBCSAE)

I'm really uncomfortable with your being here now

(invented example)

However, only the first example is a direct speech act because the directive, *go away*, is in the form of an **imperative sentence**, a form conventionally associated with a directive. The other two examples are indirect. The second sentence is a yes/no question. Typically, such structures elicit a yes or no response. But in this context, the speaker is asking an individual to leave but in a less direct manner. The third example is even more indirect. It is in the form of a declarative sentence, a form most closely associated with, for instance, a representative. But in the appropriate context, this example too could have the intent of asking someone to leave, though its high level of indirectness would certainly leave room for ambiguity and potential misinterpretation.

In English, indirectness is very common with directives and is typically associated with yes/no questions, particularly those of the form *could you* or *would you*:

Okay would you open the front uh the screen door for me please

(SBCSAE)

Would you mind just moving the screen back

(BNC H9C 3769)

Could you grab me a box of tea

(SBCSAE)

Could you take your coats off please and come into the blue room

(BNC F77 3)

In other cases, declarative sentences are used that contain modal verbs of varying degrees of indirectness. By using the modal verb *should* in the example below, the speaker is suggesting fairly strongly that the addressee take an introductory composition class.

You should take Intro Comp next semester.

(MICASE ADV700JU047)

However, if *might want to/wanna* is used instead, the command becomes more of a suggestion:

Well you might wanna major in English

(MICASE ADV700JU047)

Indirectness in English, as will be demonstrated in a later section, is very closely associated with politeness, since issuing a directive requires various strategies for mitigating the act of trying to get someone to do something, an act that can be considered impolite if not appropriately stated.

Finally, speech acts can be literal or non-literal. Many figures of speech in English are non-literal in the sense that the speaker does not really mean what he/she says. It is quite common in English for individuals to postpone saying or doing something by uttering an expression like *I'll explain why in a minute* (BNC F77 450). However, the person uttering this example does not literally mean that his/her explanation will be forthcoming in precisely sixty seconds. Likewise, in *Yes I know it's taken me forever to write you* (ICE-GB W1B-001 106), the speaker uses *forever* as a means of acknowledging that his/her letter has been long forthcoming; in *and I mean there's millions of ligaments and millions of tendons you know well not millions but I mean* (SBCSAE), the speaker actually explicitly states that his utterance is non-literal: the human body does not really contain millions of ligaments or tendons.

In other cases, literalness can be more ambiguous. For instance, it's quite common to open a conversation with an expression such as *So how are you* or *How's everything*. However, the person uttering these examples does not necessarily want to know how the addressee is feeling. And embarrassment can result if the addressee does indeed respond by telling the speaker how badly, for instance, he/she is feeling. The utterance *We live close enough for goodness sake let's get together one night* (BNC KBK 3549) is similarly ambiguous. Does the speaker really want to get together with the addressee, or is this simply a way of closing a conversation?

Felicity/appropriateness conditions

For a speech act to be successful, it needs to satisfy a series of conditions referred to as either **felicity** or **appropriateness conditions**. Searle (1969) proposes four such conditions: propositional content, preparatory, sincerity, and essential. To understand how these conditions work, it is useful to see how they apply to a very common type of speech act, the apology.

According to Thomas (1995: 99f.), an apology, schematized within Searle's typology, would have the following structure:

Propositional act: S [speaker] expresses regret for a past act A of S
Preparatory condition: S believes that A was not in H's [hearer's] best interest
Sincerity condition: Speaker regrets act A
Essential condition: Counts as an apology for act A

Propositional condition: Any speech act has to have propositional content, i.e., be expressed in a form conventionally associated with the speech act. Apologies, as noted earlier, are typically marked with either the performative verb *apologize* or an expression such as *I'm sorry*:

I apologize for the urgency on this, but to get it through to the Department of the Environment it has to be lodged at the beginning of February and then up to them by by March

(BNC JA5 593)

Preparatory condition: Before making an apology, the speaker obviously has to believe that he/she has done something requiring an apology. In the above example, the speaker makes an apology because she believes that requiring her work staff to do a considerable amount of work on short notice requires an apology.

Sincerity condition: A key component of any apology is that the speaker be sincerely sorry for what he/she has done. Because the above statement is made in a work context, where the speaker is higher on the power hierarchy than the people to whom the apology is directed, many might doubt the speaker's sincerity and dismiss the apology as perfunctory, i.e. as something said by a superior in passing. Obviously, whatever interpretation is made would be heavily dependent on the superior's relationship with her workers, their past perceptions of her, and so forth.

Essential condition: If the apology is not perceived as sincere, then the speech act will ultimately fail: while it may have the form of an apology and be directed towards some past situation requiring an apology, if it is not accepted as an apology, the speech act becomes meaningless.

Although all speech acts must satisfy each condition to be successful, many speech acts are distinguished by the different ways that they satisfy the individual conditions. For instance, the propositional condition for a representative is that it must be a statement that can be confirmed as either true or false:

Between 20 June 1294 and 24 March 1298 England and France were formally and publicly at war

(ICE-GB W2A-010 003)

I went and saw their house the other night

(SBCSAE)

That looks like succotash to me it's got peas and lima beans

(SBCSAE)

Other speech acts, in contrast, do not have this constraint. A request, a type of directive, cannot be true or false, since the act of asking for something has no truth value:

On behalf of Nether Wyresdale Parish Council I request that the following alterations/improvements be made to the play equipment on Scorton Playing Field

(BNC HPK 114)

Oh what are you doing? Oh shut up. Go away.

(BNC KBH 747)

Requests differ further from other kinds of speech acts because, as Searle (1969: 66) notes, "*Order* and *command* have the additional preparatory rule that *S* must be in a position of authority over *H*." Thus, the effectiveness of both of the directives above depends crucially upon whether the individuals uttering the directives have power over those to whom the directives are issued.

The cooperative principle

The philosopher H. Paul Grice proposed the cooperative principle to explain how conversation involves a certain level of "cooperation" among communicants:

Our talk exchanges do not normally consist of a succession of disconnected remarks, and would not be rational if they did. They are characteristically, to some degree at least, cooperative efforts; and each participant recognizes in them, to some extent, a common purpose or set of purposes, or at least a mutually accepted direction.

(Grice 1989: 26)

Grice proposed four maxims to explain how people cooperate when they speak: Quantity, Quality, Relation, and Manner. When a maxim is violated (or "flouted"), a conversational implicature results, i.e., the utterance receives an interpretation that goes beyond the words that are spoken. For instance, the conversational exchange below occurred at the end of an interview with three individuals – Michael Shapiro, Michael Moshan, and David Mendelson – who had created a musical CD to help prepare high school students in the United States to take the verbal section of a standardized test, the SAT (Scholastic Aptitude Test).

Linda Werthheimer (interviewer): How well did the three of you do on the verbal section of the SAT?
David Mendelson: Michael Shapiro did really well [laughter]
(Weekend Edition, NPR, Saturday, January 6, 2007)

Quite naturally, the interviewer is interested in how the creators of the study guide did on the very test for which they are attempting to help students succeed. But because Mendelson does not really answer her question, instead commenting on how well one of his co-authors did on the exam, he has violated Grice's maxim of Quantity: he has not made his contribution to the conversation informative enough. He has said too little. And the implicature – the additional layer of meaning in his response – is that he did not do well on the exam. The laughter following his statement clearly indicates that the other speakers had recognized his violation of the Quantity Maxim and understood the meaning of what he was saying.

Table 3.1 lists Grice's four maxims, provides brief definitions of them, and then lists Grice's full definitions. To best understand the

Table 3.1. Maxims of the cooperative principle

Maxim	Summary	Grice's (1989) description
Quantity	Don't say too much; don't say too little	1. Make your contribution as informative as is required (for the current purposes of the exchange) 2. Do not make your contribution more informative than is required (quoted from p. 26)
Quality	Be truthful	1. Do not say what you believe to be false 2. Do not say that for which you lack adequate evidence (p. 27)
Relation	Stay on topic; don't digress	Be relevant (p. 27)
Manner	Make sure what you say is clear and unambiguous	1. Avoid obscurity of expression 2. Avoid ambiguity 3. Be brief (avoid unnecessary prolixity) 4. Be orderly (p. 27)

maxims, it is useful to examine some examples that adhere to and violate them.

Quantity

All communicants must strike a balance between providing too much and too little information when they speak or write. In the example below, both speakers achieve this balance because they directly answer each of the questions they are asked.

A: Have any of the supervisors been in
B: Oh yeah I've had a lot of visitors lately um I went downstairs to get something to eat and somebody was waiting at the door today
A: Who was it
B: John Wood do you know him
A: No
B: He was um
A: Is he an old guy
B: No no kind of a young black guy

(ICE-USA)

Speaker B, for instance, directly answers A's question about whether any supervisors had come in. B provides slightly more information than necessary, saying that many visitors had come in. But this extra information does not exceed the amount of detail that would be provided in a conversation of this nature.

In the next example, in contrast, too much information is provided. In this example, a former Democratic Congressman in the United States, Richard Gephardt, is responding to a question from a reporter asking him whether he thought that George Bush was the legitimate president of the United States, since Bush's election victory in 2000 followed a highly contentious and controversial recount of votes in the state of Florida. Instead of giving a simple yes/no response to the question followed by a brief explanation, Gephardt provides a very lengthy answer:

The electors are going to elect George W. Bush to be the next president of the United States, and I believe on January 20, not too many steps from here, he's going to be sworn in as the next president of the United States. I don't know how you can get more legitimate than that.

Gephardt could have simply replied, "Yes, I think that George W. Bush was legitimately elected." However, because his party, the Democrats, had vigorously contested Bush's election and lost a legal challenge to the Republican party, many will interpret the length of his utterance as meaning that he does not think that George Bush is the legitimate president of the United States.

Quality

When we communicate, there is a tacit assumption that what each communicant says or writes will be truthful. For instance, when speaker A below asks B who she is going to spend the evening with, A expects B to give a truthful answer.

A: So who are you going out with tonight
B: Koosh and Laura

(SBCSAE)

This may seem like a fairly obvious point, but conversational implicatures definitely result when an utterance is judged as not being truthful. The excerpt below was taken from the first page of a marketing survey enclosed with a child's toy:

Please take a moment to let us know something about yourself. Your valuable input enables us to continue to develop our advanced learning tools.

Following this statement were a series of questions eliciting informa-tion not just about the quality of the toy but about the occupations of household members, their annual income, the kinds of automobiles they drove, and so forth. In this context, many people will interpret the above statement as less than truthful: the manufacturer is not solely interested in improving its "advanced learning tools." Instead, it wants to gather demographic information about the parents who purchased the toy so that they can be targeted in the future with advertisements for other toys.

Even though communicants place great faith in the truth of the asser-tions that they make and hear, there are certain situations when violating the Quality Maxim is considered acceptable. For instance, if someone asks you "Do you like my new hairstyle?", it would be highly inappropriate in most contexts to reply "No," since this could result in hurt feelings. Therefore, in most communicative contexts, many people would reply "Yes" or "It's great," even if their replies are untruthful. Of course, the per-son to whom the reply is directed would undoubtedly judge the reply as truthful. But as will be noted in a later section, politeness is such an important pragmatic concept in English that it overrides other pragmatic considerations.

Relation

The notion of what is relevant in discourse will vary from one context to another. For instance, in the conversation below, speaker B asks A if he started his new job. However, a few turns later, B changes the topic entire-ly, cutting off any further discussion of A's job and shifting the topic to a phone call B had received the previous night:

B: Are you um how's your new job did you start
A: I just was painting and I do a little carpentry a little gutter work and
    stuff
B: Uh huh
A: So I've been doing that
B: Someone called for you last night

A: Really

B: Yeah

A: Who was it

B: But I told him you were you weren't working here anymore

(ICE-USA)

In casual conversation, such topic shifts are normal, since there are no real pre-planned topics that people intend to discuss when they converse casually and in many instances we are free to change topics, digress, etc., without violating the maxim of relation.

In other contexts, however, it is expected that speakers/writers stay on topic. Note how in the two examples below, which were taken from class lectures, instructors specifically note that they are going to go off topic by uttering statements like *let me digress a little here* that tell their students explicitly that they are aware that what they say next will not be directly relevant to the previous topic of discussion:

okay then obviously basic biology failed **let me <SS LAUGH> digress a little here**. um, there is no fundamental physical set of principles to describe, the precise effect, of temperature on enzyme catalyzed reactions in real organisms.

(MICASE LES175SU025)

okay. any other questions? if not let me leave this model, and i wanna start talking about the Static Neoclassical Model. but before i do that **i wanna digress for a second** and talk about aggregate production functions, which will be a piece of the Static Neoclassical Model.

(MICASE LEL280JG051)

The reasons why these instructors so explicitly mark their digressions is that if they do not, students might not only become confused but think their instructors are disorganized, confused, and not good at teaching. In formal writing, violations of the maxim of relation are even more strictly penalized, and are seen as markers of poor writing.

Manner

Clarity of expression is highly valued in what we say and write. For instance, someone going to a public forum on global warming expects information on this potentially technical topic that is understandable to a general audience, not scientists already quite familiar with the subject. This is why the excerpt below on this topic contains so much metadiscourse – expressions, such as *My talk will be split into four sections*, that comment directly on how a particular piece of discourse is being organized (other examples of metadiscourse are in boldface):

But **what I'd like to talk to you about** uh this afternoon just uh briefly because we only have forty-five minutes is uh studying climate change from space. And **my talk will split into four uhm sections. I'll spend a few minutes talking about the climate system** and uh then having sort of looked at that **we'll ask the question and hopefully answer it** uh why observe from space. There are many parts of the climate system that we could discuss uhm but uh **I thought I would concentrate on** polar ice, and any of you who saw ITV's News at Ten last night uh will have will have a foretaste of at least one of the things that I uh will address. And then **I'll say a few words about** where do we go next, uh what's going to happen in the future. **So we'll start with** what is the climate system.

(ICE-GB S2A-043 009)

The speaker so explicitly tells her audience what she will discuss because she knows that the people to whom she is speaking do not have a written text at hand to refer to, and she wants to provide them with a global framework for her talk so that they will be able to anticipate what she will be discussing.

In other contexts, such signposting is unnecessary. It would be odd to begin a spontaneous dialogue with statements such as "First, I'm going to discuss the weather and then my visit with my father" because, as mentioned earlier, such dialogues have a fairly loose organizational structure. In many kinds of written texts, it is considered bad style to include commentary such as "In this paper, I will ..." because it is expected of authors that they organize what they say in a less heavy-handed manner: what they write should be implicitly well organized and not require constructions that reveal the structure.

While the previous examples focus on the maxim of manner as it applies to entire discourses, it applies to single utterances as well. Much prescriptive advice about writing focuses on telling writers how to write clear sentences. Kirkman (1992: 50) advises writers to avoid "excessive 'nominalization' – excessive use of 'noun-centered' structures ... [and to instead use] A crisper, 'verb-centred' style ..." Thus, he argues that the first example below, which contains three nominalizations (*functions*, *allocating*, and *apportioning*) as well as a verb in the passive voice (*are performed*), is much less clear than the second example, which is in the active voice and contains verbal equivalents (*allocates* and *apportions*) of two of the nominalizations in the first example:

The functions of allocating and apportioning revenue are performed by the ABC.

The ABC allocates and apportions the revenue.

While Kirkman's (1992) advice might seem purely prescriptive, Hake and Williams (1981: 445–6) describe psycholinguistic research and an experiment they gave that suggests that the nominal style is much more difficult to process than the verbal style. However, Hake and Williams (1981) also report that in certain contexts, readers will judge essays written in the nominal style as "better" writing than equivalent essays written in the verbal style. Consequently, clarity of expression is often valued less than the high level of abstraction associated with the nominal style, which many associate with intellectual maturity. This contradiction calls into question just how consistently speakers adhere to the maxim of manner.

Problems with the cooperative principle

Determining whether an individual has violated or adhered to a maxim of the cooperative principle is largely a matter of interpretation. As a result, different people will reach different conclusions about the same utterance. In the example below, Floyd Landis is commenting on the results of two drug tests he took following his winning the Tour de France in 2006 that revealed elevated levels of testosterone:

I have never taken any banned substance, including testosterone. I was the strongest man in the Tour de France and that is why I am the champion.

Those who believe Landis' claims of innocence will obviously not think that he violated the maxim of quality. Those who do not believe him will think he did violate this maxim, and the implicature that they will draw is that he is a liar trying to protect his reputation.

In other situations, it is not clear whether one or more maxims have been violated. In an utterance discussed earlier in this section, an interviewee did not directly answer a question about whether he had done well on a standardized test: he said nothing about his own performance but instead commented on how well one of the other interviewees had done. Because his answer was incomplete, he violated the maxim of quantity. But by violating this maxim, he arguably made his contribution unclear as well. Does this mean that he violated both the maxims of quantity and manner simultaneously? Again, there is no way that this question can be definitively answered, since how people interpret an utterance is often a highly subjective and personal matter.

The positing of four maxims of the cooperative principle raises another question: why these four maxims and not more or fewer maxims? To address the criticism inherent in this question, Sperber and Wilson (1995) have proposed a general theory of relevance. This theory is grounded in Grice's notion of speaker intentions, but instead of expressing these intentions through separate maxims, the theory is centered on the idea that when people communicate, they try to determine the relevance of what is said to them:

Intuitively, an input (a sight, a sound, an utterance, a memory) is relevant to an individual when it connects with background information he has available to yield conclusions that matter to him: say, by answering a question he had in mind, improving his knowledge on a certain topic, settling a doubt, confirming a suspicion, or correcting a mistaken impression.

(Wilson and Sperber 2006: 608)

Relevance, Wilson and Sperber (2006: 609) argue, is a scalar phenomenon, with highly relevant utterances having higher "positive cognitive effects" and less relevant utterances increasing "the processing effort expended." Thus, as they note, if a woman who is allergic to chicken calls the host of a dinner party she is attending to inquire what will be served for dinner, the reply *We are serving chicken* will be much more relevant than *We are serving meat*, since the first utterance provides her with a highly informative response to her question and also entails the second utterance.

This does not necessarily mean that all communication will be as highly relevant as the first reply to the woman's question. Instead, speakers strive to achieve what Wilson and Sperber (2006: 612) characterize as "optimal relevance." For instance, if I ask you whether you enjoyed the dinner I just cooked for you, and you reply *It was fine*, this response rather than *I loved it* may be all you are willing to tell me. And I may infer from your response that you did not like the dinner all that much – a correct inference because had your response been more relevant, it would have been highly impolite. Politeness, as the next section will demonstrate, overrides many of the pragmatic principles discussed thus far.

Politeness

In their highly influential cross-linguistic analysis of politeness conventions in language, Brown and Levinson (1987: 60–1) argue that politeness in language is centered around the notion of **face** – "the public self-image that every member wants to claim for himself" – and the efforts made by interlocutors to "maintain each other's face." Polite usage of language comes into play whenever a speaker has the potential to produce a **face-threatening act (FTA)**, an utterance that undermines the tacit understanding that all language should preserve face. In determining the exact level of politeness that will be employed to mitigate an FTA, Brown and Levinson (1987: 15) propose three considerations: the power relationships existing between speakers, their social distance, and the level of impoliteness that the FTA would create. Although numerous alternative views of politeness exist (see Watts' (2003: 49–53) survey of them), Brown and Levinson's work remains one of the more detailed and comprehensive treatments of politeness.

Power relationships and social distance

In any social group, there will be differing power relationships among people. In a classroom, for instance, there will be a **disparate** power relationship between teacher and students: the teacher will be a **superordinate** (i.e. higher on the power hierarchy) and the students **subordinates** (i.e. lower on the hierarchy). Most of the students will be **equals**: no power imbalance will exist between them. However, even among students, it is possible to find disparate relationships if, for instance, students form study groups, and one or more students in the groups hold power over the others. Whether individuals are disparates or equals will affect how they communicate. Students may use honorifics such as *Professor* or *Doctor* to address their teachers as a way of explicitly marking the disparate power relationship that exists between a student and a teacher. In contrast, students may use their first names to address one another as a way of indicating that they are equals.

In addition to *Professor* and *Doctor*, English has a limited number of other referent honorifics: expressions that show deference and respect to individuals by referring either directly or indirectly to them. In the first two examples below, the honorifics *Mrs* and *Professor* are titles used before the names of individuals being discussed in the third person. In the second two examples, in contrast, *Dr* and *Mister* are used before the names of individuals who are being directly addressed:

Another witness **Mrs** Angela Higgins said she saw the defendants shouting and behaving stupidly.

(BNC HMA 298)

it is a particular pleasure, for me today to introduce our honored speaker, **Professor** Gary Glick who is Professor of Chemistry and Professor of Biological Chemistry, and who was named to the Werner E Bachmann Collegiate Professorship of Chemistry in nineteen ninety-nine.

(MICASE COL200MX133)

Dr Vernon, is this the way to make depressed people happy?

(BNC HV1 17)

Thank you **Mister** Smith for calling Pacific Bell.

(SBCSAE)

English has other titles used as honorifics (e.g. *Miss, Ms, Sir, Madam, General, Colonel, President, Prime Minister,* and *Officer*) as well as terms of address that have very restricted uses: *your hono(u)r, sir,* and *madam* (which in Southern American English can be shortened to *ma'am*). *Your hono(u)r* is used in a court of law to address a judge:

That is the agreement, **your honor**, and on behalf of Mr. Downey, we would now withdraw all pending motions of demur that are now pending before the court.

(archives.cnn.com/2001/LAW/07/16/downey. probation.cnna/index.html, accessed January 22, 2007)

Sir and *madam* (*ma'am*) are found in face-to-face conversations where speakers are disparates and the subordinate wants to show a high degree of deference to the other. These expressions are also found in the salutation of highly formal letters. In the examples below, *sir* and *ma'am* are used by servers to address customers in a restaurant:

Have you been helped, **sir**?

(MICASE SVC999MX104)

And what did you want **ma'am**

(SBCSAE)

In the next example, *madam* is used to address a caller on a radio talk show:

I'm terribly sorry **madam**, I'm terribly sorry madam, you might die if you take this drug

(BNC HV1 447)

In the final example, the highly formulaic *Dear Sir(s)* begins a letter:

Dear Sirs,

   You ought to be aware of a potentially serious problem caused by a recurring leak ...

(ICE-GB W1B-016 102)

In personal letters, in contrast, people tend to address each other by first name, an indication that both writer and addressee are equals and that little social distance separates them.

Dear John,

   A day of hectic activity. Julie and I took Emily and her 2 boys who are aged 5 and nearly 3 swimming this morning ...

(ICE-GB W1B-008 034)

Social distance specifies the extent to which individuals have a close or a more distant relationship. Although the notions of social distance and power relationships are related – disparates, for instance, tend to be more socially distant from one another than equals – the categories are nevertheless distinct. While all communicants will be either equals or disparates, some may be **intimates** as well. Intimates are individuals between whom there is little social distance: children and parents, spouses, partners, close friends, and so forth. Intimates can be either equals or disparates. For instance, parents are higher on the power hierarchy than children; spouses could be either equals or disparates, depending upon whether a power imbalance exists between them. Whether individuals are intimates will affect the way they communicate as well. Close intimates will often use terms of endearment:

Oh **honey** I miss you

(SBCSAE)

How are you **my little-one**?

(ICE-GB W1B-001 043)

Come here **sweetheart**.

(BNC GYD 93)

Could I beg your indulgence, **my dear**?

(SBCSAE)

Their topics of conversation will vary too. Intimates are more likely to talk about family, health issues, and problems than non-intimates. The conversation below, for instance, would only occur between intimates, since it deals with very personal topics: familial problems, suicide, divorce and remarriage.

Speaker C: Is that why he changed his name because he was going to be picked on?

Speaker A: Yeah ... because of his name but also because just the kind of person he is; he's just a, he's a very unhappy kid

Speaker B: Well, Susan got remarried and they moved and all the stuff was happening

Speaker A: Then his father committed suicide

Speaker B: Yeah, so they figured this would be a good thing for him to
           kind of like have a new start for himself; he can go to his new
           school but it didn't work
Speaker A: He still got picked on

(SBCSAE)

As the social distance between speakers increases, the greater the requirement for polite usage of language: calling one's boss *sweetheart*, for instance, is likely to be perceived as highly inappropriate and impolite, unless the boss and employee know each other well and over time have developed a close relationship.

It is clear that the words people use and the topics they discuss are in large part determined by their social relationships: whether they are disparates, equals, or intimates. However, in many languages, these relationships affect the choice of second person pronouns as well: the so-called T/V distinction. This distinction is named after the pronouns *tu* and *vous* in French, which are used in, respectively, informal and formal contexts: *tu* when there is less social distance between speakers, *vous* when there is greater social distance. English, however, makes no such distinction: the pronoun *you* is used in all contexts, regardless of the power relationships existing between speakers or their social distance. At one time in its history, English did make the distinction. As Blake (1992: 536) notes, although usage was inconsistent, during the Middle English period, *thou* and *thee* were used to denote "intimacy or contempt," while *ye* and *you* "were neutral and polite." By early Modern English, the distinction was no longer made, making English one of the only Indo-European languages lacking an informal and formal second person pronoun.

Levels of impoliteness, face-threatening acts, and tact

While power relationships and social distance are important influences on levels of politeness that speakers of a language will use, an equally important consideration is the extent to which a speaker is willing to commit an FTA. If I have a guest over for dinner who is overstaying his welcome, I can simply say *You've been here long enough. Leave*! if I am unconcerned about producing an utterance that is highly impolite. In most circumstances, however, people will mitigate the directness of an utterance such as this, using strategies that convey their intentions but in ways that are more indirect: *I have to get up early for work tomorrow. Let's call it a night and get together again really soon.* The difference between this utterance and the one above is directly related to Geoffrey Leech's (1983) notion of "tact" as expressed through his tact maxim, one of six maxims that comprise his politeness principle.

Tact, according to Leech (1983: 109), has two polarities:

Negative: Minimize the cost to *h* [hearer]
Positive: Maximize the benefit to *h*

The tact maxim, in turn, applies to two of Searle's speech acts: directives, which attempt to get someone to do something (*I order you to ...*), and less commonly commissives, which commit the speaker to doing something (*I promise to ...*). Speech acts in each of these categories form a cline that

Leech describes as a cost–benefit scale. Thus, an imperative sentence such as *Peel these potatoes* violates the tact maxim and is (at least potentially) highly impolite, since the cost to the hearer of doing what this sentence requests is high and the benefit very low. In contrast, the imperative sentence *Have another sandwich* adheres to the tact maxim and is at the appropriate level of politeness: there is little cost to the hearer and considerable benefit.

Of course, context rather than the particular form of an utterance will ultimately determine where on the cost–benefit scale it will rank. For instance, if two people are working together to prepare a meal and one inquires *What should I do next*, it would be perfectly appropriate for the other person to reply *Peel the potatoes* without appearing to be too direct and impolite. But in communicating with one another, speakers do rely on a variety of strategies to mitigate the directness of their utterances:

(1) Directives can be mitigated by several expressions that help "soften" the imposition that the directive causes. These expressions include *please*:

Let's get started. Quiet **please**.

(MICASE LEL115JU090)

Sit down **please**, on your bottom.

(BNC F72 522)

Okay folks step right in the elevator **please**

(SBCSAE)

excuse me:

Excuse me you don't have a stapler like behind the desk that I could use?

(MICASE SVC999MX104)

and *thank you* (or its shortened equivalent *thanks*):

Thank you for not smoking.

What are the cheapest seat tickets? I suppose getting tickets for the Oxford game is going to be out of the question? **Thanks in advance** for any help, Andy K.

(BNC J1C 1089)

Both *excuse me* and *thank you* have additional uses beyond those given above. *Excuse me* is used in contexts where the speaker wishes to offer a kind of mild apology for some inconvenience he/she has caused:

Excuse me I've got a rather heavy cold.

(BNC FUU 116)

Oh sorry about that **excuse me**.

(MICASE LAB175SU026)

Thank you is somewhat pragmatically odd in a directive, since its typical use is to offer thanks for some act that has already been completed:

Yes, **thanks** very much for that information.

(BNC FMP 817)

But *thank you* in a directive anticipates that the addressee will actually do what the directive requests. Hence, the use of *in advance* in the expression *thanks in advance*.

(2) English has a formulaic yes/no question beginning with the modals *could* or *would* that is an alternative to equivalent imperative sentences and that is conventionally associated with polite requests.

> okay i'll give you a minute or two to fill out these forms for Deborah, and uh, then we'll get started. um okay uh guys **could you** pass them uh this way?
>
> > (MICASE LEL220JU071)

> **Could you** ring her back when you've got a moment?
>
> > (BNC AOF 257)

> **Would you** look at page forty-three?
>
> > (ICE-GB S1B-061 068)

To further mitigate the directives in these constructions, *please* can be added as well as certain kinds of adverbials, such as *possibly* or *perhaps*:

> Marilyn, **could you please** answer that?
>
> > (ICE-GB S1B-009 103)

> So **could you possibly** backdate it to Monday?
>
> > (BNC H50 12)

(3) Speakers can use constructions that are even more indirect in their intentions than the formulaic questions given above. They can go "off record," as Brown and Levinson (1987) note, by giving the hearer "hints" or "be[ing] vague or ambiguous" (p. 214) and therefore "invit[ing] conversational implicatures": additional meanings in their utterances that are not overtly stated. For instance, if one roommate asks another for help moving a couch and receives the reply *After I'm done with my coffee*, it would be possible a few minutes later for the roommate requesting the help to utter *Are you done with your coffee yet?* This question serves as a non-threatening way of reminding her roommate that it is time to move the couch.

The example below could be interpreted as a request to "shut the window" (Brown and Levinson 1987: 215) or turn on the heat, even though the utterance is a declarative sentence that could be a simple statement of fact.

It's cold in here.

The next example avoids directly ordering members of a swim team to attend practices by using a passive verb with no agent and a somewhat ambiguous lexical verb, *expected*:

Attendance is expected from all swimmers
> (Memo, YMCA, Cambridge, MA, January 24, 2007)

Does *expected* mean that swimmers have to attend practices? This is left purposely ambiguous to avoid the potentially face-threatening act of insisting that swimmers come to practice.

The example below was spoken by several waitpersons at a dinner reception to individuals mingling in groups eating hors d'œuvres and drinking wine as an indirect way of getting them to sit down for dinner.

You're invited to sit down for dinner.

The disparate power relationship between waitpersons and guests obviously led to the indirectness of the utterance.

Although the two examples below are considerably less indirect than the ones above, they nevertheless attempt to mitigate the imposition of asking a server to bring more wine, or a host to provide a guest with a cup of coffee:

We're going to need another bottle of wine.

(invented example)

I wouldn't mind some coffee actually

(ICE-GB S1A-045 214)

While hearers would undoubtedly correctly interpret the intentions of the above examples, the more indirect the utterance, the greater the likelihood the hearer will not infer its correct meaning. But for many speakers, this is a risk worth taking, since they would rather be misunderstood than produce a less than tactful utterance.

Other kinds of politeness

Tact is not the only consideration motivating polite language usage. There are additional motivating factors as well.

Gratitude for favors (either accepted or declined) and compliments are typically expressed through variations of the lexeme *thanks*. In the examples below, gratitude for favors accepted is conveyed through use of the verb *thank* as well as the expressives *thank you* and *thanks*, often intensified with adverbials such as *very much*:

i'd like to **thank** my wife Rachel for her kindness and her loving support and understanding of the husband that at eight o'clock goes back to his office five nights a week, and to Hannah and Jeremy.

(MICASE COL200MX133)

Thanks very much indeed for your call Nelly.

(BNC FX5 329)

Thank you Mister Smith for calling Pacific Bell

(SBCSAE)

If an offer of something is turned down, the addressee is placed in an awkward situation, since declining someone's generosity can lead to a potential FTA. In the examples below, the expressives *no thank you* or *no thanks* help mitigate the FTA by explicitly marking the addressee's gratitude. The speaker in the second example goes one step further by actually explaining why he is turning down an offer of orange juice.

Speaker A: Do you want any more cake?
Speaker B: No thank you.

(BNC JBB 591)

Speaker A: Juice, Warren?
Speaker B: No thanks, I can't drink OJ anymore

(SBCSAE)

Compliments can also be awkward for the addressee, since they work against Leech's (1983: 136–8) modesty maxim, which stipulates that speakers should "minimize praise of self; maximize dispraise of self." *Thank you* as well as other communicative strategies can be used to mitigate violations of this maxim. For instance, in the example below, the speaker thanks someone who had complimented his business practices. But in addition to simply offering thanks, he also attempts to minimize his accomplishments by describing the compliment as "too generous" and noting that other companies had done work similar to what he had done.

Thank you. Well, thank you for the kind remarks. I think they're perhaps, if anything too generous because er, I will remind you as I said of the, at least three hundred companies who are doing pretty effective work in this area

(BNC JNL 92)

In addition to modesty, Leech (1983) describes other communicative acts calling for various levels of politeness. His generosity maxim –"minimize benefit to self; maximize cost to self" (p. 133) – explains why while it is perfectly acceptable to lend something to someone (the first example below), if individuals want someone to lend something to them, then they have to use heavily mitigated forms such as *please* and *I promise I'll pay you back* at the end of the second example:

Well see, if you're desperate for a machine I'll **lend you** one something to do doodles on.

(BNC KB9 4640)

Do you think you can **lend me** some money, please, I promise I'll pay you back

(BNC KP6 2689)

Leech's (1983: 135) approbation maxim ("minimize dispraise of other; maximize praise of other") explains why when speakers and writers criticize the Iraq war, they often go out of their way to praise the individuals fighting the war and their families so that criticism of the war is not inadvertently linked to criticism of those fighting the war:

Decisions by President Bush offer little hope that our **brave soldiers** and Marines will face anything but more death, maiming and grief for their **loving families**.

(Letter to the Editor, *Arkansas Democrat-Gazette*, January 17, 2007)

"America's **honorable soldiers** and their families, and the security of our country, must not be jeopardized based on the false and unachievable hopes that if we stay just a little bit longer everything will work itself out in Iraq. The evidence is clear that that is not the case," [Representative George] Miller said.

(*San Francisco Chronicle*, November 29, 2006, p. A1)

In fact, praising the soldiers in Iraq is so important that then-Senator Barack Obama (Democrat, Illinois) was forced to apologize for making the statement below during a speech:

We now have spent $400 billion and have seen over 3,000 lives of the **bravest** young Americans **wasted**.

(February 11, 2007)

While Obama adheres to the Generosity Maxim by describing the soldiers as "the bravest young Americans," he simultaneously violates it by describing their efforts as "wasted."

Leech (1983) proposes other maxims of politeness, but his approach raises an important issue, summarized below in one of Brown and Levinson's (1987: 4) criticisms of Leech's maxims of politeness:

if we are permitted to invent a maxim for every regularity in language use, not only will we have an infinite number of maxims, but pragmatic theory will be too unconstrained to permit recognition of any counter-examples.

In other words, if one encounters examples that do not fit into existent maxims, one simply invents a new maxim. As noted in an earlier section, a similar criticism was leveled against Grice's four maxims of the cooperative principle.

Speaker variables

The discussion so far in this chapter has focused on a series of pragmatic principles – speech acts, the cooperative principle, and politeness – and how these principles determine how people speak in various communicative contexts. Language use of this nature is characterized by James Milroy and Lesley Milroy (1997: 50) as "*contextual style ... the speaker's relationship to the resources of language and of the situational context in which the speaker finds himself at different times.*" Other variation, however, is more inherent to speakers themselves. For instance, while the form *Could you please pass the salt* is more polite than *Pass the salt*, it is also the case that studies have shown that females tend to use polite linguistic forms more frequently than males. Gender is thus one of a number of speaker variables: particular characteristics of speakers that affect how they use language. Other speaker variables include geographic mobility, age, social class, ethnicity, education, and social networks. The study of speaker variables is the cornerstone of research done in sociolinguistics, an area of linguistics concerned with the study of social variation in language.

Although speaker variables appear to be mutually exclusive categories, they overlap considerably. While age and social class are not related, social class and education are more clearly connected, since the social class of which one is a member will very often determine the amount of education that individual receives. In addition, some of the variables are exceedingly difficult to define. Commenting on sociolinguistic treatments of gender, Cameron (1995: 15–16) remarks:

Whereas sociolinguistics would say that the way I use language reflects or marks my identity as a particular kind of social subject – I talk like a white middle-class woman because I am (already) a white middle-class woman – the critical account suggests language is one of the things that constitutes my identity as a particular kind of subject. Sociolinguistics says that how you act depends on who you are; critical theory says that who you are (and are taken to be) depends on how you act.

In other words, do women speak more politely because they are female, or does polite language usage define one as a female? In addition, gender is not simply a biological phenomenon; it is an ideology as well that is tied in very closely with sexual identity: whether one is heterosexual, gay, lesbian, bisexual, or transgendered. Thus, when sociolinguists make claims about how males and females use language, it is important to realize that their conclusions reflect a significant simplification of the effect of gender on language usage.

But despite this simplification, and the complexity inherent in speaker variables, it is nevertheless the case that how individuals speak is directly influenced by the speaker variables that define them. To provide concrete examples of the role that speaker variables play in language usage, this section examines how they affect the speaking styles of two hypothetical individuals: Michael A., an 18-year-old Caucasian male living in Quincy, Massachusetts, and Teresa B., a 42-year-old African-American woman living in Atlanta, Georgia.

Michael A.

Michael A. has lived his entire life in Quincy, a suburb immediately south of Dorchester, one of the many neighborhoods of Boston. His parents moved to Quincy in the late 1970s from the Charlestown neighborhood of Boston during a period when there was considerable white flight from Boston to many of the communities on the south shore. Although Michael A. plans to apply to a local community college when he graduates from high school, neither his parents nor his older siblings attended college. Both of Michael's parents are second-generation children of Irish immigrants to Boston. His father is an electrician and his mother works for the state of Massachusetts as a clerk in a municipal court. Michael A. speaks with what locals would describe as a Boston accent. For instance, his speech is **non-rhotic**: he does not consistently pronounce **post-vocalic** /r/, the sound /r/ preceded by a vowel in the same syllable. As a result, he would typically pronounce a word such as *never* as /nɛvə/ rather than /nɛvɝ/ because the final syllable of this word contains the vowel /ə/ (commonly referred to as **schwa**); in this context, the following /r/ can be optionally deleted.

Michael A.'s speech is /r/-less because of the region of the country in which he resides and the social class of which he is a member. This pronunciation is confined to the eastern seaboard of the United States primarily for historical reasons. The Massachusetts area was one of the earliest parts of the United States to be colonized, and the original colonists brought with them their speech patterns, in this case the omission of post-vocalic /r/. Ironically, in Modern British English, Michael A.'s pronunciation of *never* is Standard British English, so-called **RP (received pronunciation)**. In the United States, however, /r/-less speech patterns have an entirely different status. As Labov documents in his now classic study "The Social Stratification of (r) in New York City Department Stores," conducted in 1962 (see Labov 1972), there is a direct correlation between a speaker's social class and his or her pronunciation of post-vocalic /r/.

Labov reached this conclusion by eliciting the pronunciation of post-vocalic /r/ from employees working in three different department stores in New York City having various levels of prestige: Saks Fifth Avenue (highest prestige), Macy's (middle-level prestige), and S. Klein (lowest prestige). Labov determined these rankings by examining, for instance, the costs of comparable items in the stores, and the targeted audience of advertisements the stores ran in local New York newspapers. Interviewers then went to the stores and asked clerks to direct them to a floor – always the fourth floor – on which a particular item could be found. The interviewer made note of the clerk's pronunciation of *fourth* in two contexts: casual style (the response given to the interviewer's first request for the floor on which the item could be found) and careful style (when the interviewer's initial request was followed by "Excuse me?," forcing the clerk to give a more deliberate pronunciation). Labov (1972: 51) found a "clear and consistent stratification of (r) in the three stores" with the highest incidence of post-vocalic /r/ in Saks (the high-prestige store) and the lowest incidence in S. Klein. By analogy, Labov's findings can be extrapolated to Boston, where omission of post-vocalic /r/ is a **social marker**: a usage of language (in this case a specific pronunciation) that identifies one as being a member of a particular social class. In Boston (and southeastern Massachusetts in general), /r/-less speech patterns are associated with the working class. Therefore, post-vocalic /r/ is more likely to be absent in Michael A.'s speech than in the speech of an individual born and raised in southeastern Massachusetts who is a member of, say, the middle class. Ironically, at one time, Michael A.'s pronunciation was associated with upper-class speech. The Boston Brahmins, descendants of the former British colonizers of Massachusetts, took great pride in their British accents. But this class of individuals has long died out in Boston as has the positive attitude towards British speech patterns in general, a trend that Labov (1972: 64) also documents in New York City, where the "Anglophile tradition" began declining following World War II.

Because of his age, Michael A. also speaks differently than his parents. Although he is familiar with many regional vocabulary items – *tonic* meaning 'soft drink' or *spa* used to refer to a convenience store – he does not actually use these expressions, since he perceives them as words used mainly by "older people." Age is an important social variable for tracking language change or studying the phenomenon of **apparent time**: linguistic constructions that pattern according to a speaker's age. In her work with the *Dictionary of American Regional English* (DARE), Hall (2004: 105) found that age was "the most distinctive social variable" in determining a speaker's use of regional vocabulary items, "since they reflect basic changes in our culture." For Michael A., older vocabulary items hark back to an earlier era, not the contemporary era in which he lives. Michael A.'s desire to be "current" is also reflected in the fact that he and other younger speakers are more likely to use **slang** than older speakers. Although slang has many popular definitions, in linguistics it is regarded as a kind of in-group language: the jazz age of the 1930s and 1940s popularized slang such as *cool* and *hip*; in the 1960s, expressions such as *groovy*, *far out*, and *bummer* permeated the culture of "hippies" and "flower children." Michael A. and his friends draw their vocabulary from hip-hop culture, which in music and movies has contributed such words as *bling bling* (noun 'elaborate jewelry'), *def* (adjective 'excellent'), and *catch a case* (verb 'get arrested') (*The Rap Dictionary*, www.rapdict.org/Main_Page). Slang can be very transitory: it is language of the moment and tends to disappear as its users move from adolescence to adulthood.

Michael A.'s use of language is also a consequence of his gender. While he uses *like* as a **discourse marker**, he does so less frequently than females his age do. The word *like* has many uses in English: it can be a verb, meaning 'enjoy' or 'be fond of' (*I like chocolate brownies*; *I like classes in English literature*); it can also be a preposition, meaning 'similar to' (*Many people like my father retire early*). As a discourse marker, however, *like* does not have a clearly identifiable meaning but a particular function in the context in which it is used. In the example below, the frequent use of *like* serves "to signal the sequential relationship between units of discourse" (D'Arcy 2007: 394):

to kids the only consequence **like** of stealing is getting, what they're stealing. **like** there's no **like** punishment and for the kid **like**, shooting that girl to him he was **like**, repaying her for hitting him cuz i think that was what the thing was ...

(MICASE DIS115JU087)

This use of *like* is one of four cases of what D'Arcy (2007: 392) terms "vernacular" uses of *like* – instances of *like* whose uses are more restricted than the use of *like* as a verb meaning 'enjoy,' which all speakers of English would use. Although both males and females use *like* as a discourse marker, it is more commonly found in the speech of females than males (D'Arcy 2007: 396), and although it occurs more frequently in the speech of individuals below 20, older speakers (even those as old as 80) use it too (D'Arcy 2007: 402). And this use of *like* has global reach, extending beyond North America to countries such as Ireland and England. For instance, Andersen (2001) found that in the Corpus of London Teenage English (COLT), the heaviest use of *like* occurred among higher-class adolescents. And most sources discussing *like* note its predominance among whites rather than other racial groups.

What these findings illustrate is that very often no one speaker variable can adequately explain the use of a particular linguistic item: one variable works hand in hand with another. But despite the overlapping nature of the variables, some variables, such as ethnicity, are so powerful that they alone can have a significant effect on language usage – a point that will be pursued in greater detail in the next section.

Teresa B.

Teresa B. lives in Atlanta, Georgia. Unlike most cities in the United States, the majority of residents in Atlanta (61 percent) are, according to 2000 census figures, of African-American origin. While Atlanta has many of the problems associated with most urban areas in the United States – 21 percent of its population lives under the poverty level and 39 percent of households are headed by a single female – it has a range of social classes and a well-established African-American middle class, of which Teresa B. is a member. Although neither of her parents went to college, they were able to open their own business, move out of a poor inner-city area of Atlanta, and thus provide themselves and their daughter (their only child) with a comfortable middle-class existence. Teresa B. went to good public schools and attended Emory University, where she received an accounting degree and ultimately an MBA. She speaks a variety of English that is commonly referred to as **General American (GA)**.

General American is an accent that does not associate an individual with a particular region of the United States, ethnic group, or social class. In the movie *American Tongues*, Ramona Lenny defines this accent by describing why people like her had to speak it when they recorded numbers to be used in directory assistance calls:

They [telephone company officials] were looking for generic speech. Or some people call it homogenized speech. Speech that would float in any part of the country and didn't sound like it came from somewhere in particular, perhaps the voice from nowhere.

(Ramona Lenny, American Tongues)

To sound as though they come "from nowhere," speakers of General American must, for instance, make sure that their speech contains post-vocalic /r/, so that they do not sound as though they come from the eastern seaboard, and they must use the diphthong /aɪ/ in words such as *fight* and *write* rather than a lengthened /aː/ (equivalent to the first vowel in *father*), so that they do not sound as though they speak some variety of southern American English. General American is simply a way of speaking that avoids identifying the speaker with speech patterns that are stigmatized.

As a working professional, Teresa B. is in contact with many other middle-class working professionals, both African-American and white. Many of her white co-workers frequently comment on how "articulate" her speech is – a kind of coded language indicating that these individuals are conscious of the fact that Teresa B. does not speak African American Vernacular English (AAVE) and that African-Americans are, in general, lacking of good verbal skills: "When whites use the word [*articulate*] in reference to blacks," Clemetson (2007) comments, "it often carries a subtext of amazement, even bewilderment. It is similar to praising a female executive or politician by calling her 'tough' or 'a rational decision-maker.'" Teresa B. is acutely aware of this attitude towards her, the way that she speaks, and AAVE in general.

Among linguists, the linguistic status of AAVE is in dispute. Some see it as having creole origins: the product of contact between slaves speaking mutually unintelligible West African languages and slave owners and traders speaking various kinds of English. Others, in contrast, believe that AAVE is simply a dialect of English resulting from contact between slaves and slave owners in the southern part of the United States. Among the public, AAVE has been controversial and polarizing, especially since the mid 1990s as a result of the Ebonics controversy. This controversy resulted in 1996 after the Oakland, California School Board declared that AAVE, which they termed "Ebonics," was a separate language, and should therefore be taught in Oakland schools both to make students speaking it aware of its structure and to help them learn Standard English. This decision created a huge uproar among educators, politicians, and journalists to the point that the Oakland School Board had to repudiate the resolution.

To understand the complex mix of attitudes and contexts that Teresa B. must navigate when she speaks, it is useful to invoke the notion of social networks. Milroy and Gordon (2003: 117) characterize social networks as "the aggregate of relationships contracted with others, a boundless web of ties which reaches out through social and geographical space linking many individuals, sometimes remotely." Teresa B. and Michael A. have very different social networks. Michael A.'s network is relatively closed and is confined primarily to his family, friends, neighbors, and co-workers – people with whom he interacts daily. Teresa A. has a larger circle of individuals with whom she interacts on a much less intimate basis: she occasionally socializes with her work colleagues, and while she resides in the city in which she was born, she no longer lives in the neighborhood in which she was raised. She returns home frequently for visits with family and friends but does not have the immediate proximal ties to them that Michael A. does. She also makes frequent business trips to many cities around the United States, further expanding the people with whom she interacts and her geographical mobility.

Because Teresa B. has to communicate with individuals in many different contexts, she is quite adept at **style shifting**: adjusting the way that she speaks according to the social context in which she is communicating. But she has paid a price for this linguistic dexterity. As an African-American, she has had to deal with the controversial status of AAVE both within the African-American community and the larger society in general. Among African-Americans, varying attitudes toward AAVE can be found. Rickford (2004: 199) comments that while AAVE was viewed with great pride within the African-American community from the 1960s to the late 1990s, following the Ebonics controversy (described earlier in this section), attitudes toward AAVE became much more negative. For instance, the African-American comedian Bill Cosby has made very negative comments about AAVE, claiming, as Dyson (2005: 72) quotes him, that speakers of AAVE "can't speak English" and "[do not] want to speak English." Dyson (2005: 72) himself has a very high opinion of AAVE, arguing that it "captures the beautiful cadences, sensuous tones, kinetic rhythms, forensic articulations, and idiosyncrasies of expression that form the black vernacular voice."

Teresa B. has been aware of her very conflicted linguistic identity from a very young age, but as she gained more education and increasing exposure to numerous different social groups, she has become acutely aware of stylistic variation – how different contexts require different uses of language – and quite adept at style shifting. Bell (1984: 145) describes stylistic variation as a type of intra-speaker variation because it "denotes differences within the speech of a single speaker" rather than differences among speakers. He proposes a model of audience design to explain stylistic variation, a model consisting of the following individuals: speaker, addressee, auditor, overhearer, or eavesdropper.

When speakers style-shift, Bell (1984: 160) claims, they are responding primarily to addressees, individuals whom they are directly addressing and who are full participants in the conversation. Secondary participants include auditors, people who are not being directly addressed but are full participants; overhearers, people who are known by the speaker but not participants; and eavesdroppers, who are neither known nor participants. Other influences on style shifting include the topics under discussion and the particular setting in which communication takes place. Thus, when Teresa B. gives a report during a business meeting at the company where she works, she shifts her style primarily in response to her department manager, her immediate supervisor; secondarily to her co-workers; and minimally (if at all) to the department secretary taking minutes, an individual playing no role at the meeting. The setting – a meeting – and the topic (a formal report) would cause Teresa to elevate the formality of her speech even more than if she were speaking one-on-one with her supervisor.

Stylistic variation is closely related to social variation, and when speakers style-shift they are more likely to move up on the scale of formality than down: Michael A. is more likely to insert post-vocalic /r/ in his speech in more formal contexts; if Teresa B. were to travel to Boston, she would not be likely to delete post-vocalic /r/ if she found herself in the company of people whose speech lacked post-vocalic /r/. Allan Bell (1984: 152) comments that this "pattern is remarkable in its consistency, appearing in study after study."

Summary

Communication is not simply the product of decoding the words in a sentence or utterance and then determining their meaning. Any parent knows that when a child utters *Dad, I'm still hungry* after finishing a snack, the child is not simply making a declarative statement: he is requesting more food. The parent reaches this conclusion on the basis of information derived from the social context itself, not simply the individual words of the utterance. And to correctly interpret the meaning of this utterance, the parent has to understand the illocutionary force of the child's utterance: the child's intentions in uttering the sentence. In determining that the child is issuing a directive, the parent draws upon a number of contextual clues, particularly the fact that he has heard this very same utterance on many occasions after his son has completed eating a snack.

Self-study activities

1. Match the construction in the left-hand column with the speech act with which it is associated in the right-hand column.

   (1) The English language originated in England
   (2) I promise to do the work
   (3) I hereby declare the meeting open
   (4) Don't take too long
   (5) I'm sorry I broke the glass

   a. Assertive/Representative
   b. Directive
   c. Commissive
   d. Declaration
   e. Expressive

2. Distinguish the grammatical meaning of *I wouldn't mind another glass of wine* from its pragmatic meaning. In discussing the pragmatic meaning of the statement, briefly describe a context in which the statement would be likely to occur.

3. Which expressions in the conversation below are utterances? Which are grammatically well formed sentences? Explain your choices.

   Speaker A: I really like chocolate ice cream.
   Speaker B: Me too. My second favorite flavor is vanilla.
   Speaker A: I don't care for vanilla. Too tasteless, in my opinion.
   Speaker B: Really? I think it has great taste.

4. Discuss whether the speech acts listed below would be direct or indirect.

   (1) A teacher says to her students: "Please leave your papers on my desk."
   (2) One person saying to another sitting next to an open door leading to the backyard of a house: "Lots of mosquitoes are getting into the house."
   (3) A son says to his mother: "I'll take out the garbage later."
   (4) A guest at a dinner party says to another guest during dinner, "Could you please pass the butter?"

5. Two speakers (Fred and Hazel) are gossiping about a third person (Christine). Fred says: "Christine is always late for work. I think she's going to get fired. She's a totally irresponsible worker." Noticing that Christine is approaching and that Fred doesn't realize this, Hazel comments: "Do you think it will rain later today?"

   (a) Which of the maxims of the cooperative principle (quantity, relation, manner, and quality) has Hazel violated?
   (b) What is the conversational implicature of this violation? That is, what additional information is Fred likely to read into Hazel's utterance?

6. Discuss how the conventions of formal written English require writers to adhere to Grice's maxims of the cooperative principle.

7. In the conversation below, a library patron has brought to the circulation desk in a library newspapers that were addressed to the library and had been taken outside the library against library policy. Discuss the extent to which the patron and library worker follow or do not follow Leech's (1983) principles of politeness.

   Library Patron: I found these newspapers in the administration building. They're addressed to the library, so I thought they must be yours.
   Library Worker: Well, if you have the time, you could take them up to the 4th floor, or you could just leave them here.
   Library Patron: You can throw them out for all I care.

8. A father says to his child: "Put your toys away now!"
   (a) Would the child and father be equals or disparates?
   (b) Has the father violated any of the maxims of the politeness principle?

9. Why are younger speakers more likely to use slang than older speakers?

Further reading

See J. L. Austin's *How to Do Things with Words* (Oxford University Press, 1962) for an early discussion of the notion of pragmatic vs. grammatical meaning. A description of speech act theory can be found in J. Searle, *Expression and Meaning* (Cambridge University Press, 1979). The cooperative principle is outlined in H. P. Grice, *Studies in the Way of Words* (Cambridge, MA: Harvard University Press, 1989). For a general overview of the field of pragmatics, see S. Levinson, *Pragmatics* (Cambridge University Press, 1983). Two differing perspectives on politeness are presented in P. Brown and S. Levinson, *Politeness: Some Universals in Language Usage* (Cambridge University Press, 1987) and G. N. Leech, *Principles of Pragmatics* (London: Longman, 1983). A discussion of social variables and other issues from a sociolinguistic perspective can be found in many of the chapters in F. Coulmas, ed., *The Handbook of Sociolinguistics* (Oxford and Cambridge, MA: Blackwell Publishers, 1998).

CHAPTER PREVIEW

The previous chapter described how the social context in which communication takes place affects the form and usage of the words and sentences that people speak and write. This chapter focuses on a different kind of context, the linguistic context, and how it also affects the way that language is structured and used. When speakers or writers create a **text**, the linguistic resources that they use – where words are placed in a sentence, for instance, or how what they say or write is organized – are very dependent upon a number of considerations. For instance, if two individuals are engaging in a casual conversation, what they say will be divided into **speaker turns:** one person will speak, followed by another, with each person observing conventions for how speakers take turns speaking when they converse.

Introduction

The study of the effects of the linguistic context on language use is tied very closely to the notion of text. While most theorists would agree that a text is a structure larger than a sentence, the specifics of exactly how a text should be defined is very "theory-dependent" (Titscher *et al.* 2000: 20). For discourse analysts, a text is both a linguistic and sociocultural construct. Thus, in the introductory section of *The Handbook of Discourse Analysis*, the editors describe a text (or a discourse, as they call it) in both linguistic and non-linguistic terms as being "anything beyond the sentence ... [that involves] language use, and ... [that is the product of] a broader range of social practice that includes nonlinguistic and non-specific instances of language" (Schiffrin, Tannen, and Hamilton 2003: 1). Within this framework, a newspaper article, for instance, is not just a collection of sentences structured and used in a way consistent with the standards of journalistic English, but the result of social practices inherent within the media in general. The cognitive psychologists Teun van Dijk and Walter Kintsch do not consider the social dimension of texts at all in their classic book *Strategies of Discourse Comprehension* (1983). Instead, they define a text in purely cognitive terms as containing a microstructure and a macrostructure: "the local structure of a text" vs. its "global structure" (Kintsch 1998: 50). From this perspective, a newspaper article contains a series of sentences tied together by various linguistic devices (its microstructure) that are part of a larger structure containing a headline, lead, and so forth (its macrostructure). And interpreting a newspaper article requires readers to draw upon their knowledge of what constitutes a newspaper article and how sentences are structured in such articles.

The linguists Michael A. K. Halliday and Ruqaiya Hasan posit similar notions of text to van Dijk and Kintsch's, but take a functional rather than a cognitive approach in their characterization of texts. For Halliday and Hasan (1985: 52), a text is a functional unit because it represents "language that is doing something in some context, as opposed to isolated words or sentences." To capture the functional nature of texts, they propose that texts have two main characteristics: unity of structure and unity of texture. Unity of structure is closely associated with the notion of register. A newspaper article is part of the more general register of journalistic English, which contains many sub-registers, such as news reportage, sports reportage, editorials, and features. Each of these sub-registers contains texts with a similar overall structure and a set of linguistic features (e.g. a certain kind of vocabulary or particular grammatical constructions) that may be unique to the register or used differently in the register than in other registers. As noted above, news reportage contains a headline, lead, and so forth, and (additionally) numerous linguistic constructions, such as the frequent use of proper nouns (the names of people discussed in news stories) and relatively short sentences, since newspapers have to appeal to a wide audience and must therefore avoid the kinds of complex structures found in other registers, such as academic prose.

Texts have texture because they contain numerous linguistic markers establishing what Halliday and Hasan (1985: 73) refer to as a "tie": some linguistic marker that links two parts of a text together. For instance, the short excerpt below, taken from a spontaneous conversation, contains an initial mention of *book* with various ties back to it as the text unfolds: two instances of *books* as well as two instances of the third person pronoun *them*.

yeah, i think that it's good practice to just kinda write questions in a **book** i always mark my **books** i mean it's a shame if you plan on selling **them** back, you know right but i always write in my **books** and keep **them** as long as i want

(MICASE ADV700JU047)

Links such as these create cohesion and ultimately coherence: a text with various cohesive ties that is clear and meaningful. Cohesion alone does not necessarily result in coherence. The second sentence in the example below contains a marker of cohesion – *consequently* – that indicates that the second sentence is a logical consequence of the first.

It is quite cold out today. Consequently, I don't plan to wear a warm jacket.

However, this short sequence is not coherent because the second sentence is actually not a logical consequence of the first: the second sentence would be logically more sound if the speaker had said that he planned to wear a warm jacket. What this example illustrates is that cohesion does not necessarily produce coherence, unless the cohesive link is used to mark a relationship that already exists in the text.

Register or genre?

Although it is common to call journalistic English a *register* and press reportage a *sub-register*, other terms, such as *genre* and *sub-genre*, are commonly used too. While these terms are often used interchangeably, the inconsistent use of them (and other terms such as *text type*) has created, as Lee (2001) notes, considerable confusion, largely because how the terms are defined varies by theory and academic discipline: a genre, for instance, means something quite different to a literary theorist than to a linguist. For Lee (2001: 46), a *register* is defined by "lexico-grammatical and discoursal-semantic patterns associated with situations (i.e. linguistic patterns)," while a *genre* consists of texts that can be classified into "culturally-recognisable categories." On the one hand, a classroom discussion is a register because texts created within this register have a particular hierarchical structure and contain a set of linguistic constructions typically associated with the register. Because participants in this register engage in the Socratic method, instructors typically ask questions (*What did the author mean in section 3?*) that students answer. If students answer correctly, instructors say so and move on to the next question; if they answer incorrectly, different instructors employ different strategies (*Not exactly. Does anyone else have an answer?*). This text structure is repeated over and over again in a class, resulting in a set of linguistic structures (e.g.

questions) that occur more commonly in this genre than in other types of spoken registers. On the other hand, a classroom discussion is also a genre: while teachers and students converse with one another in many cultural contexts (e.g. the United States, Great Britain), in other contexts they do not, since in many educational systems students and teachers do not engage in dialogues: teachers merely lecture. Since the goal in this section is to discuss unity of structure from a purely linguistic perspective, the term *register* will be used throughout.

Registers also differ, as Lee (2001: 48) notes, in terms of their specificity, and comparison of varying systems for categorizing registers reveals numerous differences. As the diagram below illustrates, there is a cline from more generally defined registers (e.g. classroom discourse) to more specific instantiations of the register (e.g. classroom discussions, study groups, and student/teacher conferences):

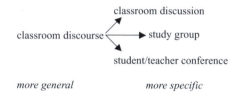

more general　　　　　　*more specific*

Thus, a classroom discussion can be regarded as a sub-register of the more general register of classroom discourse. The notion of sub-register is very important because research has shown that some registers can be quite different from one another. For instance, Biber (1988: 171) found that the various sub-registers of academic writing (natural sciences, medicine, mathematics, etc.) exhibited considerable linguistic differences.

Because many corpora aim to include as many different registers as possible, different corpora will contain different registers as well as different systems for classifying registers. For instance, the International Corpus of English (ICE) and British National Corpus (BNC) classify academic writing in somewhat different ways (sub-registers are in parentheses):

ICE:　Written texts→printed→informational→learned (humanities, social sciences, natural sciences, technology)

(Nelson 1996: 30)

BNC:　Written texts→academic prose→(humanities/arts, medicine, natural sciences, politics/law/education, social and behavioral sciences, technology/computing/engineering) (Lee's (2001: 57) reclassification of this register, which differs from the original BNC system of classification)

The ICE system makes more overt distinctions than the BNC system, for instance classifying academic writing as printed and informational, categories absent in the BNC system. The BNC includes many more sub-registers than ICE. While the differences may appear superficial, they reflect at a deeper level different conceptions of what the register of academic writing is like and how it differs from other systems. In the ICE system, emphasis is placed on differences among the written registers: printed writing is distinguished from non-printed writing (such as personal letters) and informational writing from instructional, persuasive, and creative writing. In the BNC system, the whole register is more broadly conceived, with a greater number of sub-registers included within the register of academic prose. Of course, there is a certain sense of artificiality to both systems of classification, since the sub-registers are not necessarily discrete: much work in linguistics, for instance, could be classified as falling in both the humanities and social sciences. Nevertheless, such systems are useful for studying how differing uses of language lead to differences in the structure of texts.

Spoken and written registers

Spoken and written registers have been traditionally regarded as distinct, since speech is produced under very different circumstances than writing. For instance, much speech, particularly spontaneous dialogue, is not pre-planned. Although some writing is also not pre-planned (e.g. notes, email messages), more formal kinds of writing are heavily planned and often go through multiple drafts. Much speech is immediate: individuals conversing with one another are together, allowing each speaker to seek clarifications, for instance, if something said is unclear. Writing is more distant: the needs of the audience to whom the writing is directed have to be anticipated by the writer, and once the reader receives the text there is no way for him or her to engage with the author if something is not clear. If all spoken and written registers are considered together, however, one finds, as Biber (1988) convincingly demonstrates in his book *Variation Across Speech and Writing*, that there is a continuum between speech and writing: some written registers, such as fiction, share many features with spoken registers; some spoken registers, such as panel discussions, share many features associated with written registers.

Biber (1988) reached this conclusion by first using a statistical test, factor analysis, to determine which linguistic constructions tended to co-occur in two corpora of spoken and written British English: the London–Lund Corpus of spoken British English and the London–Oslo–Bergen (LOB) Corpus of written British English. Biber (1988: 13) conducted this analysis in the belief that if particular linguistic constructions co-occurred, they were serving similar linguistic functions: that the co-occurrence together of, say, passive verbs and **nominalizations** (i.e. verbs such as *create* converted into abstract nouns such as *creation*) was not coincidental but an indication that these two constructions (and others) were serving a similar function. After examining the co-occurrence patterns of sixty-seven different linguistic items, Biber (1988: 9) created six textual dimensions, which specify "continuums of variation rather than discrete poles." Biber (ibid.: 110) found that nominalizations (and nouns in general) were linked to texts associated with Informational Production on Dimension 1 and Explicit Reference on Dimension 3 below. Passive verbs were found in texts with features clustering around the Abstract Information position on Dimension 5.

Dimension 1: Involved vs. Informational Production
Dimension 3: Explicit vs. Situation-Dependent Reference
Dimension 5: Abstract vs. Non-Abstract Information

Registers associated with texts illustrating information production, exhibiting explicit reference, and containing abstract information include official documents, professional letters, press reviews, and academic prose. These distributions make perfect sense if registers are viewed, as Halliday and Hasan suggest (see above), as contexts in which language is doing something. One function of the passive, for instance, is to place emphasis on what is being done rather than on who is doing it – a communicative goal that all of the above registers share. The example below, taken from a university memorandum outlining faculty responsibilities, contains an agentless passive (*are required*), a passive in which the doer of the action is omitted, because the focus is on who is responsible for providing a syllabus, not on who is setting the requirements:

Faculty members **are required** to provide a syllabus for each course that they teach.

(Memorandum, *Minimum Faculty Responsibilities*,
University of Massachusetts, Boston)

The next example, taken from the same memo, contains four nominalizations. Texts that are highly informational, Biber (1988: 104–8) comments, are highly nominal. Thus, the expression *have the obligation* is used rather than the verbal equivalent *are obligated*.

Faculty members have the **obligation** to restrict the **administration** of final **examinations** to the official **examination** period

Biber (1988) provides many additional examples of linguistic constructions associated with the dimensions above as well as the three other dimensions. For instance, casual conversation is on the Involved rather than the Informational end of Dimension 1, primarily because when people engage in conversation their goal is generally not to exchange information but to engage with one another. Therefore, they will use linguistic constructions, such as *I* and *you*, that enable them to achieve this communicative goal.

Unity of structure

In their discussion of the structure of registers, Halliday and Hasan (1985: 39–40) distinguish **closed registers**, which have a very fixed hierarchical structure, from **open registers**, which have a looser hierarchical structure. A service encounter, for instance, has an almost stereotypical structure. When people buy something from someone, such as lunch meat at a delicatessen, both sellers and buyers go through the same routine every time. The seller typically begins with a greeting followed by something like *What can I get you?* The buyer, in turn, will respond *I'd like...* After the seller has filled the buyer's order, he or she will say *Will there be anything else?* If the answer is yes, the seller will repeat the previous routine; if the answer is no, the text will move towards closure, with the seller saying

That will be [gives cost] followed by, for instance, some kind of salutation. The language may vary from what is given above, but the point is that speakers know the routine – it is a kind of ritual – and go through each stage of it every time this type of business transaction takes place.

Spontaneous dialogues, in contrast, are one of the more loosely organized registers. However, they do have structure, as Halliday and Hasan (1985: 40) note: they are "never totally open-ended ... [but possess] strategies and styles of meaning." Speakers can, for instance, change topics rather suddenly, or overlap their speech with the speech of those with whom they are communicating. But this does not mean that conversation is without structure: spontaneous dialogues have a flexible but discernible hierarchical structure, and conventions for determining how and when speakers take turns speaking.

To illustrate how registers vary in unity of structure, this section describes two kinds of spoken texts – spontaneous dialogues and telephone conversations – and one sub-register of journalistic prose: press reportage.

Spoken registers

Because speech is the primary mode of communication, it is worth investigating in detail some of the major spoken registers existing in English. Figure 4.1 lists different types of spoken registers as they are classified in the International Corpus of English (ICE).

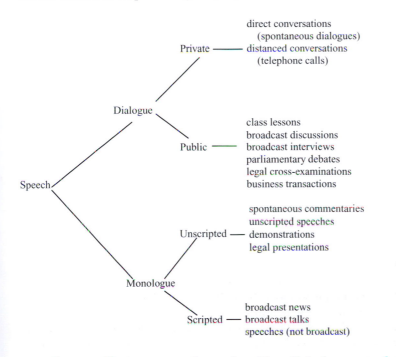

FIGURE 4.1
Spoken registers in the International Corpus of English (adapted from Nelson 1996: 29).

As Figure 1 illustrates, speech can be either dialogic or monologic. If speech is dialogic, it will involve two or more speakers conversing privately – over dinner in someone's home, for instance – or publicly, e.g.

as participants in an interview on a radio or television broadcast. Interestingly, while telephone calls are classified as private, the use of cell (mobile) phones outside the home or work place has made such calls semi-public, a change in the status of telephone calls since the ICE categories were created in the early 1990s. If speech is monologic, in contrast, it will involve a single individual speaking extemporaneously or from a prepared script. A lawyer giving a final statement at the end of a court trial, for instance, may work from notes but on the whole speaks spontaneously. On the other hand, when an individual gives a formal speech, he or she will simply read from a prepared text and may, in fact, produce a text differing little from a formal written paper.

The differing types of speech in Figure 4.1 do not exhaust the types of spoken texts that exist in English, nor does the figure provide the only way that spoken English can be categorized. Messages left on telephone answering machines are not included, and other typologies of text classification (such as Lee's (2001: 57) system for the British National Corpus) do not include, for instance, the private/public distinction. In addition, while the ICE system draws a clear line between dialogic and monologic speech, some of the registers are mixed. For instance, broadcast news includes scripted monologic speech, as when the news is read from a prepared text, and spontaneous dialogic speech, as when a newsperson conducts an interview with another individual. Nevertheless, the categories do reveal factors that directly influence how spoken texts are structured, a point that will be illustrated through the analysis of a very common type of spoken text: spontaneous dialogues, which includes face-to-face conversations and telephone calls.

Spontaneous dialogues.   Although linguists of all theoretical persuasions have studied the structure of conversation, some of the most significant research has been conducted by sociologists and ethnographers doing research in **conversation analysis**. In one of the earliest works on the structure of conversation, "A Simplest Systematics for the Organization of Turn-Taking for Conversation" (1974), Harvey Sacks, Emanuel A. Schegloff, and Gail Jefferson provide one of the first detailed discussions of the systematic nature of face-to-face conversations, positing the notion of speaker turn and describing how speakers engage in **turn taking** when they converse.

Because conversation analysis has a strong empirical basis, all analyses are based on transcriptions of recorded speech. As soon as one sets out to transcribe speech, it becomes necessary to develop a system of transcription. The excerpt below was taken from a face-to-face conversation in the Santa Barbara Corpus of Spoken American English (SBCSAE) and annotated with markup used in spoken texts included in the International Corpus of English (ICE), of which the SBCSAE is a part. Although many different transcription systems exist, most capture the basic elements of speech annotated in the conversation below. For instance, all systems divide conversations into speaker turns and have some way of indicating who is speaking when. In the example below, the symbols <$A> and <$B> distinguish speaker A's contributions from speaker B's:

<$A> <#> God I said I wasn't gonna do this anymore <,,> <#> Stay up late <,,> <#> Kinda defeats the purpose of getting up in the morning <,,>
<$B> <#> I know <,> <#> And it's a hard habit to break

The ICE system uses the symbol <#> to divide what speakers say into text units, which correspond roughly to the notion of utterance (meaningful units of language) introduced in Chapter 3. Although many systems do not annotate any features of intonation, short and long pauses are marked by <,> and <,,>, respectively, in the ICE system. ICE texts contain other types of annotation – for instance, ways to mark **overlapping speech** (two or more people speaking simultaneously) – but the general problem with annotation is that it greatly reduces the readability of a spoken text. Therefore, in the sections below, annotation will either be presented selectively or changed in a manner that enhances readability. Table 4.1 contains a definition of the annotation used in this section.

Table 4.1. Select annotation used for spoken texts in the International Corpus of English (ICE) (adapted from Nelson 2002)	
<$A>, <$B>, *etc.*	Speaker IDs: mark the beginning of a speaker turn
<#>	Text unit: delineates the beginning of a meaningful unit of language (see **utterance**)
<O>...</O>	Untranscribed text: encloses extralinguistic information (e.g. a speaker clearing his/her throat)
<?>...<?>	Uncertain transcription: transcriber is uncertain about what speaker said
<>...</.>	Incomplete word: speaker utters only part of a word
<[>...</[>	Overlapping string: start and end of entire sequence of overlapping speech
<[>...</[>	Overlapping string set: start and end of each speaker's part of an overlapping string
<>	Short pause: one syllable in length
<,>	Long pause: more than one syllable in length
<&>...</&>	Editorial comment: commentary by transcriber
<@>...</@>	Changed name or word: new name or word for reasons of privacy
<unclear>...</unclear>	Unclear word(s): transcriber cannot understand what speaker has said

In their discussion of how individuals take turns speaking in conversations, Sacks, Schegloff, and Jefferson (1974: 700–1) describe a number of general characteristics of face-to-face conversations. For instance, at any given time in a conversation, generally "one party talks at a time"; two or more people speaking simultaneously is "common" but overlaps tend to "be brief." Much of the structure of a spontaneous dialogue "is not fixed, but varies": there are no constraints on the topics discussed, for instance, or the order of turns (who speaks when); speakers can say as little as they want (a single word), or as much as they want (within the limits of what other speakers will tolerate before they will insist on talking). But while variation exists in any conversation, there tends to be more structure at the beginning and end of a conversation than in the middle of a conversation, where conventions for turn-taking tend to be the dominant organizational principle.

Many texts have clearly identifiable openings and closings. Although a spontaneous dialogue does not require an opening – sometimes conversations just begin – many spontaneous conversations begin with a greeting:

<ENV> <#> <O>DOOR_OPENING_AND_CLOSING</O>
  <$A> <#> Hi sweetie <,,>
  <$B> <#> Hey <,>

(SBCSAE)

The initial annotation indicates that the text opens with someone entering a room and opening and closing a door. Speakers A and B then greet each other. A greeting is a type of **adjacency pair**: a two-part utterance in which the first part elicits the second part. All greetings have two parts, in this case an initial *Hi sweetie* followed by *Hey*. As the beginning of a conversation continues, it is also common for speakers to ask how the other party is doing:

  <$A> <#> Sweetie frumptions <,,> <#> This is kinda open <,,>
  <$B> <#> Yep <,,> <#> How was work
<ENV> <#> <O>CLOSET</O>
  <$A> <#> I'm so tired <,,>
  <$B> <#> Tired
  <$A> <#> It was <unclear>word</unclear> <#> It was okay I left my bag
        there <,,> <#> I left my bag and all my money and all my things
        <,,>

Because A is returning from work, B asks how work was. While opening a closet door and (probably) hanging up her jacket, A replies that she is "tired." This leads to a discussion of what happened to A at work. In many conversations, this section will be more perfunctory, with one person saying something like *How's everything?* and the other replying *Fine*. As was noted in Chapter 3, these utterances are not necessarily literal: the first speaker most likely does not want to know how the second speaker actually feels. But such utterances are expected at this juncture in a spontaneous dialogue, and speakers invariably make them without much thought, largely because they are instances of phatic communication: language whose function is to establish social bonds between speakers rather than to convey meaningful linguistic information.

A telephone call, another type of spontaneous dialogue, has a different kind of opening, largely because such conversations are distanced, and people making phone calls need to insure at the start of the conversation that they reach the party to whom they wish to speak. The opening of a telephone conversation is therefore one instance of what Schegloff (2002: 333) refers to as a summons–answer sequence: a ringing phone literally "summons" someone to engage in a conversation.

Exactly how the callee responds to the summons is very dependent upon the formality of the call and the extent to which the caller and callee recognize each other's voices. In the example below, the callee answers the phone and opens the conversation with the word *Hello*, the most common way that a phone call starts. The caller then greets the callee. At this juncture, the caller could have identified himself (*Hi Sean, this is Justin*), but does not do so, probably because he anticipates (correctly in this case) that the callee will recognize his voice.

<$A> <#> Hello
<$B> <#> Hi Sean
<$A> <#> Hello Justin
<$B> <#> You all right
<$A> <#> Yeah
<$B> <#> Good good

(ICE-GB:S1A-100 73–78)

The conversation then proceeds as any spontaneous dialogue would.

In the next example, instead of saying *Hello*, the callee opens the conversation by giving his name. The two callers then greet each other, with the caller not identifying himself, since the callee obviously recognizes his voice.

<$A> <#> Bill Lewis here
<$B> <#> Hi
<$A> <#> Hi <#> How's things
<$B> <#> OK

(ICE-GB:S1A-096 001–5)

While it is possible in British English to open a phone call by giving one's name, the use of *Hello* is more common in American English.

Other structures are employed in more formal contexts where neither party is sure of the identity of the other party:

Callee: Hello
Caller: Could I speak with Sue Henderson, please?
Callee: Yes, speaking.
Caller: This is Henry Jamison calling

Or where the party being called is not present to accept the call:

Caller: Is Sue Henderson in?
Callee: I'm afraid she isn't here. Could I take a message.
Caller: Sure, tell her that Henry Jamison called.

With the proliferation of cell (mobile) phones and caller ID, these kinds of openings are becoming more restricted in usage, since when making or receiving a call, the identity of the caller or callee is already known. Hence, there is little need to go through the kinds of "ritualistic" openings given above: instead of saying *Hello*, the callee may simply open the conversation by saying *Hi, John, what's on your mind?*

Speakers also employ specific strategies for closing texts. In the example below, the end of the conversation is foreshadowed by what is referred to as a **pre-closing sequence**. Speaker A's statement *Good to see you* is followed by an invitation to B to *Come see me, you know, whenever you're in town*. A few turns later a more explicit series of farewells occurs: *See you* and *Bye-bye* and then three instances of *Okay* affirming the closure of the conversation.

<$A> <#> Good to see you <,,> <#> Come see me <#> You know whenever you're <{><[> in town </[>
<$B> <#> <[> I will </[></{> <,,>
<$A> <#> And uh <,,><O>in</O> let me know what you get into I'm sure it'll be something fun <,>
<$B> <#> I hope so <,,>
<$A> <#> I think it will <,,> <#> See you
<$B> <#> Bye bye
<$A> <#> Okay <,>
<$C> Okay <,> <$C> <#> Just <,> let us know <,,> if you need anything <,>
<$B> <#> Okay <,>
<$C> <#> Okay

(SBCSAE)

Closing a conversation can be difficult and awkward for all parties involved. Thus, pre-closing sequences serve to ease the transition to the end of a conversation.

While openings and closings have identifiable components, the middle of a conversation – where most conversation takes place – is typically much less structured. As a result, this section of a conversation can consist of little more than speakers following various principles of turn-taking. As Sacks, Schegloff, and Jefferson (1974: 702) note, a speaker turn consists of "various unit types": from structures as large as a sentence to as small as a word. The excerpt below contains various kinds of structures. The first turn, for instance, contains one partially formed *why*-question followed by a complete formulation of the question. The second and last turns, however, consist of phrases: two noun phrases (*all the blood* and *Katie*), an adverb (*probably*), and an interjection (*mhm*):

S1: so why is the other picture, why is the other picture more disturbing?
S4: all the blood probably.
S1: yeah i think so. the amount of blood.
S12: yeah i i think like just the fact of like, showing, a notebook and, and something like that just like remnants it's, [S1: mhm] really, grotesque to me.
S1: mhm. Katie?

(MICASE LES220SU140)

Speakers are "initially entitled," Sacks, Schegloff, and Jefferson (1974: 703) continue, "to one such unit [per turn]." At the end of the unit, one finds what is known as a **transition relevance place** (**TRP**), a juncture where a potential change of speaker can occur. Thus, a change of speaker could have occurred following any of the five structures described above. However, as the excerpt illustrates, a change in speaker is not mandatory at a TRP: the current speaker can continue to speak unless he or she "selects" another individual to speak, or someone not speaking "self-selects"; that is, employs a strategy that allows for a change in speaker.

The current speaker can select the next speaker by uttering the first part of an adjacency pair. As noted in an earlier section, if one speaker greets another, the second speaker is expected to reciprocate with a greeting as well. In the exchange below, the first speaker compliments the second speaker, causing her to offer thanks for the compliment:

S2: good to see people still smiling at this time of year.
S3: yeah <S3 LAUGH> thanks

(MICASE ADV700JU047)

If the current speaker asks someone a question, the person to whom the question is addressed is compelled to answer. The brief exchange below consists of three question/answer adjacency pairs, with the last sequence consisting of two questions – *Oh do you want some more* and *What do you think* – before an answer is provided.

<$A> <#> Mom did you want me to to <,> cook the rest of the of the <,,>
    the red uh <,><.>tam</.> uh <,,> chilis <,,>
<$B> <#> <O>COUGH</O><O>COUGH</O> <,,>
<$C> <#> I don't know <,,>
<$A> <#> Where are they
<$C> <#><.><unclear>word</unclear>I<|.><.><unclear>word</unclear>
    I</.> <,,> <#> I put the chilis over there or <.>in</.><,> in here <{><[>
    already </[>
<$A> <#> <[> Oh do you </[></{> want some more <,,>
<$C> <#> What do you think <,,>
 <X> <#> <O>SNIFF</O>
<$C> <#> It's pink enough

(SBCSAE)

If the current speaker does not select another party to speak, the other parties can self-select themselves as speakers: they can begin speaking at the point of a gap in the conversation, or they can speak simultaneously with the current speaker, creating an instance of overlapping speech. Both strategies for taking the floor are found in the excerpts below. In each of the excerpts, all annotation was removed from the original transcription except for speaker IDs, text unit markers, pauses, and segments of overlapping speech; instances of overlapping speech are highlighted in boldface to increase readability.

The first excerpt was taken from a conversation that A and B were having that focused on how to put horseshoes on a horse. In this section of the conversation, B is obviously the dominant speaker: his first two turns, for instance, contain numerous TRPs, which are marked in many cases by pauses. To take the floor from B in B's first turn, A overlaps his speech with the two words (*right here*) occurring just prior to one of B's TRPs.

<$B> <#> You're always bent over <,> <#> And like in the front <#> You stick the horse's hoof <,> between your leg you know <,,> Kinda like that and you kinda you go like this you kinda bend down like this and you have the horse's hoof <{><[> **right here** </[>
<$A> <#> <[> **It's hard on your back** </[></{>
<$B> <#> It's really hard on your back <,> <#> Like <,> I noticed that girl's back muscles were just tremendous <#> too you know <,,> <#> Couldn't believe it <,,> <#> She had like on this <,> really kinda short shirt you know <#> There's this <,,> I think that's cold <,,>
<$A> <#> Just don't <,> <#> it's <#> if you rub something against it it's just <,>
<$B> <#> Makes a sound <,,> <#> Nkay <,,>
<$A> <#> So what <,> <#> what were you gonna do out there today

(SBCSAE)

However, A does not keep the floor for long as B echoes what he says (*It's really hard on your back*) and continues speaking until A takes the floor again at a TRP following *cold* that is marked with a long pause. B resumes speaking when A pauses following *it it's just* and B finishes the sentence that A was having difficulty completing: *It makes a sound.* B's helping A finish his sentence is an instance of an other-initiated repair: one person correcting another person's speech, in this case by supplying A with words he was having difficulty articulating. The other kind of repair, a self-initiated repair, occurs when a speaker corrects him or herself. For instance, A's second turn has two false starts – *Just don't* and *it's* – before A adjusts his syntax and composes a subordinate clause: *if you rub something against it.*

In the next excerpt, which occurred at the start of a conversation that A and B were having, A utters three text units. B takes the floor at the TRP that ends the third unit and is accompanied by a long pause.

<$A> <#> God I said I wasn't gonna do this anymore <,,> <#> Stay up late <,,> <#> Kinda defeats the purpose of getting up in the morning <,,>
<$B> <#> I know <,> <#> And it's a hard habit to break <#> <{><[> **Usually I don't** </[>
<$A> <#> <[> **It is** </[></{>
<$B> <#> <.>s</.> <unclear>word</unclear> Usually I don't stay up late <,,> <#> <O>in</O> But it's like if I'm up after midnight <#> <O>laugh</O><,> It's just like

(SBCSAE)

A tries to get the floor back by overlapping the beginning three words of one of B's units: *Usually I don't.* However, B does not yield the floor but instead begins his unit again: *Usually I don't stay up late.* This part of the exchange reveals an important point about overlapping speech: overlaps are, as Sacks, Schegloff, and Jefferson (1974: 706) note, "common but brief." That is, the competition for the floor that overlaps create is usually resolved fairly quickly, with either the current speaker keeping the floor or a new speaker taking it over.

Not all overlaps, however, are attempts by a speaker to take the floor. On two occasions in the excerpt below, B overlaps A's speech with the interjection *Mhm*:

<$A> <#> Turn on the fire alarm that would do it <#> These kids <.>were</.> came in and <,,> I was <,> like we're closing <#> In a few minutes they said well we'll <#> We'll wait until you kick us out <#> Cause they didn't really want to buy anything <{><[> **they just wanted** </[> to look
<$B> <#> <[> **Mhm** </[></{>
<$A> <#> And I said okay <,,> we're closed <,,> <#> Out <#> <,,> so I was moving them like making them go <{><[> **out**
<$B> <#> <[> **Mhm** </[></{>
<$A> <#> **and** </[> they were <,> trying to be cute and <,> say sweet things and <,,> <#> To stay in <,>

(SBCSAE)

These instances of overlaps are referred to as **back channels**: they are verbal affirmations that B is offering to A and serve to demonstrate to A that B is listening and that she is sympathetic to the story that A is telling. The overlaps are not an attempt by B to take the floor from A.

Of course, the linguistic characteristics of speaker turns covered in this section only touch upon the linguistic structure inherent in turns. For instance, in addition to having an overall structure, speaker turns tend to begin and end with certain structures. In an analysis of two corpora of spoken English, Tao (2003: 190–1) found that a mere twenty different forms began 60 percent of the turns he studied. Two of the constructions beginning turns in the excerpt above – *and* and *mhm* – ranked fourth and fifteenth, respectively, on Tao's list. The frequent occurrence of the forms stems largely from the function that these forms play in conversation: *mhm* as a back channel and *and* as a marker of addition (a use of *and* that will be described in greater detail in the section below on unity of texture).

Written registers

Figure 4.2 schematizes the major written registers in the British National Corpus as they are classified by David Lee. Lee (2001: 53) developed this system of classification because of "the broadness and inexplicitness of the [original] BNC classification scheme." For instance, in the original system, the sub-registers under "Fiction" in Lee's system (drama, poetry, and prose) were all classified within a single register – imaginative prose – even though drama, poetry, and prose exhibit significant linguistic differences.

Figure 4.2 lists eight major registers of written English that differ along a number of parameters. Writing can be academic or non-academic, with the same sub-registers within each of these registers. The assumption behind this classification is that writing in the natural sciences, for

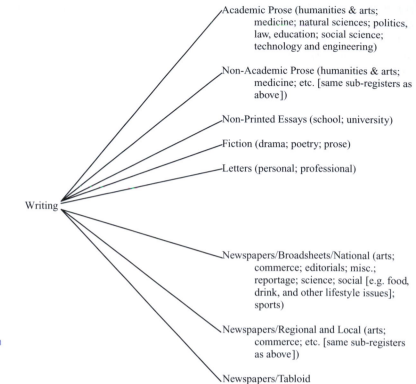

Academic Prose (humanities & arts; medicine; natural sciences; politics, law, education; social science; technology and engineering)

Non-Academic Prose (humanities & arts; medicine; etc. [same sub-registers as above])

Non-Printed Essays (school; university)

Fiction (drama; poetry; prose)

Letters (personal; professional)

Writing

Newspapers/Broadsheets/National (arts; commerce; editorials; misc.; reportage; science; social [e.g. food, drink, and other lifestyle issues]; sports)

Newspapers/Regional and Local (arts; commerce; etc. [same sub-registers as above])

Newspapers/Tabloid

FIGURE 4.2
Major written registers in the British National Corpus (based on Lee 2001: 57–8).

instance, will differ from writing in the social sciences, and that the audience towards whom the writing is directed – academic vs. non-academic – will also affect the way that language is used. As was the case with the spoken registers in Figure 4.1, there is an attempt to cover a wide range of written registers. Thus, national, regional, and local newspapers are included as well as broadsheets, tabloids, and the many different types of writing found in newspapers: reportage, editorials, and so forth. Not all of the written registers in the BNC are included in Figure 4.2; a number of registers without sub-registers, such as administrative and advertising writing, can be found as well. Some of the sub-registers, it should be noted, are not as discrete as the categorizations in Figure 4.2 would suggest. While literary criticism is traditionally regarded as fitting within the sub-register of humanities/arts, much literary criticism draws upon work in psychology or the social sciences to interpret literary texts. Many written texts will therefore exhibit characteristics of more than one register or sub-register.

Because the BNC was released in the mid 1990s, it does not contain newer types of registers, such as blogs. Also, with the proliferation of email, which is included in the BNC, the register of handwritten letters, both personal and professional, is now becoming somewhat archaic. There are also additional written registers, such as legal writing, not included in the BNC. Many modern corpora exclude legal English because it is a rather specialized register that has a very restricted use and has not changed much over the years.

Like spoken registers, written registers vary in terms of how rigidly they are organized hierarchically. While no written text has as loose a structure as spontaneous dialogues, a personal letter, for instance, will not have as clearly identifiable a hierarchical structure as a biology lab report. Since press reportage is such a common written register with which all literate people will be familiar, this sub-register of newspaper writing will be described in the next section.

Press reportage. Newspapers, as Figure 4.2 demonstrates, are composed of texts taken from a number of different sub-registers. These sub-registers differ primarily because language has a different function in each. Editorials, for instance, express opinions and therefore are persuasive in nature. Articles on the arts, on the other hand, could be descriptive (e.g. a discussion of a new exhibit at an art museum) or evaluative (e.g. a movie review). But at the core of any newspaper is reportage: texts that inform the readership of a newspaper about current local, national, or international events. And as van Dijk (1988: 52–9) demonstrates, news reportage has a very specific hierarchical structure to which news writers must adhere and which readers anticipate when they read a news article. Reportage, van Dijk (1988: 55) claims, consists of two major sections: a brief "Summary" followed by a lengthier "Story." Each of these two sections contains many subsections, such as a lead, background information, and verbal comments from people with knowledge about the story. Because newspaper articles are presented in narrow columns, typography and layout are prime considerations too. Headlines are larger than the rest of the text, and paragraphs are typically shorter than in other kinds of writing, sometimes no longer than a single sentence. The discussion below highlights some of the major components of the summary and story sections of news report.

Summary: A news article opens with two obligatory elements – a headline and a lead – and several optional elements: a date, a byline, and the name of the city in which the news event took place:

Housing lawsuit vs. state dropped

By Jonathan Saltzman
GLOBE STAFF

Three of the largest public housing authorities in Massachusetts, citing a pledge by Governor Deval Patrick to adequately fund public housing, said yesterday they have dropped a lawsuit that accused the Romney administration of shortchanging the state's nearly 250 local authorities by millions of dollars.

(*Boston Globe*, March 28, 2007, p. B1)

Because the above excerpt was taken from an article in the Metropolitan section of a Boston newspaper, no city name is given. Had the article been about an event taking place outside Boston, a city name would have been provided. No date is given because the article appeared in the print edition of the newspaper, where the date is given on each page. The Web versions of news articles will always contain dates, since such articles are often retrieved individually by search engines, making the date an important piece of information. The author's name is given, since he is a staff member of the newspaper in which the article appeared. Many articles from news services, such as Associated Press, do not contain the names of authors.

Not all of these optional elements, however, are crucial to the opening of a news article. Most important are what van Dijk (1988: 53) characterizes as the two essential elements of the Summary: the headline and the lead, which provide in capsule form exactly what the news story is about. Headlines are always written in telegraphic speech: an abbreviated language lacking **function words**. The above headline, "Housing lawsuit vs. state dropped," lacks the definite article *the* before *Housing* and *state* and omits the auxiliary verb *is* before *dropped*. Headlines are also typically in larger fonts than the main text; the kind of language they contain depends upon whether they appear in a broadsheet or tabloid. Because the *Boston Globe* is a broadsheet, the language of the lead is neutral and factual: "Three of the largest public housing authorities in Massachusetts ... dropped a lawsuit." Tabloids, in contrast, often contain headlines that employ various literary devices, such as "rhyme" and "punning" (Malmkjær 2005: 165), and that are often highly sensationalistic. For instance, the headline "No Way, Hillary" appeared in a news story in the *New York Post* (March 28, 2007) discussing the results of an opinion poll reporting that 50 percent of those surveyed would not vote for Hillary Clinton if she ran for president of the United States. In the *Daily Mirror* (March 28, 2007), a British tabloid, the headline "Nut skis down tube escalator" opened a story about an individual skiing down an escalator at a London Underground station.

The Story: While the opening of a news article is relatively short, the remainder of the article – termed the "Story" by van Dijk (1988) – can be considerably longer, depending upon the complexity of the event being reported and the amount of space that the newspaper has to devote to the event. The Story has two main components: the "Situation" and a second section, "Comments," containing comments, often in the form of quotations, about the situation. The Situation will follow the lead and contain a narrative recounting, called the "Episode," of exactly what transpired. The excerpt below was taken from an article entitled "F&C to sell Canadian business" and contains the lead followed by a few paragraphs from the beginning of the Situation:

Cincinnati flavor-maker F&C International Inc. has agreed to sell its Canadian subsidiary, including its snack seasonings business, to an Irish food company for up to $ 7.7 million.

The sale agreement, subject to a public auction slated for Sept. 22, would be the largest asset sale in F&C's effort to emerge from bankruptcy reorganization.

Bankruptcy Judge J. Vincent Aug Jr. Wednesday granted F&C's request to expedite the sale of the Canadian business to Kerry Ingredients of Canada, a unit of Kerry Group plc, subject to creditor objections ...

(ICE-USA)

The first part of the Situation provides essential information about the sale: that the sale is part of a "bankruptcy reorganization" on the part of F&C, was authorized by a "Bankruptcy Judge," and would involve a particular company: Kerry Ingredients of Canada. Within the Situation it is also common to find background information. A few paragraphs later, it is noted that F&C was "once a hot stock on Wall Street" and that its former chairman had been terminated following the disclosure of "inventory discrepancies estimated at up to $8 million." Background information is crucial in a news story because newspapers assume that potential readers may not be familiar with all of the events leading up to the story, and will therefore need background information to fully understand the events discussed in the story.

At various junctures in the Situation, different kinds of commentary will be provided, either by the writer or by the people interviewed for the story. The excerpt below contains two direct quotations taken from an article entitled "Prospects good for new oil well."

New Zealand Oil and Gas announced yesterday that a second test on the well near Inglewood had showed flow rates between 220 and 280 barrels a day.

Flow testing continued yesterday.

A first flow test at Ngatoro-2 on the weekend had flowed up to 170 barrels of oil a day.

"I would be most surprised if they don't make it commercial because of its locality," an industry source said yesterday.

The well, 4km south-west of Inglewood, was close to the infrastructure necessary to develop it.

"Anything in these sorts of order (of flow rates) is starting to look very attractive from NZOG's point of view."

(ICE-New Zealand W2C-001)

The excerpt begins with three short paragraphs describing two tests done on an oil well at two different times, and noting that the second test had revealed increasing amounts of oil being produced by the well. Two quotes follow and serve to provide a perspective from an expert that the well has considerable commercial potential. Quotes add credibility and perspective to a news story. While the source in this story is not named – he or she is simply referred to as "an industry source" – in other contexts names of sources are included, especially if the source is a highly knowledgeable and credible source of information.

Commentary can also come from "the journalist or newspaper itself" even though, as van Dijk (1988: 56) correctly observes, "newsmakers share the ideological view that fact and opinion should not be mixed." In several sections of commentary in an April 3, 2007 article in the *New York Times* ("Justices Say E.P.A. has Power to Act on Harmful Gases," p. A1) the choice of wording is highly evaluative. This article dealt with two Supreme Court rulings in the United States that authorized the Environmental Protection Agency (E.P.A.) to regulate automobile emissions. The ruling is characterized as "one of its [the Supreme Court's] *most* important environmental decisions in years" (evaluative language is emphasized here and in the other two examples). Because the Bush Administration did not want the E.P.A. to regulate emissions, the ruling is described not just as a loss for the Bush Administration but "a *strong rebuke*." Advocates of regulating gases were not simply pleased with the ruling but "*exultant*." The choice of language in these examples is not just descriptive but helps convey the editorial perspective of the newspaper in which they occur.

While the headline and lead are obligatory and occur in a specific order, there is more variability in the Story section of a news story. The Episode will come first but where the Background and Comments are placed can vary, as can exactly how much information is placed in each of these sections. One source of this variability is that the length of an article is often constrained by the amount of space that is available for an article. Thus, editors can always cut out or trim sections of the Story if necessitated by space limitations.

Unity of texture

For a text to achieve coherence, it is not enough that it have a hierarchical structure. Additionally, all of its component parts must fit together in a manner that is recognizable to the hearer or reader. The individual parts of a text – the sentences and clauses within it – must also be linked. Various devices work together to achieve what is referred to as unity of texture: constituents within a clause are ordered in a specific way so that the thematic structure of the clause promotes the easy flow of information from clause to clause, and relationships between clauses are indicated by various markers of cohesion, such as logical connectors like *therefore* or *however*. Without specific linkages between clauses, hearers and readers would have to infer how everything is related, making comprehension difficult if not impossible.

Thematic structure

In traditional grammar, sentences are often divided into a subject and a predicate. In the very simple sentence *The boy walked the dog*, *The boy* is the subject and *walked the dog* the predicate. The notions "subject" and "predicate" are related to syntax (the topic of the next chapter): how constituents are ordered within a sentence or, more basically, a clause. The above example is a **main clause** that is also a **declarative sentence**.

Elements in clauses, however, can be viewed from a different perspective, specifically in terms of how their placement in a clause contributes to the flow of information in a text and helps connect one clause with another. Viewing clauses from this perspective involves the study of their thematic structure.

The study of thematic structure is rooted in work on functional sentence perspective (FSP) conducted originally by Prague School linguists such as Frantisek Daneš (1974) and Jan Firbas (1992) and adapted for English by the British linguist Michael A. K. Halliday (see Halliday and Matthiessen 2004). The theory of FSP explains why speakers/writers pick one word order over another – why, for instance, they would say or write

The boy walked the dog vs. its passive equivalent, *The dog was walked by the boy*. Instead of viewing a clause as containing a subject and a predicate, FSP divides the clause into the **theme** and the **rheme**. In the first example above, the theme is the first major element in the clause, namely the subject: *The boy*. The rheme is everything else. In the second example, the theme shifts to *The dog* and the rheme, again, is everything else.

There are various factors that will influence the placement of constituents in the theme and the rheme, specifically what is **given (or old) information** in the clause and what is **new information**. There is a general principle in English and other languages that, wherever possible, old information should precede new information. For instance, in the example below, the writer uses two constructions containing passive verbs: *It was built* and *it was purchased by Phyllis and Keith*:

Stanhope Hall must be one of the most extraordinary houses in this book. It **was built** way back in 1135 as a fortified manor house. In 1976 it **was purchased** by Phyllis and Keith who restored it, quite miraculously, from an almost derelict state to its present form in which it resembles its original appearance to an extraordinary degree.

(BNC CJK 1806)

The writer could just as easily have used equivalent constructions with verbs in the active voice: *Someone built it* and *Phyllis and Keith purchased it*. However, in this context, the passive constructions place the old information – the pronoun *it* – in the theme, and the new information – everything else in the two sentences – in the rheme. Old information is information recoverable from the prior linguistic context. Thus, *it* is old information because its **referent**, *Stanhope Hall*, occurs in the first sentence. New information is information introduced into the text for the first time. The words following the first instance of *it* – *was built way back in 1135 as a fortified manor house* – are new information because they have no prior mention in the text; the same holds true for the words following *it* in the second example. The tendency to place new information towards the end of a clause is referred to by Quirk *et al.* (1985: 1357) as **end-focus**.

The patterning of old followed by new information in a clause greatly enhances cohesion: old information in the theme provides a link to information introduced previously. And because passivization is a syntactic process that moves constituents around in a clause, clauses in the passive voice occur quite commonly in texts, despite the fact that many style manuals recommend against the use of the passive. Advice not to use the passive must be weighed against the advantages of using the passive to promote cohesion and the appropriate placement of new and old information.

In speech, degrees of prominence are marked not just by word order but by intonation as well. Speech is segmented into **tone units**: sequences of words in which one unit – usually the last part of the rheme – receives the highest pitch and consequently the greatest prominence. The example below contains a single tone unit. Because this is a declarative sentence, the pitch will rise, peak on the first syllable of *mother*, and then fall, ending the tone unit and potentially starting a new tone unit.

He told his MÒTHer|

(adapted from Quirk *et al.* 1985: 1599)

In an **unmarked tone unit** (i.e. the most frequent and common type of tone unit), the last stressable syllable will receive the greatest stress, since placing greater stress on this syllable serves to highlight the new information in the unit. Typically, the prominent syllable in a tone unit will be a **content word** (e.g. a noun or verb) rather than a function word (e.g. a preposition or article), since content words carry more meaning than function words. Function words will only be stressed if prominence on them is contextually warranted. For instance, the example below is one possible response to the question *Did Harriet do the work?*:

NÒ | Ì did the work |

The reply contains two tone units. In the second tone unit, the highest pitch occurs on the function word *I* to emphasize the fact that the person uttering this clause did the work rather than the person referred to in the question. This is an example of a **marked tone unit**: one that is less common. Had this been an unmarked tone unit, the most prominent syllable would have been the one on *work*.

Writing, it should be noted, has nothing approximating the complexity of intonation for highlighting prominent pieces of information. At best, punctuation and other kinds of typography provide a crude representation of intonation. The two examples below both contain instances of the logical connector *thus*:

Thus, Irish nationalism is conceived by most members in an abstract way, but it has concrete import for key groups.

(BNC A07 221)

Thus hard braking should be avoided, particularly if the glider has started to swing.

(BNC AOH 543)

In a rough sense, placing or not placing a comma after *Thus* mimics the intonation choices that speakers have when this word occurs clause-initially: they can either give *Thus* prominence by placing it in a tone unit by itself, or deemphasize it by integrating it into a larger tone unit containing the words following it. In writing, a comma after *thus* adds emphasis to it; no comma decreases its prominence in the clause. The effects in writing, of course, are much less pronounced than in speech, since writing is a mainly visual medium, and punctuation can provide at best only a rough representation of the intonation patterns that would exist if the written text were read aloud.

In addition to passivization, there are other syntactic processes that serve to focus items in a clause or add extra emphasis to them. One process, already mentioned in Chapter 2, is topicalization, which involves moving information out of its normal positioning in the rheme to the front of the clause. The example below focuses on many characteristics of Max Bialystock, all occurring in a series of noun phrases at the end of the first sentence. Although the theme of the second sentence – *a mensch* – is new information, its form – indefinite article + noun – is parallel to the other noun phrases. Moving it out of the rheme therefore adds emphasis to it and also promotes cohesion.

Max Bialystock is many things – a stinking liar, a crook, a shameless noodge, a stud muffin for the elderly and infirm. And of course a big fat Broadway producer. But **a mensch** he is not.

(*NY Times*, Jan. 19, 2007, p. B2)

The final sentence in the next example contains a clause beginning with *How* that is parallel in form to the two clauses ending the preceding sentence and that contains some old information, the pronoun *that*:

"They're [Iraqi militants] watching us carefully," he [Maj. Gen. Joseph F. Fil Jr.] said. "There's an air of suspense throughout the city. We believe, there's no question about it, that many of these extremists are laying low and watching to see what it is we do and how we do it. **How long that will last**, we don't know."

(*NY Times*, Feb. 16, 2007, p. A6)

Placing the *how*-clause in the theme links the second sentence with the prior sentence.

Two types of clauses – the **pseudo-cleft** and the **cleft** – can also contribute to focus and emphasis. These types of clauses tend to occur most frequently in speech because the item being focused or emphasized receives heavy stress. A pseudo-cleft is a paraphrase of a declarative sentence; the pseudo-cleft begins with *what* and contains a form of the verb *be*:

Declarative Sentence: I like organic food.
Pseudo-Cleft: **What** I LÌKE **is** organic food.

In the above example, the pseudo-cleft construction places heavy stress on the verb *like* and allows the speaker to emphasize the fact that she likes organic food.

In the example below, the pseudo-cleft places emphasis on *do*, stressing that the speaker does his own stretching rather than relying on treatment by a physiotherapist, whose availability cannot be counted on.

You know I I think you still need to go back uhm maybe do something at least once a week but that's not always available because there're so many people who need phi physiotherapy Uhm so **what I've always tended to** *do* **is to do my own stretches at home**

(ICE-GB:S1A-003 26–29)

In the example below, stress could be placed on either the first syllable of *happening* or *time*, again depending upon which of these two words the speaker wishes to emphasize.

Uhm I think a lot of the way that that the arts and dance are progressing is uhm is towards an awareness that part of art and dance, a central part of art and dance is to do with the recovery of the whole person uhm to do with making people whole that that's the role of art and dance And uhm I think **what's been** *happening* **for** for a quite a period

of *time* is that therapy has been uhm put on one side dance on another

(ICE-GB S1A-004 91–94)

A similar effect can be achieved in a cleft sentence. A cleft sentence has the structure of *it+be+[ ]+*relative pronoun (e.g. *who* or *which*) with some item stressed and emphasized following *be*:

Declarative Sentence: My brother called me yesterday.
Cleft: **It was** my BRÒther **who** called me yesterday.

Instead of using a cleft sentence in the second example below, Speaker A could have answered her own question by saying *You told me that, didn't you* with falling pitch rather than rising pitch on *didn't you* to indicate that A came to the realization that B had indeed brought certain information to her attention.

B: I thought they were playing the borderline
A: Yeah was it you who told me that? **It WÀS you that told me that wasn't it**

(ICE-GB S1A-099 271–2)

But by using a cleft sentence instead, with stress on *was,* this realization is highlighted more explicitly. In the cleft structure below, the speaker could highlight the first syllable of either *study* or *architecture*:

B: On what did you I mean did you decide at that stage to continue in architecture
A: No not really I kind of I mean I I started the course thinking that uhm I'd sort of do the full seven years and stuff but like I'm just going through the course I just just realised that **it was actually the study of architecture I really enjoyed**

(ICE-GB S1A-034 17:1:B)

With stress on *STÙdy*, he is telling B that he realized that he liked studying architecture rather than practicing it; with stress on *ÀRchitecture*, he is saying that he preferred studying architecture rather than some other subject.

Markers of cohesion

While cohesion is promoted through focus and emphasis, it can also be achieved by a series of processes that establish explicit connections between clauses. Whenever speakers or writers use a word such as *therefore*, for instance, they are explicitly signposting a relationship between sections of the text that they are creating, indicating that what comes next in the text is a logical consequence of what has previously been said. This kind of link, called a cohesive tie, is part of a process called **Conjunction**, one of five types of cohesion proposed for English by Michael A. K. Halliday and Ruqaiya Hasan in their highly influential 1976 book *Cohesion in English*. In this book, Halliday and Hasan comprehensively describe how cohesion is achieved by conjunction and four other processes: **Reference**, **Substitution**, **Ellipsis**, and **Lexical Cohesion**.

Reference. Because the study of reference is typically done within the field of semantics, a full discussion will be deferred until Chapter 6. But for purposes of establishing cohesive ties in a text, Reference is a process whereby a construction such as a third-person pronoun links parts of a text that have the same referent. In the example below, *she* and *her* refer back in the text to *Maria*, a proper noun that refers to a particular female in the external world named Maria.

Maria was last seen shouting for help inside a military jeep that evening. **Her** family heard **she** had been taken to the Regional Command Military camp in Legaspi City. **She** has not been seen since. Members of **her** family have received death threats.

(BNC AO3 527)

Similar links can be created with other third-person pronouns, such as *he/him/his*, *it/its*, or *they/them/their* as well as with **demonstrative pronouns** such as *this/that* and *these/those*. The conversational exchange below opens with mention of an individual referred to as *some guy*. Throughout the exchange, reference back to this person is made with the pronoun *he*, until the last turn where he is referred to as *this kid*, with the demonstrative pronoun *this* pointing back ultimately to the initial mention of *some guy*.

<$A> <#> **Some guy** came out and **he** was
<$B> <#> Oh
<$A> <#> **he** was trying to sell us *cologne*
<$B> <#> No **he** wasn't trying to sell us cologne
<$A> <#> Well it <#> No I guess **he** was trying to like lure us to a place where they would sell like imitation cologne but **he** said *it*'s not imitation because
<$E> <#> I got a deal
<$B> <#> Yeah
<$E> <#> you can't refuse
<$A> <#> because *it*'s made by the same people
<$B> <#> I mean **this kid** was # He looked like a (SBCSAE)

Also in the excerpt are two instances of *it* contracted with *is* that refer back to the earlier mention of cologne. The word *cologne*, it should be noted, is repeated twice before it is referred to with the pronoun *it*. This repetition is an instance of Lexical Cohesion, which will be discussed in greater detail below.

While demonstratives such as *this* or *that* can occur before nouns, they can also occur alone and have very **broad reference**. The instance of *This* in the second sentence below refers back to all of the information conveyed in the sentence that precedes it.

The use of coinage in Roman Britain appears to have ceased *c.* 420 A.D. almost at the same time that the pottery factories ceased production. **This** was probably the direct consequence of the withdrawal of the Roman army and administration.

(ICE-GB W1A-001–70-71)

Substitution.   Substitution and Reference are similar in the sense that both processes involve some linguistic item substituting for another item occurring in the prior linguistic context. Substitution differs from reference, according to Quirk *et al.* (1985: 864), in that it is less contextually dependent: in the earlier example above, interpreting who the pronoun *she* refers to depends upon knowledge of who *Maria* is. In addition, substitution involves a wider range of constructions: not just nouns and pronouns but verbs and adverbs as well.

The pronoun *one* (or its plural form *ones*) very commonly substitutes for a previously mentioned noun. In the first example, *one* in the last turn substitutes for *particle* in the second turn:

S3: yes we use, we simply use the arrow to say which is the positron so the arrow denotes the direction of, electric charge, this way it's negative that way it's positive. yeah? yes?
S5: does the **W** *particle* have mass?
S3: which **one**?

(MICASE COL485MX069)

Likewise, *ones* in E's turn substitutes for *kids* in B's turn:

<$B> <#> And I like withheld recess from several **kids** on on Thursday
<$E> <#> Well did you give candy to the **ones** that got excellents

(SBCSAE)

While *the same* in the last sentence below is a noun phrase, it does not substitute for another noun phrase but instead a much larger structure: everything the speaker says the mother did in the utterances preceding *the same*:

Yeah. I mean, your mother sat by the fire for years Yes, yeah, controlling everything. Yeah, oh yeah, so she thought. Yeah, yeah. And you did **the same** did you?

(BNC K65 1102)

The next two examples contain the adverb *so* which occurs along with the verbs *do* and *thought* (as well as *too* in the second example). In the first example, *so* substitutes for the predication *generate the bulk of our money supply*.

The need for state interference in this market springs from the fact that it is no longer the state but the commercial banks which **generate the bulk of our money supply**. They do **so** by creating credit.

(BNC A3T 386)

In the second example *so* in S1's turn substitutes for everything said by S2 in the preceding turn:

S2: um huh, so everyone in the community goes to the high school play that's very interesting
S1: yeah i thought **so** too.

(MICASE OFC115SU060)

Ellipsis.   Ellipsis is like Substitution except that it involves deleting information recoverable from some prior context rather than replacing the information with a word like *do* or *so*. For instance, in the example below, the speaker begins by mentioning that he thinks *Oxford United* has experienced *one best thing*:

Basically what I, I think the best thing that's happened to Oxford United this season. Well there are **two**.

(BNC KRT 4288)

However, rather than repeating this information in his second utterance following *two*, he simply leaves it out. It might seem counterintuitive that the omission of linguistic material creates a cohesive tie. However, in order to correctly interpret the second utterance above, the hearer has to recover the missing information from the prior context.

Halliday and Hasan (1976: 154) comment that words such as *two*, which are members of the class of numeratives (i.e. words that describe quantities of something), commonly precede the positions where ellipsis takes place, as do certain kinds of pronouns, such as *these* and *any* in the examples below (the elliptical material is italicized in brackets):

In same cases additional amounts are available for particular needs. The optician will include **these** [*additional amounts*] when appropriate.

(ICE-GB W2D 117–118)

\<$B\> \<#\> Can I grow some basil from seed
\<$C\> \<#\> Yes that's how I've \<#\> I don't have **any** [*basil*] this year but I've
    grown it other years

(SBCSAE)

While the previous examples illustrated ellipsis within noun phrases, larger structures can be elided too. In the first two examples below, verbs and other elements are deleted:

When you buy a used vehicle the seller may agree to include a current licence in the sale. If the seller does not [*include a current licence*] you must use form V10, or form V85 for goods vehicles weighing over 1525 kgs unladen.

(ICE-GB W2D-010 101–2)

\<$C\> \<#\> Take this to the table please
\<$B\> \<#\> \<[\> Okay I will [*take this to the table*] \<#\> just wait a minute

(SBCSAE)

In the next example, the subject and contracted verb in the last turn are elided:

\<$B\> \<#\> Okay \<#\> Two weeks ago I'm watching TV and David Horowitz
    is going to have this former car radio thief on
\<$A\> \<#\> It's her boyfriend
\<$B\> \<#\>Yeah [*it's*] her ex boyfriend

(SBCSAE)

Lexical Cohesion.   The types of cohesion discussed so far "move hand and hand," Halliday and Hasan (1985: 83) note, with Lexical Cohesion, which establishes a link with the prior context by, for instance, repeating a word mentioned earlier or using a **synonym** of the word. For instance, in an example such as the one below, the reader/writer has a number of options to link the second sentence with the first:

I turned to the ascent of the peak.
$$\begin{bmatrix} \text{The ascent} \\ \text{The climb} \\ \text{The task} \\ \text{The thing} \\ \text{It} \end{bmatrix}$$
is perfectly easy.

(Halliday and Hasan 1976: 279)

One way to create a link with *the ascent* is to simply repeat the phrase. However, if such repetition is undesirable, a synonym such as *climb* can be used instead. Other options include using progressively more general words, such as *task* or *thing*, or simply a pronoun such as *it*, which involves an earlier type of cohesion, Reference, rather than Lexical Cohesion.

Exactly which choice is made is guided on the one hand by clarity – the need to use an expression that clearly refers back to something mentioned earlier – and the avoidance, where possible, of repetition. The excerpt below illustrates how these two considerations work.

Democratic presidential hopefuls sparred genially last night on details of ***the Iraq war***, healthcare, and guns, but **they** stood resolutely united in blaming President Bush for getting the country into ***the war*** and in agreeing on the need to end ***it***.
   In the first national debate of the 2008 presidential season, **the eight contenders** all denounced ***the war***, with two of **the group** – former senator John Edwards of North Carolina and Senator Christopher Dodd of Connecticut – acknowledging outright that their 2002 votes to authorize the war were the biggest professional mistakes of their lives.

(Milligan 2007)

The excerpt opens with the introduction of two items of new information – *Democratic presidential hopefuls* and *the Iraq war* – that each begin what Halliday and Hasan (1985: 84) refer to as a cohesive chain: a series of expressions all related to each other. *Democratic presidential hopefuls* are first referred to by the referential pronoun *they* ("*they* stood resolutely") and subsequently by two instances of Lexical Cohesion: the synonymous expression *the eight contenders* and the more general expression *the group*. *The Iraq war* is first referred to with the more general expression *the war*, which is followed a few words later by the referential pronoun *it*, and then at the start of the second paragraph by the repetition of the expression *the war*.

Personal pronouns will be used when it is clear in the context exactly what is being referred to: *it* refers clearly back to *the war* because there is no intervening noun that *it* could refer to. However, as a text progresses, and more nouns are introduced, it becomes necessary to either repeat an expression or use a synonym or more general expression. Thus, in the second paragraph *Democratic presidential hopefuls* are referred to as *the eight contenders*. Using a synonymous expression such as this both preserves clarity and provides for variety of expression; that is, it avoids both ambiguity and potentially undesirable repetition.

Conjunction. Conjunction is different from the types of cohesion discussed so far. It does not depend on linguistic items occurring in the prior context. Instead, it involves the inclusion of various kinds of expressions that mark relationships between what occurred previously in a text and what follows. In this sense, the expressions that are part of this type of cohesion – words such as *also* or *therefore* and phrases such as *on the other hand* – act as signposts, specifically marking how various segments of the text are logically related.

Although there are different ways to describe the relationships that words within the category of Conjunction mark, Halliday and Hasan (1976: 242–3) propose four different relationships: additive, adversative, causal, and temporal. Within each of these general groups are a series of grammatical items expressing different variations on how additive relations, for instance, can be expressed in texts.

In its purest form, addition is signaled in texts by the **coordinating conjunction** *and* and transitional expressions such as *also* and *in addition*. Additive *and* is particularly common in spontaneous dialogues; such dialogues are unplanned and *and* serves as a way for speakers to signal that they are adding something new to what they said previously:

I'd always wanted to go to Australia. **And** I met this Australian in London **and** I lived with him for a year and went to Australia. But something happened. **And** I don't this is the big thing I don't know. I felt we had to break up **and** that we just couldn't stay together **and** sort of our sex life disappeared **and** for years we were just completely platonic.

(ICE-GB-S1A–050–5–10)

In written registers, such uses of *and* would not occur, since writers have the opportunity to more carefully plan what they are going to write next.

Exemplification is another kind of additive relationship. Expressions such as *for instance* or *for example* indicate that a specific example of some previously mentioned general point is forthcoming. In the example below, *for instance* introduces an example of how the Volga provinces differed from other parts of Russia:

In general, conditions of land tenure, communal arrangements, and cultural traditions differed considerably in the Volga provinces from those in the West and the centre of European Russi. **For instance**, members of Volga communes were apt to be more outward-looking than those in Kursk guberniia because of their wider market ties and better transport facilities.

(BNC A64 1015)

Adversative relationships are marked by the coordinating conjunction *but* and other expressions such as *however*, *instead*, and *in contrast* that serve to mark some kind of difference or contrast between sections of a text. Towards the end of the excerpt below, *however* indicates that there are two views on postmodernism: that it is either a "break from modernism" or a "continuation of" it:

Some theorists have thought about postmodernism as a kind of radical break from modernism, so a radical shift from, the kind of, sort of stylistic, and theoretical example set by somebody like Mies van der Rohe. Others **however** argue that it's merely a continuation of modernism.

(MICASE LEL320JU147)

Causal and temporal relationships are marked, respectively, by expressions such as *therefore*, *as a result*, and *so*, and *first*, *finally*, and *then*. Because the passage below is a narrative, the three occurrences of *then* mark the progression of time in the story. In addition, *so* in the third text unit indicates that because two women were sitting and available, the individual being referred to decided to walk up to one of them and begin talking to her.

<$C> <#> He was sitting there there were two guys sitting at a table right where you are <#> And **then** these two women are sitting here <#> **So** uh he comes over there and is talking with that woman <#> I don't know about what but **then** like ten minutes later she and her friend are over at their table <#> And **then** twenty minutes later they were kinda like all over each other <#> You know <#> kissing et cetera et cetera

(SBCSAE)

So is a highly informal marker of causation. In more formal texts, *therefore* or *as a result* would be used instead.

Summary

Although definitions of a text will vary, most linguists would agree that for a text to achieve coherence, it must exhibit unity of structure and unity of texture: it must have a clearly identifiable beginning, middle, and end, and the clauses within it must be linked together by various cohesive devices. While it is possible, as the next chapter will demonstrate, to offer a precise definition of a sentence, how texts attain structural and textural unity is subject to considerably more variation. In both open and closed registers, speakers and writers will ensure that the texts they create have textural unity by appropriately placing new and given information; using various constructions to add emphasis where necessary; and drawing upon cohesive devices to help tie sentences, clauses, and utterances together.

Self-study activities

1. Why do some feel that email has features of both spoken and written English?
2. Name some contexts better suited to writing than to speech, and vice versa. For instance, are there situations when you'd rather send someone an email than talk to them on the phone?
3. Would the conversation a patient and doctor have during an annual medical examination be part of an open or closed register?

4. In the sentences below, which expressions would be considered old information?

    Lately, the Boston area has been hit with a number of ice storms. These storms have caused numerous traffic accidents. They have also made sidewalks very slippery to walk on.

5. Style manuals frequently criticize the use of sentences in the passive voice, advising writers to prefer the active voice instead. Is this good advice? Are there occasions when the passive voice is necessary?

6. Find two different types of cohesion in the passage below. Explain your choices.

    Ordinarily, earthworms are considered gardeners' most trusted helpers, natural plows that churn dirt and deposit nutrient-rich beads of soil that feed plants. But the wrigglers have a darker side ... they are now so numerous and widespread that they are dramatically changing the forest ecosystem, devouring a layer of the forest floor that native wildflowers, beetles, and other species need to survive.

    (*Boston Globe*, Monday, Dec. 11, 2006, p. C1)

Further reading

For a discussion of general differences between speech and writing as well as differences between registers of speech and writing, see D. Biber, *Variation Across Speech and Writing* (New York: Cambridge University Press, 1988). Differences between spoken and written registers found at universities are described in D. Biber, *University Language: A Corpus-based Study of Spoken and Written Registers* (Amsterdam: Benjamins, 2006). A more cognitively based approach to text structure can be found in W. Kintsch, *Comprehension: A Paradigm for Cognition* (Cambridge University Press, 1998). An overview of conversational analysis is presented in E. A. Schegloff, *Sequence Organization in Interaction: A Primer in Conversation Analyis*, Vol. I (Cambridge University Press, 2007). Two key books on unity of structure and texture are M. A. K. Halliday and R. Hasan's *Cohesion in English* (London: Longman, 1976) and *Language, Context, and Text: Aspects of Language in a Social-Semiotic Perspective* (Victoria, Australia: Deakin University Press, 1985). An overview of the Prague School approach to communicative dynamism is described in J. Firbas, *Functional Sentence Perspective in Written and Spoken Communication* (Cambridge University Press, 1992).

5 English syntax

CHAPTER PREVIEW

This chapter is concerned with one facet of structure, English syntax: how words are grouped and ordered within sentences, clauses, and phrases. For instance, English places adjectives before nouns (e.g. *beautiful house*) rather than after them (**house beautiful*), a feature of English syntax that distinguishes Germanic languages from Italic languages, which generally favor the placement of adjectives after the nouns that they modify (e.g. Italian *casa bella* 'house beautiful').

KEY TERMS

Clause functions

Clauses

Constituency

Form/function

Formal/notional definitions

Linear/ hierarchical structure

Phrases

Sentences

Word classes

Introduction

This chapter marks a major transition in the book. It moves the discussion from a focus on principles of pragmatics to a description of rules of grammar. In other words, instead of describing *why* particular structures are used in specific contexts, the discussion will focus more explicitly on *how* particular constructions are formed. At the center of any discussion of syntax is the notion of **constituency**: the idea that syntactic units are not simply arbitrarily grouped and ordered but form identifiable units. Traditionally, syntacticians have identified four different levels of structure at which constituents can occur:

sentences $\rightarrow$ clauses $\rightarrow$ phrases $\rightarrow$ words
largest   smallest

The largest constituent is the sentence; the smallest is the word. Between these two extremes are clauses and phrases, though as will be demonstrated later, sometimes sentences and clauses are identical: a declarative sentence, for instance, may consist of one **main clause**.

There are two different types of constituents: immediate constituents and ultimate constituents. Exactly which elements constitute immediate constituents depends upon what level of structure (sentence, clause, phrase) is being considered. To illustrate this point, consider the sentence below:

Robbin Mayfield and his graffiti-removal crew drive an old Wonderbread truck

(ICE-USA W2C-002)

At the highest level, the sentence itself is a constituent. But within the sentence, one can find several immediate constituents: separate units into which a given structure can be divided. For instance, the sentence can be divided into two immediate constituents: the **subject** (*Robbin Mayfield and his graffiti-removal crew*) and the **predicate** (*drive an old Wonderbread truck*). The predicate, in turn, contains two additional immediate constituents: the verb (*drive*) and the noun phrase (*an old Wonderbread truck*). At the level of the word, the lowest level of structure, we find the ultimate constituents: the individual words themselves (*Robbin*, *Mayfield*, *and*, *his*, etc.). The details of exactly how notions such as subject and verb are defined will be described in greater detail in subsequent sections of the chapter. At this stage, however, it is reasonable to consider why *an old Wonderbread truck* is considered a constituent, but *his graffiti-removal crew drive an* is not.

To identify constituents, it is possible to apply specific tests. One test for constituents that Huddleston and Pullum (2002: 21) describe involves the insertion of a moveable adverb into the sentence, since an adverb such as *probably* can only be placed at constituent boundaries. Notice that in the above example, the adverb *probably* can be inserted between immediate constituents (the subject and predicate), but not within a constituent itself (e.g. between *old* and *Wonderbread*):

Robbin Mayfield and his graffiti-removal crew probably drive an old
Wonderbread truck

*Robbin Mayfield and his graffiti-removal crew drive an old **probably**
Wonderbread truck [an asterisk placed before a sentence indicates that
the sentence is ungrammatical]

Other tests for constituency include whether one word can be substituted for another (e.g. a pronoun for a noun) and which constructions can
be moved when systematic changes are made to a sentence. In the example below, the pronouns *it* and *them* could be substituted for the first and
last part of the sentence, indicating that these two parts of the sentence
are constituents, specifically noun phrases:

One of the best known models was constructed by J. A. Howard and J. Sheth
(BNC G3F 1121)

It was constructed by **them**

This example is also in the passive voice. If the sentence is changed to the
active voice, the noun phrase following *by* is moved to the subject position
in the sentence:

J. A. Howard and J. Sheth constructed one of the best known models

If the original sentence is made into a question, the subject switches
places with the verb *was*:

Was **one of the best known models** constructed by J. A. Howard and J.
Sheth?

What insertion, substitution, and movement tests illustrate is that at
the level of syntax, certain structures form units but others do not.
Those structures that do form units are not an arbitrary and ad hoc collection of constructions, but constructions that can be assigned formal
grammatical descriptions – descriptions that identify a finite set of
grammatical constructions that form the building blocks of English
syntax. The remainder of this chapter describes and defines these
constructions. But before the constructions are defined, it is necessary
to describe the two primary ways that grammatical categories are
defined.

Formal vs. notional definitions

Grammatical descriptions are of two types: formal or notional. Formal
descriptions focus on specific characteristics of a grammatical construction. For instance, the word *truck* in English can be classified as a noun
because it shares with many (but not all) nouns in English the ability to be
pluralized by the addition of orthographic *s*: *trucks*. Notional definitions, in
contrast, are more semantic in nature and define constructions in terms of
general qualities that they possess. Notionally, nouns are defined as anything that is a person, place, thing, or idea. *Truck* is a noun because it is a
"thing."

Modern linguistics favors formal over notional definitions, largely because formal descriptions provide a better means of identifying constructions than notional descriptions. As an illustration of this point, consider the opening lines of Lewis Carroll's *Jabberwocky*:

> 'Twas brillig, and the slithy toves
> Did gyre and gimble in the wabe:
> All mimsy were the borogoves,
> And the mome raths outgrabe.

This poem is often cited as evidence that when readers or listeners parse sentences (i.e. identify nouns, verbs, and so forth), they rely not on notional definitions of grammatical categories but on formal definitions instead. Because readers unfamiliar with the poem will not know what *toves* means, they will be unable to determine whether it is a person, place, thing, or idea. Instead, they will have to rely on more formal criteria: *toves* ends in the plural marker -*s* and follows the adjective *slithy*. And even though readers will also not know what *slithy* means, they will be able to identify it as an adjective because it follows the article *the*; precedes the noun *toves*, the precise position in the noun phrase where adjectives in English typically occur; and ends in -*y*, a word ending associated with adjectives (e.g. *filthy* and *hefty*). Now, there may seem to be considerable circularity in the reasoning here: both *slithy* and *toves* are simultaneously interpreted as an adjective and noun, respectively. But this is the essence of syntactic analysis: how constructions are parsed depends crucially upon where they occur in a sentence or clause in relation to other constructions.

While some kind of notional, or semantic, analysis can complement purely formal analyses, notional analyses alone are way too vague to provide definitive definitions of grammatical constructions. For instance, in many notional grammars, verbs are characterized as expressing either action (e.g. *walk*, *talk*, *run*) or a state of being (e.g. *am* as in *I am tired*). However, while this definition works in many cases, in some instances it leads to an incorrect analysis. The word *handshake* expresses an action: the movement of hands involved in the act of shaking someone's hand. But this word is not a verb but a noun, a determination that can be reached on purely formal grounds. In the example below, although *handshake* cannot be pluralized, it occurs after the possessive pronoun *His*, which occurs in the same position prior to the noun that the article *the* does:

His handshake was dry and firm and his smile reached his clear grey eyes.

(ICE-GB W2F-004 061)

Because notional definitions do not always yield correct analyses, most linguists rely primarily on formal definitions of grammatical constructions, a methodology that will be followed throughout this chapter.

If notional definitions are so problematic, it is worth asking why they persist. One reason is that they have a long tradition in English grammar, largely because grammars of English are based on the terminology found in classical Greek and Roman grammars. For instance, the notional definition of a sentence as a "complete thought" can be traced back to Dionysius Thrax's Greek grammar written ca. 100 BC. Linguists of the modern era have modified this terminology as a result of advances in linguistic science and the need to have terminology that describes languages that are very different from Greek, Latin, English, and other Indo-European languages – the languages upon which **traditional grammar** is based. Thus, many of the modern, more scholarly grammars of English, such as Randolph Quirk *et al.*'s (1985) *A Comprehensive Grammar of the English Language*; Rodney Huddleston and Geoffrey Pullum's (2002) *The Cambridge Grammar of the English Language*; and Douglas Biber *et al.*'s (1999) *The Longman Grammar of Spoken and Written English*, will contain a mixture of more traditional and more recent terminology.

Advances in linguistics, however, have led to the development of a fairly extensive and sophisticated vocabulary of linguistic terms – terms that are far too advanced for the potential audience for discussions of English grammar. Hence, notional definitions persist in many school grammars. School grammars are different from scholarly grammars in that they are written for school-age children and young adults. They contain primarily notional definitions because it is thought that more formally based definitions are too advanced for students at this level: simple and straightforward definitions are more important than those that are theoretically more accurate. This trade-off has led to considerable controversy among educators, since there is extensive evidence that students taught purely notional definitions never fully learn grammar. Moreover, in the study of foreign languages, notional definitions become even less valuable: to learn how gender is marked in Spanish or French, for instance, one needs formal knowledge of articles and of gender endings for nouns. Notional definitions of gender will not suffice in this instance, since beginning learners of languages do not know enough vocabulary to be able to determine, for instance, whether something is a person, place, thing, or idea.

The linear and hierarchical structuring of constituents

English has constraints on both the linear ordering of constituents and on their hierarchical groupings. As an illustration of the difference between the linear and hierarchical nature of syntax, consider the expression *foreign language specialist*, which exemplifies the notion of structural ambiguity: two different meanings depending upon how the words in the expression are grouped.

How *foreign language specialist* is interpreted depends not just on how the words are ordered but upon whether *language* is grouped with *foreign* or *specialist*, as schematized in (a) and (b) below:

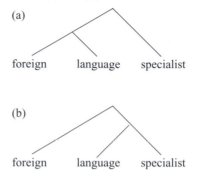

(a)

foreign   language   specialist

(b)

foreign   language   specialist

In (a), because *foreign* and *language* are grouped, the phrase has the meaning of 'a specialist in foreign languages.' In (b), in contrast, the grouping of *language* and *specialist* creates the meaning of 'a language specialist who is foreign-born.'

Groupings of this nature constitute the core of English syntax, and along with constraints on the linear order of constituents, they allow linguists to describe the form and function of various kinds of constructions in English, from the sentence down to the word.

Form and function

Constituents can be described in terms of their form and their function. In the clause *The child is healthy*, *healthy* has the form of an **adjective phrase** and the function of a **subject complement**. The form of some constituents can be determined by the particular suffixes that they contain as well as their positions relative to other constituents. *Healthy* contains an ending, *-y*, that is used to convert nouns to adjectives. Thus, *healthy* is derived from *health*, *tasty* from *taste*, *wealthy* from *wealth*, and so forth. *Healthy* is also a predicative rather than an attributive adjective: it occurs following the **linking verb** *is* rather than directly before the noun, as in *the healthy child*. *Healthy* is functioning in the clause as a subject complement because it follows the linking verb *is* and describes the subject of the sentence, *the child*.

The kinds of criteria applied above to identify adjectives and subject complements can be applied to all forms and functions in English. Such an analysis reveals that constituents have forms at all four levels of structure:

Word Classes: noun, verb, adjective, adverb, preposition, etc.
Phrases: noun phrase, verb phrase, adjective phrase, adverb phrase, prepositional phrase
Clauses: main, dependent
Sentences: declarative, interrogative, imperative, exclamatory

While all types of phrases, clauses, and sentences are given in the list above, only a sampling of word classes is given, since additional classes exist in English (e.g. articles, pronouns, conjunctions).

English has far fewer functions, and these functions are restricted to elements occurring within clauses (both main and subordinate). Thus, the functions below are often referred to as clause functions:

Subject
Predicator
Complement (subject and object)
Object (direct and indirect)
Adverbial

Since constituent forms and functions are key components of syntax, the next two sections provide an overview of some of the important form classes in English and the particular clause functions that these particular forms can have.

Word classes and phrases

Word classes and phrases are very closely linked. First of all, a phrase is named after the word class that acts as **head** of the phrase. A head is a word upon which everything in a phrase is centered. In a phrase such as *full of hope*, for instance, all parts of the phrase are associated with the adjective *full*. Therefore, this construction is called an adjective phrase. Likewise, in the phrase *might have mattered*, everything is associated with the **lexical verb** *mattered*, making this a verb phrase. In fact, word classes and phrases are so closely linked that there are cases where a single word can constitute a phrase. In the sentence *Necessity is the mother of invention*, *necessity* is both a noun and a noun phrase. It is a noun, as will be demonstrated in the section immediately below, because it contains the suffix *-ity*, one of a series of suffixes that occur on nouns. It is a noun phrase because it is functioning as subject of the sentence, one key function of noun phrases that will be described more fully in a later section on clause functions.

To describe both word classes and phrases, the discussion in this section will focus on two of the more important phrase types – noun phrases and verb phrases – and the other types of phrases (such as prepositional phrases) that can occur within them.

Noun phrases

All noun phrases (NPs) are centered on either a head noun or pronoun (more on pronouns later in this section). One key characteristic of nouns is that most exhibit **number**: they have a singular or plural form often marked in writing by orthographic *s*. (In speech, as will be demonstrated in Chapter 7, there are actually three different pronunciations of *-s*.) However, as Table 5.1 illustrates, not all nouns fit into this pattern.

Nouns have traditionally been distinguished as being **count** or **non-count**. Count nouns are literally "countable": we can think of a table as either a single (one) or plural (more than one) entity. Although most count nouns take the regular plural ending, some like *ox* take an irregular plural ending (*oxen*); others exhibit a change in vowel going from the singular to

Table 5.1. Count and non-count nouns in English	
Category	Examples
Count Nouns	
• regular plural marker: *-s*	table(s), clock(s), desk(s), bus(es)
• archaic plural marker	ox(en), child(ren), foot/feet, mouse/mice, tooth/teeth
• borrowed plural marker	criteri(on)/criteri(a), dat(um)/dat(a), stimul(us)/stimul(i)
• same form for singular and plural	deer (sg.)/deer (pl.), fish (sg.)/ fish (pl.), sheep (sg.)/sheep (pl.)
• no singular form	pants, scissors, glasses (i.e. eyewear), shorts
Non-count Nouns	furniture, freedom, water, money, evidence, music

the plural: singular *goose*, for instance, becomes plural *geese*. Typically, the examples in this category preserve forms going back to Old English: *-en* ended a number of nouns during this era; the vowel changes, resulting from the process of umlauting, were common too. Number can also be marked by:

- Singular and plural forms borrowed from other languages. The endings on singular *criterion* and plural *criteria*, for instance, were borrowed into English from Ancient Greek. Sometimes borrowings of this type will have both regular and irregular forms: *concerto* was borrowed into English from Italian and can either be pluralized with English *-s* (*concertos*) or Italian *-i* (*concerti*). Sometimes borrowed forms have lost their foreign suffix and become a regular English plural: although *gymnasium* was borrowed from Latin, it is more common to see *gymnasiums* than *gymnasia*.
- No overt plural markers at all (e.g. one *deer*, two *deer*). Occasionally, nouns in this category will have a regular plural form too. For instance, biologists often use *fishes* rather than *fish*.
- No singular, but only a plural form (e.g. *scissors* but not **scissor*). These forms are generally found on objects having two parts, such as the two blades on a pair of scissors, or the two legs on a pair of pants.

There are also non-count nouns, which make no distinction between a singular or plural form. Thus, it is possible to talk of *furniture* – which would include a group of items, such as chairs, couches, beds, etc. – but not **furnitures*. Some nouns have both count and non-count forms. In the first example below, *water* is a non-count noun, since it is being used to describe a liquid of unknown quantity:

Medical care was virtually non-existent, food and **water** often withheld,
and torture rife.

(BNC AO3 224)

In the next example, however, because *waters* refers to more than one lake
or river, it is being used as a count noun in this context:

The northern squawfish ... has caused substantial depletions of juvenile
salmonids in various **waters**

(ICE-USA-W2A-022)

Nouns can also be marked by various suffixes. For instance, the suffix
-ion can be added to verbs to form an abstract noun called a nominalization: *create* → *creation* or *fascinate* → *fascination*. Other noun suffixes
include *-er* or *-or*, which are added to verbs to create nouns for someone
who does something (e.g. *wait* → *waiter*, *act* → *actor*), and *-ence* or *-ance*,
which are also added to verbs to create nouns (*exist* → *existence*, *tolerate* →
tolerance). Other nouns, particularly those that are animate, can take possessive *'s*: *the man's watch*, *the teacher's book*.

Personal pronouns in English, which can also serve as the head of a
noun phrase, make distinctions not found on nouns. Table 5.2 lists the
various forms that personal pronouns take in English.

Table 5.2. Personal pronouns in English					
Person	Subjective	Objective	Reflexive	Possessive	Indefinite
1st	I (sg.) we (pl.)	me us	myself ourselves	my/mine our/ours	
2nd	you (sg. and pl.)	you	yourselves	your/yours	
3rd	he, she, it (sg.) they (pl.)	him, her, it them	himself, herself, itself themselves	his, her(s), its their(s)	somebody, someone, everyone, all, none

Like nouns, most personal pronouns (with the exception of *you*) are
marked for number (e.g. singular *she*, plural *them*). The pronoun *you* is
quite anomalous in this regard. It appears to be marked only for plural
number because it always takes a plural verb:

And you are Mrs McDougall?

(BNC CKF 214)

However, in the example above, *you* is clearly being directed toward a single individual. In earlier periods, English did have both a singular and plural form, but over time the distinction was lost. To explicitly pluralize *you*
in Modern English, it is only possible to use a circumlocution such as *all
of you*:

First of all I'd like to thank **all of you** for agreeing to be on the committee, reading the draft, and coming to the defense.

(MICASE DEF500SF016)

Plural forms of *you* do exist, but in restricted contexts: *y'all* in Southern varieties of American English, and *youse* in some non-standard varieties of English.

Pronouns make many more distinctions than nouns:

- Pronouns have three persons. First person pronouns are directed towards the speaker or writer, second person pronouns toward the addressee, and third person pronouns to someone or something being discussed.
- First and third person pronouns have subjective and objective forms – the second person pronoun *you* does not. The subjective forms are used when the pronouns are functioning as subject of a clause (e.g. *I like pizza*, **She** *jogs daily*). The objective forms are used when the pronouns are functioning as objects in a clause or as objects of prepositions (e.g. *My mother called* **us**, *The burden of proof is on* **them**).
- All pronouns have reflexive and possessive forms. Reflexive pronouns refer back to a co-referential noun or pronoun, as in *The children amused* **themselves** or *We must remind* **ourselves** *to arrive early tomorrow*. Possessive forms occur either before a head noun in a noun phrase (e.g. **my** *book*, **your** *watch*) or as head of a noun phrase (e.g. *That cookie is* **mine**, *Those glasses must be* **hers**).
- Indefinite pronouns, such as *someone* or *none*, occur only in the third person and have only a single form. Unlike first and second person pronouns, they do not change form in subject or object positions.

The internal structure of noun phrases.   While it is possible for a noun phrase to contain only a single head noun or pronoun, other form classes can optionally occur before or after the head noun. The diagram below schematizes some common form classes occurring in noun phrases and their positions relative to the head noun:

Determinative Phrases	Adjective Phrases	Head Noun	Prepositional Phrases/ Relative Clauses
the	expensive	house	on the hill
every	beautiful	city	that we visited

The first position in the noun phrase contains a class of words called **determinatives** (Huddleston and Pullum 2002: 368–99), which are part of determinative phrases. These words include the articles (*a*, *an*, and *the*), demonstratives (e.g. *this*, *that*, *these*, *those*), indefinite pronouns (e.g. *all*, *every*, *most*, *many*), and cardinal numbers (e.g. *one*, *two*, *three*).

The second position (if the noun phrase contains a determinative phrase) is occupied by adjective phrases, which immediately precede the head noun. Like nouns, adjectives can sometimes be identified by the suffixes that they contain. Degree adjectives (i.e. adjectives that can be measured on a scale) that are one or two syllables in length will have comparative and superlative forms ending in, respectively, *-er* and *-est*: *small, smaller, smallest; nice, nicer, nicest*. Adjectives that are lengthier will take *more* or *most* instead: *beautiful, more beautiful, most beautiful; conservative, more conservative, most conservative*. Adjectives also sometimes have suffixes found only on adjectives, such as *-ic* (e.g. *electric, fantastic, diabetic*), *-able* (e.g. *reasonable, comfortable, tolerable*), *-ive* (e.g. *festive, conducive, restive*), or *-al* (e.g. *diabolical, rational, seasonal*).

In the examples in the diagram above, adjective phrases consist of a single adjective. However, it is also possible for adjective phrases to contain more than one adjective as head, as is the case with *quick* and *just* preceding *victory* in the example below:

It was in the U-S government's interest to present Desert Storm as a **quick** and **just** victory

(MICASE LEL220JU071)

The head adjective can also be preceded by an intensifying adverb, such as *very* or *somewhat*:

The people in the wheelchairs in the group are already ***very* proficient** dancers.

(ICE-GB S1A-001 076)

This ***somewhat* idiosyncratic** interpretation is no doubt coloured by the specificities of French history

(BNC AOK 21)

The final position in the noun phrase, which follows the head noun, can optionally contain either a prepositional phrase or a **relative clause** (a type of clause discussed in a later section on subordinate clauses). Unlike nouns and adjectives, prepositions have no particular form: no suffix, for instance, that uniquely marks a word as a preposition. In addition, prepositions cannot usually stand alone but require an object, typically a noun phrase such as *the hill*, in *on the hill*, but also clauses. In the first example below, the preposition *in* is followed by a clause beginning with *keeping*. In the second example, *of* is followed by a clause beginning with *what*:

It plays a key role **in *keeping city streets on the move*** and is even the object of the best modern designers' desire.

(BNC A3M 67)

So we have this idea **of *how well they're closing and opening***.

(ICE-GB S2A-056 056)

The semantic classes in which prepositions can be classified are quite complex. Two of the more basic meanings that prepositions express are time and location. In *on the hill*, *on* specifies location. In other contexts, however, it can express time: *on time, on my birthday*. Other prepositions can likewise express both time and space: *in a moment/in the garden; at noon/at my father's house; by tomorrow/by the bookcase*. However, while these meanings are easy to discern, others are more difficult. For instance, the preposition *in* preceding *keeping city streets on the move* in the above example has no easily

Table 5.3. Idiomatic combinations of prepositions with nouns, verbs, and adjectives

Category	Examples
Nouns	an expert *in* aerodynamics, an authority *on* golf, a fight *over* money, the pick *of* the litter
Verbs	call *off* the meeting, tear *up* the contract, get *on* with your life, cave *in* to their demands, talk *through* his problems, track *down* the order
Adjectives	prone *to* anxiety, low *on* money, jealous *of* his brother, satisfied *with* the results

identifiable meaning. Instead, its use is more a consequence of its following the head noun *role*, which purely for reasons of idiom takes the preposition *in*. English contains many idiomatic combinations of prepositions with nouns, verbs, and adjectives. Table 5.3 contains some examples. Of course, this is a mere sampling of the various idiomatic combinations represented in the table. Verb–preposition combinations are so common in English that they are sometimes referred to as phrasal verbs or prepositional verbs. One difference between the two constructions is that while the preposition can be moved in a phrasal verb –

I've got to **take down** all that wallpaper.

(CIC)

... **take** all that wallpaper **down**.

– in a prepositional verb, it cannot:

She **looked at** Ethel, who had secured a notebook and pencil.

(BNC AOD 2249)

*She **looked** Ethel **at**, ...

Embedding and recursion. The occurrence of a prepositional phrase within a noun phrase is one example of a more general phenomenon in syntax, **embedding**: the inclusion of one structure within another structure. The noun phrase below contains multiple instances of embedding:

... acts of successful mob violence against the authority of the church and nobility

(ICE-USA W2A-001)

The head noun of the phrase, *acts*, is followed by an embedded prepositional phrase beginning with *of*. This prepositional phrase, in turn, contains an embedded noun phrase, *successful mob violence*. Embedded in the head of this noun phrase, *mob violence*, is another prepositional phrase beginning with *against*, whose object, *the authority*, contains an additional embedded prepositional phrase: *of the church and nobility*.

    The process of repeatedly embedding similar structures in other structures is known as **recursion**. In theory, recursion is potentially endless,

since in an example such as the one above, one could embed prepositional phrases in noun phrases *ad infinitum*. In practice, however, there
are obvious limitations on embedding: excessive embedding leads to
lengthy constructions that are not just stylistically awkward but difficult
to interpret.

The verb phrase

In general, linguists and grammarians have offered fairly similar definitions of the noun phrase. However, there are two varying perspectives on
the verb phrase: one providing a relatively constrained definition of the
verb phrase, the other a more expansive definition.

For Quirk *et al.* (1985), the verb phrase contains two components: an
obligatory **lexical verb** (or "full verb," to use their terminology), which
acts as head of the verb phrase, and one or more optional **auxiliary verbs**.
If there are any auxiliary verbs in the verb phrase, they will always precede
the lexical verb, with **modal auxiliaries** coming first and **primary auxiliaries** second. In the example below, the verb phrase begins with the
modal auxiliary *can*, which is followed by the primary auxiliary *be* and
then the lexical verb *read*:

Certainly, a lot **can be read** into a hairstyle.

(BNC A7N 698)

Lexical verbs are an **open class** – new lexical verbs are continuously
being added to the English language – and can be classified as **regular** or
irregular. Table 5.4 lists the five forms that all lexical verbs take and contains examples of regular verbs as well as irregular verbs.

Table 5.4. Forms for regular and irregular verbs					
	Base	-s form	-ed past	-ed participle	-ing participle
Regular Verbs					
	walk	walks	walked	has walked	am walking
	move	moves	moved	has moved	am moving
	love	loves	loved	has loved	am loving
Irregular Verbs					
	drink	drinks	drank	has drunk	am drinking
	ring	rings	rang	has rung	am ringing
	bet	bets	bet	has bet	am betting
	sit	sits	sat	has sat	am sitting

Regular verbs have two characteristics: they will always contain the
same set of verb endings (-s, -ed, etc.), and their stems will never change.
The verb *walk*, for instance, will have a **base form** (sometimes called the
infinitive form) that has no verb ending and that is the form that would
be used following the infinitive marker *to*: *to walk*. In addition, there are

four forms used to mark **tense** and **aspect** (semantic notions that will be discussed in the next chapter). *Walk* has an *-s* and an *-ed* form used to mark the present tense (*walks*) and past tense (*walked*), respectively. The *-s* form, however, only occurs with third person singular subjects: *He walks, She walks, It walks*. With first person *I* or second person *you*, for instance, no ending is used: *I walk, You walk*. The *-ed* and *-ing* participle forms are used with the various forms of the primary auxiliaries *have* and *be* to mark **perfective aspect** (*have/has walked*) and **progressive aspect** (*am/was/were walking*).

Irregular verbs do not always have the same endings as regular verbs. In addition, the stems of irregular verbs do not remain constant but sometimes contain internal vowel changes: *fight*, for instance, becomes *fought* in the past tense. But despite irregularities such as these, irregular verbs do follow certain patterns. Quirk *et al.* (1985: 104–14) posit seven different classes of irregular verbs based on such criteria as the number of different forms a verb has as well as similarities in the change of vowels that the verb undergoes. For instance, *drink* and *ring* in Table 5.4 have five different forms. In addition, the vowel changes that the stems undergo are identical. The verbs *bet* and *sit* are similar in that they have only three distinct forms: the fewest number of forms that a verb can have in English. In contrast, the verb *be*, as Table 5.5 illustrates, has the greatest number of forms – eight – of any verb in English.

Table 5.5. The eight forms of the verb *be*

Base	-s form	-ed past	-ed participle	-ing participle
be	(I) am (we) are	was	have been	am being
	(you) are	were		
	(he/she/it) is (they) are			

Be has so many forms because it makes distinctions that other verbs do not. For instance, while regular verbs in the present tense end in *-s* only when they occur with third person singular subjects, *be* has three different forms in the present tense that vary by person (e.g. *am* with first person *I* and *is* with third person *he, she, it*). In addition, *be* has two different past tense forms – *was* and *were* – for singular and plural subjects, a distinction not made on regular verbs.

In contrast to lexical verbs, auxiliary verbs are members of a **closed class** rather than an open class. As a result, auxiliary verbs in English are finite in number and can simply be listed, as is done in Table 5.6.

As Table 5.6 illustrates, the primary auxiliaries *be* and *have* are marked for number, and they indicate, as was noted earlier, the progressive and perfective aspect, respectively. However, the primary auxiliary *do* has a different function: it mainly occurs in certain kinds of questions and negated sentences. In the first example below, *did* occurs with the lexical verb

Table 5.6. Primary and modal auxiliaries in English		
Auxiliary Type		
Primary	Present Tense	Past Tense
be/been/being	do(es)	did
	am/are/is	was/were
	has/have	had
Modal	**Central**	**Phrasal**
	may/might	
	can/could	
	will/would	be going to
	shall/should	ought to/need to
	must	have to

fight in a **wh-question**. In the second sentence, *did* occurs with the phrasal verb *pick up*.

Why **did** the Vietnamese ultimately *fight* on?

(MICASE LES495JU063O)

I **did** not *pick* her *up*

(ICE-GB S1A-020 004)

In both of the examples above, *did* has no real meaning: it is merely used to form a question or negate a sentence. For this reason, in some grammars it is referred to as dummy *do*. The exact details of why the sentences above are formed the way that they are will be discussed in the next section on clauses and sentence types.

Do has one additional use. In the example below, it is used to emphasize the fact that the speaker does indeed like to hear the addressee talk:

I **do** like to hear you talk.

(BNC GO7 625)

Without *do – I like to hear you talk* – the statement is far less emphatic.

There are two types of modal auxiliaries: central and phrasal. Table 5.6 lists all the central modals in English, plus some select phrasal modals. An expression such as *be going to* is considered a modal because, like *will*, it express future time and occurs at the beginning of the verb phrase. In the examples below, both *will* and *is going to* mark future time and occur before the lexical verb *leave*:

Joanne's commitment to the next 12 months **will** *leave* her little time for the hobbies that she enjoyed before tennis came along.

(BNC AOV 1096)

Joanne's commitment to the next 12 months **is going to** *leave* her little time for ...

However, while *will* and *is going to* are interchangeable in this context, in other contexts they are not.

Unlike primary auxiliaries, modal auxiliaries are typically not marked for either number or tense. The modal *must*, for instance, has the same form whether its subject is singular or plural:

The **machine must** serve the customer, not the other way around.

(ICE-GB W2E-009 084)

The **machines must** ...

In addition, the difference between modals such as *can* and *could* is usually one of meaning, not of tense. In the example below, substituting *could* for *can* does not change the tense in the sentence but instead the meaning:

Can you give us the title of the book?

(MICASE COL999MX040)

Could you give us the title of the book?

By using *can*, the speaker is asking the addressee whether she can actually supply the name of the book: this is a question requiring a yes or no answer. However, if *could* is substituted for *can*, the sentence becomes a polite request for the book title. In other words, the speaker assumes that the addressee knows the title of the book and is indirectly asking her for the title. This use of *could* was extensively discussed in Chapter 3 in sections on indirect speech acts and politeness.

While only one modal can occur in a verb phrase at a time, more than one primary auxiliary is possible. In examples below, two primary auxiliaries (*have been*) follow the modal auxiliary *may*.

Detectives said Mrs Page-Alucard **may *have been* murdered** as early as Friday morning, more than 24 hours before her body was discovered.

(BNC A49 659)

While it is possible to find up to three primary auxiliaries, such examples are rare. The example below contains three primary auxiliaries – *has*, *been*, and *being* – preceding the lexical verb *discussed*:

That er, er, little action has been taken in the last thirty forty years since this ***has been being discussed***, erm, I think the first international conference erm, produced their own report in nineteen sixty.

(BNC JJG 542)

Only two examples of verb phrases like this occurred in the 100-million-word British National Corpus.

Expanding the scope of the verb phrase. Because Quirk *et al.* (1985) restrict the verb phrase to consisting of only an obligatory lexical verb and one or more optional auxiliaries, they would schematize the verb phrase in the sentence *I called my mother* as diagrammed in Figure 5.1.

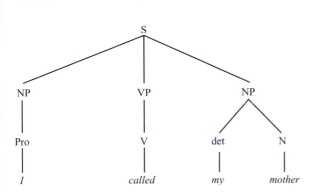

FIGURE 5.1
The verb phrase in Quirk *et al.* (1985).

According to the tree diagram in Figure 5.1, the two noun phrases and the verb phrase are separate constituents in the sentence (labeled as *S*): the final noun phrase, for instance, is not embedded in the verb phrase. Others, however, have claimed that post-verbal noun phrases such as *my mother* are not separate constituents in the sentence but embedded in the verb phrase, as diagrammed in Figure 5.2.

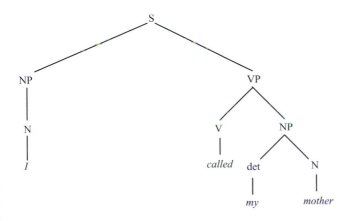

FIGURE 5.2
Alternative view of the verb phrase (Aarts and Haegeman 2006).

Aarts and Haegeman (2006: 130) argue for this analysis on the grounds that *called my mother* is a single unit rather than separate constituents in the sentence. As support for this claim, they note that if the pro-verb *do* were used to substitute for a part of the above sentence, *do* would substitute for both the verb and noun phrase, not just the verb. Therefore, if someone inquired "Did you call your mother," a possible reply would be "Yes, I did" with *did* substituting for *called my mother*. Substitution, as noted earlier, is one test for constituency.

Aarts and Haegeman (2006) provide additional evidence for including other elements in the verb phrase, such as adverb phrases. In an earlier discussion of the adjective phrase, it was noted that certain kinds of adverb phrases can occur within the adjective phrase and be used to intensify adjectives, as *very* does in the adjective phrase *very nice*. However, there is a second kind of adverb phrase that is quite moveable in a clause and as a result can occur in many different positions. For instance, consider the positions in which the adverb *only* occurs in the examples below:

I was the **only** teacher in the whole school who did not have textbooks

(SBCSAE)

The planner is set up so you can **only** choose one action for each state.

(MICASE DEF270SF061)

In the first example, *only* is focusing the head noun *teacher*, stressing that the teacher was the only instructor in the school without textbooks. Because *only* occurs between the article *the* and the head noun *teacher*, it makes sense to say that *only* is part of the noun phrase. In the second example, *only* occurs between the modal auxiliary *can* and the lexical verb *choose*. By the same logic, one would have to claim that *only* is part of the verb phrase. To claim otherwise (i.e. that *only* is outside the verb phrase), Aarts and Haegeman (2006: 129) argue, one would have to allow for a verb phrase that is "discontinuous"; that is, that *can* and *choose* in the above example are literally split in two and would constitute separate verb phrases separated by an adverb phrase containing *only*. Since such a con-stituent structure is implausible, it makes sense to say that verb phrases must be expanded to include adverb phrases as well.

Adverbs, which serve as heads of adverb phrases, are a very heteroge-neous form class. As Huddleston and Pullum (2002: 563) comment, "the adverb is a miscellaneous or residual category – the category to which words are assigned if they do not satisfy the more specific criteria for nouns, verbs, adjectives, prepositions, and conjunctions." Although Huddleston and Pullum (2002: 264) attempt to limit the number of items included in the class of adverbs, the class is still very large and diverse.

While many adverbs end with the suffix *-ly*, this is not always the case. For instance, the sentence below contains four adverbs ending in *-ly*:

A single-volume history has **recently** been **courageously** and **skillfully** attempted by Hugh Honour and John Fleming, which **inevitably** suffers from the problem of compression.

(BNC AO4 450)

The first adverb, *recently*, is a time adverb, a class including other adverbs ending in *-ly*, such as *momentarily* and *temporarily*. However, other time adverbs, such as *now* and *then*, do not end in *-ly*. Moreover, some words end-ing in *-ly*, such as *lovely* and *lonely*, are not adverbs at all but attributive adjectives, because they occur before nouns:

It's a **lovely** dress.

(BNC FS1 1260)

The remaining adverbs illustrate other adverb-types. The words *coura-geously* and *skillfully* are manner adverbs: adverbs that can be paraphrased as 'in a courageous manner' or 'in a skillful manner.' The last adverb, *inevitably*, is part of a large class of adverbs that Quirk *et al.* (1985: 620) label as content disjuncts: adverbs that enable a speaker or writer to "comment on the content of what he [or she] is saying [or writing]." In the above example, the writer uses the adverb *inevitably* to express his view that because the book was only one volume in length, it did not contain enough detail.

Although it is common for adverb phrases to be one word in length, if the adverb head expresses degree it can be intensified with the same adverbs used to intensify adjectives: **very** *recently*, **somewhat** *skillfully*, **quite** *erratically*. While intensifiers occur only before the adverbs that they intensify, other adverbs are moveable. However, different types of adverbs often have preferred positions within a clause. For instance, if place and time adverbs occur together, the place adverb (*here* in the example below) will always precede the time adverb (*yesterday*):

I saw that some of you were **here yesterday**.

(MICASE STP545JU091)

The adverb *hopefully* is both a disjunct (or **stance adverb** in some grammars) and a manner adverb. As a disjunct, it means 'It is hoped' and occurs either first in a sentence or shortly thereafter:

Hopefully it will improve Neil a bit but I think he's happier where he is now.

(ICE-GB S1A-025 285)

Well **hopefully** I won't be with Natalie by then so

(SBCSAE)

As a manner adverb, however, it means 'in a hopeful manner' and will tend to be positioned after the verb:

Loretta waited **hopefully**, anxious to hear more about Veronica's relationship with Puddephat.

(BNC HTR 2384)

Since manner adverbs are so closely related to the verb in a clause, they tend to occur either close to the verb or sentence-finally.

Conjunctive adverbs, such as *therefore* or *however*, occur very close to the start of a clause:

SU-m: So is that the review questions, all the review questions?
S1: Yeah um **however**, you can rest assured that the questions that were on the midterm will not be on the final.

(MICASE LAB175SU033)

As was noted in Chapter 3 in the section on cohesion, adverbs such as *however* establish links between parts of a text – links that are best established early in a clause. As a result, conjunctive adverbs occur towards the beginning of a clause.

The factors influencing the positioning of time adverbs such as *here* or conjunctive adverbials such as *consequently* apply not just to adverb phrases but to other phrases, such as prepositional phrases, as well: like *consequently*, the prepositional phrase *as a result* will occur towards the start of a clause. While these constructions have different forms, they have the same function: adverbial. The next section describes the notion of clause function in detail, and also elucidates the structure of two additional form classes: clauses and sentences.

Clauses, sentences, and clause functions

Like words and phrases, clauses and sentences have a specific form. For instance, the declarative sentence *The child rode a bicycle* consists of a noun phrase (*The child*) and a verb phrase (*rode a bike*) within which there is another noun phrase (*a bike*). However, clauses and sentences differ from words and phrases in that they can additionally be analyzed into clause functions: subject, predicator, object (direct or indirect), complement (subject or object), and adverbial. In the above example, *The child* functions as subject, *rode* as predicator, and *a bike* as direct object. Similar forms can have different functions because the function that a particular form has is relative to other forms with which it occurs. In the sentence *The police officer questioned the child*, *the child* now has the function of direct object, not subject of the sentence.

Of all the clause functions, the predicator is most important, since the lexical verb within the predicator determines the argument structure of a clause: the number and type of clause functions other than the predicator that can appear within a given clause. For instance, because the verb *died* is **intransitive** (i.e. does not allow an object), it can occur in a clause with as little as a single argument, the subject noun phrase *the patient* in the example below:

Although technically the health authority bears responsibility, in practice the funeral arrangements are made by the staff of the hospital where **the patient died**.

(BNC AOY 258)

In the next example, in contrast, because the verb *gave* is **transitive** (i.e. permits up to two objects), it allows for more arguments than *died*, in this case three arguments: a subject (*I*), an indirect object (*him*), and a direct object (*a red pepper*):

I gave **him** a red pepper

(SBCSAE)

While the verb within the predicator dictates which clause functions can occur within a clause, how functions such as subject and object are defined is determined by a series of linguistic characteristics that each function possesses and that distinguish one function from another. One characteristic is positional: subjects tend to occur before the verb, objects after the verb. However, this generalization does not always hold true: when objects are topicalized (as in *Beans I like*), they occur before the subject. For this reason, to adequately define a given clause function, more than one linguistic characteristic is typically associated with the function. Many sentences containing direct objects, for instance, can often undergo passivization, with the direct object becoming subject of a corresponding sentence in the passive voice. Thus, in the sentence *The police officer questioned the child*, the direct object – *the child* – becomes subject of a corresponding sentence in the passive voice: *The child was questioned by the police officer*.

To define clause functions as well as the form of the clauses and sentences in which they occur, this section begins with a discussion of the difference between main and subordinate clauses, describes how such clauses can be coordinated, and then defines the various clause functions as they occur in the four main types of sentences in English: declarative, interrogative, imperative, and exclamatory.

Main and subordinate clauses

All sentences consist of an obligatory main clause and one or more optional subordinate clauses. To begin describing main and subordinate clauses, it is useful to distinguish between finite and non-finite verb forms, and to discuss the various kinds of **subordinating conjunctions** that occur in subordinate clauses.

Although a single main clause can theoretically contain many different clause functions, the defining characteristic of all main clauses is that they must contain a predicator consisting of a finite verb. The predicator is a clause function that includes all of the elements making up Quirk *et al.*'s (1985) definition of a verb phrase: an obligatory lexical verb and one or more optional auxiliary verbs. In the three examples below, the predicators occur in a single main clause and are, respectively, *walks*, *talked*, and *was thinking*:

She just **walks** away.

(BNC A74 3045)

We **talked** about this yesterday too

(MICASE COL285MSSX038)

I **was thinking** of Turkish yoghurt

(ICE-GB S1A-063 018)

Each of the predicators, in turn, consists of either a lexical verb or auxiliary that is finite, some verbal element that is marked for tense: *walks* is marked for present tense, *talked* and *was* for past tense. Because each of the examples contains a finite verb and no markers of subordination, each of the examples qualifies as a main clause.

A clause becomes subordinate if it:

(1) lacks a finite verb and instead contains one or more non-finite verbs; or
(2) is headed by a subordinating conjunction such as *when, if, because,* or *who*.

In the verb phrase *was thinking*, while *was* is finite, *thinking* is non-finite. The verb *thinking*, an *-ing* participle, is non-finite because it is marked for **aspect**, not for tense. Because tense and aspect are semantic notions, they will be discussed in greater detail in the next chapter. But an analysis of the verb phrase *was thinking* will briefly illustrate the difference between the two notions. In this phrase, because the auxiliary *was* is marked for past tense, it locates the activity of "thinking" at some time in the past. The lexical verb *thinking*, in contrast, does not situate the act of "thinking" at any specific point of time. Instead, it focuses more on the "temporal flow" of the utterance, as Huddleston and Pullum (2002: 117) describe aspect, indicating that the activity of "thinking" was a continuous process. If the auxiliary *am* is used instead of *was*, the idea of a continuous activity persists, but the time frame of the "thinking" shifts to the present.

English has two aspects: the progressive and the perfective. The progressive, as noted above, is associated with *-ing* participles, the perfective with *-ed* participles. When these two participles occur in a clause without an accompanying finite verb, the clause will always be subordinate. To illustrate how subordination works, consider the example below, which contains two clauses: a subordinate clause (enclosed in brackets) followed by a main clause:

[**Thinking** he was taking a call from the FBI liaison man in London to announce Simon Cormack's release,] Michael Odell did not mind the hour: 5 a.m. in Washington.

(BNC CAM 1828)

As the term 'subordinate' suggests, a subordinate clause is always part of a main clause. In the example above, the opening clause (repeated as [a] below), which contains the non-finite participle *thinking*, is subordinate to the main clause ([b] below), which is marked by the finite auxiliary *did*, which is in the past tense:

(a) Thinking he was taking a call from the FBI liaison man in London to announce Simon Cormack's release ...
(b) ... Michael Odell did not mind the hour: 5 a.m. in Washington.

Theoreticians will differ over whether the subordinate clause is part of the main clause or separate from it. But the important point is that a subordinate clause is always associated with a main clause.

Clauses containing *-ing* participles are one of three types of non-finite verbs that Quirk *et al.* (1985: 150–1) identify as occurring in subordinate clauses. A second type contains a non-finite *-ed* participle. In the two examples below, the irregular *-ed* participles *driven* and *taken* head the subordinate clauses enclosed in brackets:

[**Driven** by disappointment in the present, concern for the future and nostalgia for the past,] feelings of nationalism flowed out again into old moulds.

(ICE-GB W2B-007–086)

So I have a Spanish um, English bilingual sample, [**taken** from a class actually of self identifying U-S Latinos.]

(MICASE STP355MG011)

In the two following examples, a third type of non-finite clause, called a **to-infinitive clause**, contains the base form of the verb preceded by the infinitive marker *to*:

[**To** choose the best model initially,] we examined main effects and interaction terms for the Armed Forces Qualifying Test composite.

(ICE-USA W2A-024)

[**To** begin to decrease this isolation] is therefore a vital part of the stress-
reduction programme.

(BNC CKS 1275)

While all of the previous subordinate clauses contained non-finite verb
phrases, it is also possible for a subordinate clause to contain a finite verb
phrase and be headed by a subordinating conjunction, such as *if*, *because*,
while, *who*, *when*, and *even though*. In the example below, the subordinating
conjunction *if* heads a subordinate clause containing the verb phrase *has
been discussed*, which is headed by the finite verb *has*:

I don't know [**if** that issue has been discussed by the um coordinating
council].

(SBCSAE)

The examples below contain additional instances of subordinate clauses with different subordinating conjunctions:

[**When** my finances are more stable] I will visit Paris.

(ICE-GB W1B-008 135)

They had a vague idea [**where** the place was].

(BNC AO3 846)

They were actually selling their beadworks [**because** they realized a lot of
Westerners were really into that.]

(MICASE LEL115JU090)

These actors are place entrepreneurs [**who** strive for maximum financial
return through investing, renting, or taxing property.]

(ICE-USA W2A-014)

The last example above with *who* is a specific type of subordinate clause
known as a relative clause. Relative clauses are embedded in noun phrases. They begin with a relative pronoun: *who(m)*, *which*, *that*, *whose*, and
(sometimes) *where* and *when*. In the above example, *who* is chosen because
it is used to replace a personal noun, in this case *place entrepreneurs*. The
relative pronoun *that* could also have been used:

These actors are place entrepreneurs **that** strive …

That can also replace non-personal nouns along with *which*. In the example below, *which* replaces the non-personal noun *cottage*:

I lived with an elderly lady in a little thatched *cottage* **which** looked like
something out of Hansel and Gretel.

(BNC BN1 2204)

The clause function of the noun phrase being relativized determines
the choice of *who* vs. *whom*. *Who* is used below because it replaces the

subject of the clause in which it occurs, a function illustrated by the fact that if a personal pronoun such as *they* or *them* is substituted for *who*, the choice is the subject form *they*:

Women **who** were never married or widows uh continue to play a major role in Pauline churches.

(MICASE COL605MX132)

Women [women were never married or widows] uh continue …
        [they were never …]

In the next example, *whom* is chosen because in this case an object is being replaced, as indicated by the choice of *them* rather than *they* to replace *those*:

Aeneas suffers perpetual isolation as he wanders from place to place, having lost those **whom** he loved.

(ICE-GB W1A-010 019)

Those [he loved those]
     [he loved them]

Because *whom* is dying out in English, it is being replaced by *who* in less formal styles:

… having lost those who he loved.

When objects are relativized, it is also possible to omit the relative pronoun altogether, creating a clause containing what is sometimes referred to as a zero-relative:

… having lost those he loved.

There is one additional type of subordinate clause, termed a verbless clause, that contains a subordinating conjunction but no predicator whatsoever. The example below contains the subordinator *when* followed by a prepositional phrase:

Franco never took major steps [**when** in doubt].

(BNC HPV 1012)

Implied in the above clause is a subject and predicator: when [*Franco was*] in *doubt*.

Coordination.   Subordinate clauses are sometimes referred to as dependent clauses because they are part of some other unit and cannot stand alone. A relative clause, for instance, is embedded in a noun phrase. With coordination, however, there is no dependency. Instead, two or more "like" units are connected by *and*, *or*, or *but*. The examples below illustrate four noun phrases coordinated by *and*:

These are an elite group comprising **Hong Kong**, **S. Korea**, **Taiwan**, and **Singapore**

(ICE-GB W1A-015 076)

two noun phrases coordinated by *or*:

The body is not **an instrument we can replace** or a **symbol we can contest**; it is inescapably us.

(ICE-USA W2A-001)

two non-finite *-ing* participle clauses coordinated by *and*:

Coming out of the libraries and **walking through the courtyard towards the gate at the other end**, you will see on your left the façade of the Church of St Mary.

(BNC APT 661)

and two main clauses coordinated by *but*:

There are a lot of ways you could you know check for inactivity but **the point is that's not a good measure of global quiescence**.

(MICASE MTG270SG049)

While *and* and *or* can connect more than two clauses, *but* is restricted to conjoining only two clauses.

While it is clear in the preceding examples that "like" units are coordinated, in some cases this notion becomes problematic. For instance, in the example below, two noun phrases are conjoined. However, the first noun phrase consists only of a forename – *Frank* – while the second noun phrase contains both a forename and surname: *Dweezil Zappa*.

However, free tempo soloing can sound great – just look at **Frank** and **Dweezil Zappa**.

(BNC C9J 2301)

To resolve the issue of non-parallelism in examples such as this, Matthews (1981: 203–7) argues that in the first conjoin of this example, the surname is "latent"; that is, its existence in this noun phrase is implied so that what is really coordinated is something like:

Frank [Zappa] and **Dweezil Zappa**

In other cases, it is necessary to propose **ellipsis**: the omission of some item that is identical to another item. The example below illustrates an instance of gapping: the deletion of some item in the middle of the second conjunct:

It looked like the sort of place where muggers **might** lurk and accidents [] wait to happen.

(ICE-GB W2F-006 #16:1)

In this example, the auxiliary *might* before *wait* in the second conjunct is deleted under identity with the instance of *might* before *lurk* in the first conjunct. By proposing ellipsis in the second conjunct, it is possible to claim that two like units – main clauses – are coordinated rather than one main clause and an incomplete second clause.

Clause functions

Clause functions are best defined in terms of their relationship to one another. While the pronouns *I* and *me* can clearly be regarded as subject and object pronouns, respectively, noun phrases in English have no such markings. Consequently, other linguistic criteria need to be considered to determine which function a particular element in a clause should be assigned. For instance, noun phrases can function as subject, object, complement, or adverbial. However, whether a noun phrase is functioning as, say, subject or direct object will depend upon the relationship the noun phrase has with the predicator. In the sentence *The child paints pictures*, the noun phrase *The child* is subject, not *pictures*, because subjects agree with predicators in number and direct objects do not. If *child* had been plural, the predicator would have had a different form: *The children paint pictures*. Of course, if the verb is changed to the past tense, agreement becomes irrelevant, since the same form, *painted*, would have been used with either *child* or *children*: *The child/children painted pictures*. This latter example does not invalidate agreement between subject and verb as an indicator of what is subject in a sentence. It simply indicates that additional linguistic criteria are needed to define each of the clause elements.

Because subject and predicator are functions that most clauses contain, these functions will be considered first as they help define the four types of sentences in English: declarative, interrogative, exclamatory, and imperative sentences. The section will close with a discussion of the remaining clause functions: objects (direct and indirect), complements (subject and object), and adverbials.

Although terms such as "subject" and "direct object" are used fairly consistently across various grammars of English, in some more traditionally based grammars other functions have different names. For instance, in some grammars, "predicate adjective" is used instead of "subject complement." For the sake of consistency, the terms used in this section (with one exception) follow those used in Quirk *et al.* (1985). The one difference concerns the term "verb," which Quirk *et al.* (1985) use to describe both the form of verbs as well as their function. Since this dual use of the term "verb" might create unwanted ambiguity, the term "predicator" is used instead to describe the function of verbal elements and "verb" reserved only to describe their form.

Subject and predicator. In an analysis of 677 sentences in 100 business letters, Pelsmaekers (1999: 266) found that 83 percent of the sentences were declarative, 11 percent imperative, and 6 percent interrogative (the frequency of exclamatory sentences was not included in the study). Although business English is hardly representative of English in general, these statistics do point to the prominence in written English of declarative sentences over imperative and interrogative sentences. In spoken English, the distributions are different. While Biber *et al.* (1999) do not give figures for the frequency of declarative sentences in spontaneous conversations, they do note that interrogatives (p. 211) and imperatives (p. 221) are more common in spontaneous conversations than in fiction, news, or academic writing, with interrogatives occurring more frequently than imperatives. These distributions obviously have a functional basis: unlike writing, conversation is interactive, resulting in speakers questioning one another more often or making more frequent use of imperatives to issue requests. Although imperatives lack subjects (except in special circumstances), the other three types of sentences contain (minimally) both a subject and predicator, making these two clause functions central clause elements.

The predicator has a fairly straightforward definition. It consists only of verbal elements: an obligatory lexical verb and one or more optional auxiliary verbs. In addition, only these elements can function as predicator, and they cannot have any additional functions. Subjects, however, are more varied in form – they can be noun phrases or certain types of clauses – and these forms can have other functions as well: noun phrases, for instance, can also function as objects, complements, or adverbials. For this reason, subjects are defined in terms of their position in a clause and their relation to the predicator.

Because the unmarked word order in English is S (subject) V (verb, or predicator) O (object), in declarative sentences the subject will most frequently precede the predicator. However, position alone is not sufficient to define the subject of a sentence because other clause elements, as noted earlier, can precede the predicator as well. In the example below, two noun phrases – *This morning* and *two workmen* – precede the predicator, *were screwing*:

This morning, two workmen were half-heartedly screwing new bulbs into the sockets.

(BNC HOF 1708)

Because the verb is plural (*were*) rather than singular (*was*), subject–verb agreement in the clause identifies the plural noun phrase *two workmen* as subject rather than the singular *This morning*. In cases where agreement is not relevant, however, the subject can be identified by comparing the structure of declarative and interrogative sentences, since systematic changes in the positioning of subjects and certain parts of the predicator occur when the structure of a declarative sentence and comparable interrogative sentence are contrasted.

In a yes/no question, one type of interrogative sentence, the subject and what Quirk *et al.* (1985: 79–81) term the **operator** switch positions within the clause. When the example above becomes a yes/no question, notice how the auxiliary *were* changes places not with *This morning* but with *two workmen*:

This morning, **were two workmen** half-heartedly *screwing* new bulbs into the sockets?

All auxiliary verbs (both primary and modal) can be operators as well as all forms of the lexical verb *be*, sometimes referred to as a **copula**. The examples below illustrate subject–operator inversion with, respectively, a modal auxiliary, primary auxiliary, and the lexical verb *be*:

Abortion *should* be illegal.

(MICASE STP545JU091)

→ *Should* **abortion** be illegal?

Both firms *have* taken a 45 per cent stake in each other's truck business.

(BNC A6W 172)

→ *Have* **both firms** taken a 45 per cent stake ...?

Some people *are* lucky

(SBCSAE)

→ *Are* **some people** lucky?

There is one additional operator that is used in questions containing a lexical verb other than *be* and no auxiliaries. The two examples below contain the lexical verbs *left* and *listens*. When the examples are made yes/no questions, the lexical verbs and subjects do not change positions (*leave she ...?). Instead, the operator *do* appears before the subject, carrying the tense of the lexical verb (past tense in the first example, present tense in the second):

She left it on the seashore.

(ICE-GB S1A-018 069)

→ *Did* **she** leave it on the seashore?

She listens to herself.

(BNC KBE 1398)

→ *Does* **she** listen to herself?

The use of so-called periphrastic *do* in the above examples is a relatively new phenomenon in English, dating back to Early Modern English. Not only is it used in questions such as the above but in parallel environments with the negative marker *not*. Consequently, when the first two examples below are negated, *not* will be positioned directly following *should* and *are*.

Should abortion be illegal?
→ Abortion **should** not be illegal.

Are some people lucky?
→ Some people *are* **not** lucky.

In the next example, however, *did* is added before *not*, just as it was added when the sentence had the form of a yes/no question:

Did she leave it on the seashore?
→ She *did* **not** leave it on the seashore.

In the other kind of major interrogative sentence in English, the **wh-question**, whether *do* is used or not with lexical verbs other than *be* is a matter of whether the question is subject-oriented or object-oriented. A **wh**-question begins with a **wh**-word such as *which*, *why*, *when*, *who*, *where*, and *how*. While a yes/no question elicits a yes or no response (except, of course, in the case of indirect speech acts), a **wh**-question requests specific information from the listener, or in written texts asks a rhetorical question of the reader:

What *do* we have in common, **what** *can* we talk about?

(ICE-USA W2A-020)

When *is* it appropriate to use a T-test and **when *isn't*** it?

(MICASE OFC575MU046)

How *have* you been since then?

(ICE-GB S1A-089 221)

Where *did* that language of exaggeration come from?

(SBCSAE)

In the above examples, the choice of an operator follows the pattern exhibited with yes/no questions and negation: *do* with the lexical verb *have* in the first example, for instance; inversion with *can* in the second example. However, this pattern differs when the focus of the *wh*-word is on the subject rather than the object. Both of the examples below contain some form of the lexical verb *go*. In the first example, the focus is on whom the person went to. A possible response to the question is *He went to her*. This is therefore an object-oriented *wh*-question and requires use of periphrastic *do*.

Who did he go to?

(BNC HTX 4084)

The next example, however, focuses on the individual who went into the room. A possible reply to the question is *She went into the room*. In contrast to the previous example, this is a subject-oriented *wh*-question. Therefore, periphrastic *do* is not used:

Who went into my room?

(BNC FS8 2110)

In addition to declarative and interrogative sentences, English also has exclamatory and imperative sentences. As Quirk *et al.* (1985: 834–5) note, exclamatory sentences (or 'exclamatives' as they term them) are very restricted in form. They begin with only two *wh*-words: either *what* or *how*. If the sentence begins with *what*, *what* will typically be followed by an indefinite article, an adjective, and a head noun, and finally a subject and predicator:

What a lovely day it was!

(BNC EFW 1763)

What a jerk you are

(SBCSAE)

How will precede an adjective and intensify it; the adjective will be followed by a subject and predicator:

How wonderful she is you know

(ICE-GB S1A-010 217)

How stupid I was!

(BNC FRX 134)

As two of the above examples illustrate, in writing, exclamation marks will end an exclamatory sentence. However, not all sentences ending in exclamation marks are exclamatory. The first example below is an imperative sentence, the second example a declarative sentence.

Please support generously!

(BNC A03 297)

YOUR COUNTRY NEEDS YOU!

(BNC CHW 342)

Exclamation marks are used more for emphasis in these examples.

While exclamatory sentences can be complete sentences, often they are abbreviated, with the subject–predicator section of the sentence implied:

What a gorgeous view

(MICASE LAB175SU026)

How stupid

(ICE-GB S1A-014 198)

The final sentence type in English is the imperative sentence. Unlike the three other sentence types, imperatives can include as little as a single predicator, such as *Leave* or *Stop*. However, in imperatives of this type there is an implied subject *you*:

(You) leave
(You) stop

While including *you* in an imperative is not common, often it is done to add emphasis to the command:

You listen carefully to what he wants.

(BNC J13 1756)

The verb in all imperatives of this type will be in the base form. It is not possible for imperatives to have other forms: *leaves* or *leaving*.

In addition to second person imperatives, there are also first person imperatives. These have a very fixed form and always begin with *Let's* followed by the base form of the verb:

Let's talk about race in terms of power

(SBCSAE)

let's sorta go through step by step what the newspaper did in that case, and whether it was ethical or not.

(MICASE LES220SU140)

Objects and complements. Objects and complements are clause functions that in unmarked clauses occur following the predicator. The particular lexical verb occurring within the predicator, in turn, determines which of these functions will occur within a clause.

There are two types of objects in English: direct and indirect. Although both objects require a transitive verb, they require different types of transitive verbs. Because a direct object can occur alone within a clause, it takes a **monotransitive verb** (i.e. a verb requiring a single object). In all the examples below, direct objects follow monotransitive verbs:

She *has written* several books.

(ICE-GB W2D-019 068)

Headland *is buying* Multisoft, a software group which makes business accounting systems designed for the personal computer market.

(BNC A1S 81)

He *named* like half a dozen viruses

(SBCSAE)

The key test for an object is that it can be made subject of a sentence in the passive voice:

Several books were written by her.
Multisoft is being bought by Headland.
Half a dozen viruses were named by him.

However, because the acceptability of a passive construction is, as was demonstrated in the last chapter, very context-dependent, often passivization of an object yields a sentence of questionable acceptability. For instance, while *similarities between the two kinds of parents* in the example below is a direct object, passivization results in a sentence that is grammatical but of questionable acceptability:

We *saw* similarities between the two kinds of parents

(MICASE SGR565SU144)

?Similarities between the two kinds of parents were seen by us.

But despite the questionable acceptability of the above example, passivization is nevertheless a good indicator of a direct object.

Like direct objects, indirect objects can also undergo passivization. However, indirect objects require a **ditransitive verb**: a verb that allows for two objects. Each of the examples below contains a ditransitive verb followed first by an indirect object (in italics) and then a direct object (in boldface):

She was showing *me* some photographs of herself and John in the Lake District

(ICE-GB S1A-009 112)

DVLA will then send *you* a new Registration Document in your name.

(ICE-GB W2D-010 026)

She poured *me* a second cup of coffee.

(BNC HR7 458)

And when they banned me from playing cricket for a month, they actually did *me* a favour.

(BNC CH8 1953)

All of the indirect objects in the above examples can be made subjects of sentences in the passive voice, as in, for instance:

I was shown some photographs
You will be sent a new Registration Document

One additional test for an indirect object is that it can often be moved after the direct object and become an object of the prepositions *to* or *for*:

She was showing some photographs **to** me.
They actually did a favour **for** me.

If the direct object is a personal pronoun, an indirect object is not possible. Instead, the potential indirect object must be moved to the object position in prepositional phrases headed by *to* or *for*:

I'm just showing it to him

(ICE-GB S1A-047 243)

*I'm just showing him it.

While these sentences are roughly equivalent in meaning to those in which the indirect object precedes the direct object, the prepositional phrases above are not indirect objects because objects can only have the form of noun phrases. As will be demonstrated in the next section, the prepositional phrases are best analyzed as adverbials.

Complements are constructions related to either the subject of the sentence or the object. Subject complements follow a specific type of verb: either copular *be* or a **linking verb** such as *appear*, *seem*, *resemble*, or *look*. In this type of construction, the complement either names or describes the subject. In the example below, the subject complement *ill*, an adjective phrase, is linked by the copular verb *is* to the subject of the sentence, *my husband*, and describes this person's state of health:

What's more, **my husband** is *ill*, and I can't afford to buy his medicine.

(BNC G3U 131)

In the next example, the copular verb *was* links the subject complement *my very first contact ...* with the subject *Radford*. In this instance, the subject complement serves to identify *Radford* as the speaker's "first contact ... with Chomsky's theories":

Yeah, **Radford** was *my very first contact with right uh okay, with, with, Chomsky's theories*

(MICASE STP355MG011)

The next two examples provide illustrations of subject complements occurring with the linking verbs *seems* and *appears*. Because the subject complements are adjectives, they describe the subjects.

The government hopes that at some point the Liberation Front can be persuaded to accept some form of autonomy short of independence, but **that** seems *unlikely* in the foreseeable future.

(BNC CR7 815)

The second of the paired versions of each signature appears *somewhat different*.

(ICE-USA W2A-031)

A similar relationship exists with object complements, which describe or name the object rather than the subject. However, while a subject and subject complement are linked by a predicator, the object and object complement are related by an implied predicator. For instance, in the example below, the object complement *infectious* describes the direct object, *her own enthusiasm for the subject*:

She has made **her own enthusiasm for the subject** *infectious*.

(MICASE COL575MX055)

Because a copular relationship exists between the two functions, the two parts function in many ways as a clause, or what some theorists, such as Aarts (1992), refer to as a **small clause**:

Her own enthusiasm for the subject is *infectious*

But because no overt predicator occurs, more descriptively oriented grammars refer to the object and object complement as separate clause functions, realized by phrases, within a clause.

Like direct and indirect objects, objects and object complements require specific kinds of verbs, such as *find* and *consider* in the examples below, capable of taking three arguments:

I find **it** *fascinating*.

(ICE-GB S1A-002 035)

Although she turns up for the interview her customary peaked-capped urchin self, she is worried that her feminist interpreters will consider **her video** *a sell-out*.

(BNC A7S 194)

While object complements are typically noun or adjective phrases, they can also be prepositional phrases headed by the preposition *as*:

If we consider **this** *as an equilibrium between two acids*, this is the stronger acid

(MICASE LEL200MU110)

It is a recipe which adopts **semiotics** *as its overall conceptual structure*.

(ICE-GB W2A-007 012)

Adverbials. Because the terms "adverbial" and "adverb" are so similar, it is easy to confuse them. An adverb is a term used to describe a particular word class. An adverbial, in contrast, is a term used to describe a particular clause function. While some adverbs can function as adverbials, other adverbs cannot. The example below contains three adverbs, which are highlighted in boldface; only two of the adverbs are functioning as adverbials:

In Santeria, the teaching of ritual skills and moral behavior happens **informally** and **nonverbally**; thus embodiment is **especially** important.

(ICE-USA W2A-012)

The first two adverbs – *informally* and *nonverbally* – are manner adverbs that are coordinated heads of an adverb phrase. Because this phrase is not part of another phrase in the clause, it is functioning as an adverbial. The third adverb, *especially*, is an intensifying adverb occurring within an adjective phrase that is functioning as a subject complement. Because *especially* is part of this phrase, it has no function in the clause and would therefore not be considered an adverbial.

Many different kinds of phrases can function as adverbials: noun phrases, adverb phrases, prepositional phrases, and clauses (both finite and non-finite). Adverbials differ from the other clause functions in three major regards. First, clauses are restricted to containing only one of the other clause functions: one subject, for instance, or one direct object. However, they can contain more than one adverbial. The clause below contains three adverbials:

A MAN was left homeless **yesterday after his pet Jack Russell puppy Sam started a fire** *at his flat*.

(BNC HJ3 218)

Second, although some adverbials favor certain positions in a clause, most can move around. In the example above, *yesterday* could move to the start of the clause:

Yesterday A MAN was left homeless

The entire clause beginning with *after* could also be shifted to the start of the sentence:

After his pet Jack Russell puppy Sam started a fire *at his flat*, a man was left homeless **yesterday.**

Of course, other clause elements can move around too. But when a direct object is made subject of a sentence in the passive voice, not only does the object change functions (from object to subject) but an entirely different type of sentence results (a sentence in the passive rather than active voice). Moving adverbials around mainly involves changes in emphasis and focus.

Finally, because of the diverse nature of adverbials, they form natural groupings. Biber *et al.* (1999: 763–5), for instance, identify three classes of adverbials: circumstance, stance, and linking. These classes are distinguished by the particular semantic relations that the adverbial expresses as well as by the extent to which the adverbial is integrated into the clause in which it occurs.

Circumstance adverbials exhibit close integration into clauses. For instance, *quickly* in the example below is very closely connected to the predicator *walked*, describing the pace at which Helen had walked.

Helen pulled on her jacket and walked **quickly** towards the door, not wanting to look at Mike.

(BNC HOF 2728)

Adverbials in this class, Biber *et al.* (1999: 763) note, answer questions "such as 'How, When, Where, How much, To what extent?' and 'Why'." Many different kinds of adverbials can answer these questions, and can additionally have many different forms. For instance, the example below contains three time adverbials answering the question "when." The adverbials are, respectively, a prepositional phrase, a noun phrase, and an adverb phrase:

At dawn **this morning** the building was seen to be damaged and there's been no power **since**.

(ICE-GB S2B-015 50)

The next two examples contain space adverbials answering the question "where." The words *up* and *there* are adverbs; the other two adverbials are prepositional phrases:

Did you take a nap **on the floor**?

(SBCSAE)

There's a lot of other terminology **up** *there* **in that document**

(MICASE LES335JG065)

The degree adverbials below, *very well* and *tremendously*, answer the question "To what extent":

I can't see **very well** from here.

(ICE-GB S2A-051 100)

and Vinnie Samways is able to calm it down put his foot on the ball steady it for Tottenham and find uh Terry Fenwick who must be enjoying this day **tremendously**

(ICE-GB S2A-015 230)

And the reason adverbials below answer the question "why." In the first example, the non-finite *-ing* clause explains that *the pupil* is better able to communicate because he has *developed these models*:

Having developed these models the pupil is in a position to communicate much more readily with other technical people who can manipulate similar models.

(BNC CLP 1054)

In the next example, the reason why Romtvedt writes is spelled out explicitly in the finite *because* clause:

I do not think Romtvedt has a careerist bone in his body; he writes poetry, or writes prose, **because that is what he needs to write**.

(ICE-USA W2A-005)

Stance and linking adverbials are much less closely integrated into the clauses in which they occur. The stance adverbials in the examples below – an adverb, prepositional phrase, and two finite clauses, respectively – enable the speaker or writer to comment directly on what is being stated. By using *certainly* in the first example, for instance, the speaker is expressing certainty in his belief about glaciation in Scandinavia:

Certainly, there was a tremendous amount of glaciation in the Scandinavian countries

(MICASE LES305MU108)

In the next example, the phrase *In essence* indicates that the writer believes that the crux of the problem in schools involves certain attitudes and behaviors:

In essence, schools are often reactive and the individuals within them victims because of a lack of management skills, procedures and perspectives.

(BNC AM7 1041)

And *I think* and *I believe* are so common in speech because they allow speakers to qualify the truth of statements that they make:

And he was too articulate **I think**.

(CIC)

And the Labour Party **I believe** want sanctions to work.

(ICE-GB S1B-35 028)

Like stance adverbials, linking adverbials are loosely integrated into the clause, largely because they indicate connections between clauses in a text. These kinds of adverbials were discussed in the last chapter in the section on cohesion; they help signpost relationships between parts of a text. The clause *What is more* in the example below is additive, indicating that a related point is being added to the previous point made. The adverb *none the less* is contrastive and introduces a point contrary to the writer's previous assertion.

Now, on the basis of a number of well-documented opinion polls, W. Harvey Cox (1985) argues that the majority in the Republic of Ireland favouring reunification is barely two to one, and that in the island as a whole it is three to two.
　　What is more, Cox suggests that support in the South is at best lukewarm. **None the less**, the characterization of catholic – nationalist ideology I have just documented would seem to fly in the face of this sort of evidence.

(BNC AO7 657)

Summary

Syntax involves the study of how constituents are grouped and ordered. Constituents can be identified through a series of tests. In the sentence *The woman wrote lots of letters*, *The woman* is a constituent because it can be pronominalized (*She wrote lots of letters*) and moved when the sentence is converted into the passive voice (*Lots of letters were written by the woman*). Constituents can be defined either notionally or formally. Constituents can also be described in terms of their linear and hierarchical structure, and the particular form and function that they have in a clause.

　　Although syntax is a discrete and separate level of linguistic structure, the discussion of adverbials at the end of the previous section indicates that it is often hard to discuss a specific syntactic category without making reference to the particular meaning that the category exhibits. The study of meaning is known as semantics, a topic that will be considered in detail in the next chapter.

Self-study activities

1. In *the new president of the company*, why is *the company* a constituent, but *president of* not a constituent?
2. If you define a verb as being a word that expresses "action" or "a state of being," is your definition notional or formal?
3. Provide a formal definition of the noun *television*.
4. In the sentence *The weather has been awful lately*, why does *The weather* have the form of a noun phrase but the function of subject?
5. Why is the word order in a sentence like *I have never taken such a good course* considered unmarked and the word order in *Never have I taken such a good course* marked?
6. Identify the head words in the phrases below
   (a) the small glass that contains 3 ounces of water
   (b) very rapidly
   (c) somewhat happy
   (d) might have wished
   (e) in the heat of the summer
   (f) farmers hoping for rain
7. Match the phrase in the left-hand column with the phrasal category in the right-hand column in which the phrase would be classified. Use Quirk *et al.*'s (1985) definition of verb phrase, which includes only the lexical verb, plus optional auxiliaries.

(1) can study	a.	noun phrase
(2) sufficiently soft	b.	verb phrase
(3) very softly	c.	adjective phrase
(4) after the movie	d.	adverb phrase
(5) an effectively presented talk	e.	prepositional phrase
(6) hard as a rock		
(7) rapidly		
(8) furniture		
(9) against the tide		
(10) difficult problem		

8. In English, adjectives come before nouns; in Spanish, they usually come after nouns. Is this difference between English and Spanish a consequence of the linear nature of syntax or the hierarchical nature of syntax?
9. In the examples below, identify all main and subordinate clauses.
   (a) The principal hired three new teachers.
   (b) Although it rained quite a bit last night, we did not experience any flooding.
   (c) The physician treated all the individuals who were in the accident.
   (d) To achieve success, people must work hard.
   (e) Working extra hours can lead to increased stress.
   (f) We left the party early because we were tired.

Further reading

The best way to find information on English syntax is to consult one of the major reference grammars of English: Quirk *et al.*'s *A Comprehensive Grammar of the English Language* (London: Longman, 1985), or Huddleston and Pullum's *The Cambridge Grammar of the English Language* (Cambridge: Cambridge University Press, 2002). Biber *et al.*'s *Longman Grammar of Spoken and Written English* (Harlow, England: Pearson Education Limited, 1999) is corpus-based, and provides both descriptive information about English syntax and the frequency with which various syntactic constructions occur in registers of spoken and written English.

The information in each of the above grammars is also available in shorter, more pedagogically oriented textbooks: Greenbaum and Quirk's *A Student's Grammar of the English Language* (London: Longman, 1990); Huddleston and Pullum's *A Student's Introduction to English Grammar* (Cambridge: Cambridge University Press, 2005); and Biber *et al.*'s *Longman Student Grammar of Spoken and Written English* (Harlow, England: Pearson Education Limited, 2002). Another, more empirically based overview of English grammar is S. Greenbaum's *Oxford English Grammar* (Oxford: Oxford University Press, 1996).

6 English words: Structure and meaning

CHAPTER PREVIEW

This chapter focuses on words: their internal structure and the ways that linguists and lexicographers (those who create dictionaries) have studied their meaning. The chapter opens with a discussion of the various ways that linguists have approached the study of meaning. It then continues with a description of the **morpheme**, the smallest unit of meaning, and how various kinds of morphemes are combined to create words. The remaining sections describe two general ways of characterizing the meanings of words: **lexical semantics** and **deixis**. Lexical semantics is concerned with the overall meaning of words. Deixis concerns the ability of words not only to have meaning but to "point."

KEY TERMS

Deixis: referential/ spatial/temporal

Derivational/ inflectional affix

Lexical decomposition

Lexical semantics

Lexicography

Morpheme

Semantic relations

Synonymy/ antonymy/ hyponymy

Word formation processes

Introduction

Words, like sentences and clauses, have a predictable internal structure. The plural marker on nouns, for instance, occurs at the end of a word (e.g. *law+s*), while what are known as derivational affixes can occur at either the beginning or the end of a word (e.g. *un+law+ful*). But the similarity between words and sentences and clauses goes beyond the fact that both have structure. As Sinclair (1991) argues, very often the use of a particular word evokes a whole series of other words. To describe this feature of language, Sinclair (1991: 110) proposes the idiom principle, the idea "that a language user has available to him or her a large number of semi-constructed phrases that constitute single choices, even though they might appear to be analysable into segments." For instance, Sinclair (1991: 75–6) comments that the phrasal verb *set about* is typically followed by an *-ing* participle taking an object and preceded by some structure expressing "uncertainty." In the example below, *set about* is preceded by the concessive conjunction *although* and followed by the *-ing* participle *creating*:

And **although** she does **set about** the task of **creating** a new life for herself and for her children, that task is complicated by failing health and persistent pursuit from those who claim her as their property.

(CIC)

In the next example, a contrast between clauses is marked by *Instead*, with the *-ing* participle *making* following *set about*:

Instead of constructing a geometrical and ideal entity for study that would never leave the bounds of the mind, he had **set about making**, on the basis of an inner and rational design, a thing that would exist outside of the mind.

(CIC)

Sinclair (1991) was interested in studying co-occurring patterns of words, or **collocations**, within the context of work he was doing with the Cobuild Project at Birmingham University, a project conducted in collaboration with Collins Publishers with the purpose of producing reference books, including dictionaries. The creation of dictionaries falls within the province of lexical semantics, an area of linguistics concerned with the study of the meaning of individual words. Because dictionaries are intended as reference guides, they do not provide theoretical statements about the nature of lexical meaning. However, lexicographers, those who create dictionaries, have developed methodologies for discovering the meanings of words and most effectively presenting these meanings to users of dictionaries.

Lexical semantics has also been extensively studied within linguistics proper. For instance, one way to describe the meanings of words in a more general sense is to categorize the various relationships existing between them: words with similar or identical meanings are considered synonyms, those with opposite meanings antonyms. Words such as *beagle* or *poodle* are co-hyponyms: words whose meanings are included within the meaning of the more general word *dog*. Another more controversial way of characterizing the meaning of words has been done in the area of **componential analysis**. This kind of analysis involves defining words by breaking them down into their component parts and assigning them semantic features. On one level, the words *puppy* and *infant* share the feature 'newly born.' These words differ in that *infant* has the feature 'human,' while *puppy* does not. However, this area of semantics has proven problematic, primarily because it is difficult to determine exactly what semantic features are needed. While it is important to discuss existent words in a language, it is equally important to study the specific processes, known as **word formation processes**, that describe the ways that new vocabulary are added to a language.

In addition to having meaning, words also have a "pointing" function. This function is known as deixis, a word of Greek origin that means 'to point' or 'to show.' In the sentence *The woman bought a clock*, not only does the word *woman* have meaning ('an adult female') but it points, or refers, to a particular woman in the external world. The ability of nouns and pronouns to refer is one type of deixis: **referential deixis**. Other types include **spatial** and **temporal** deixis. For instance, spatial deixis is indicated by prepositions such as *in* and *on* or demonstratives such as *this* or *that*, which situate what is being discussed either close to the speaker/writer (*This wine is giving me a headache*) or away from him/her (*That person always bothers me*). The sentence *I walked a mile yesterday* contains two temporal markers that anchor this sentence in the past: the past tense marker on the verb *walked* and the adverb *yesterday*. Other time frames are indicated by the present tense marker in English as well as the two aspect markers (perfective and progressive).

But before discussing the internal structure of words and how their meaning can be described, it is necessary first of all to define exactly what is meant by the notion of "meaning": what philosophers of language often describe as "what it means to mean."

Varying definitions of meaning

In Chapter 3, two types of meaning were distinguished: grammatical meaning and pragmatic meaning. Grammatical meaning was concerned with the meaning that could be derived directly from the words, phrases, clauses, and sentences in which language was encoded. Thus, at this level of meaning, a sentence such as *The woman called her husband* is meaningful because, for instance, the word *woman* designates an adult female and the past tense marker on the verb indicates that the act of calling took place at some time in the past. The other words in the sentence could be subjected to a similar analysis. This is meaning as it is represented at the level of grammar.

Pragmatic meaning, in contrast, describes meaning as a product of the social context in which language takes place. Consequently, when a father says to his two children *We're going to be late*, the full meaning of this statement is more than the sum of the words it contains. Instead, it is a polite way for the father to tell his children to "hurry up." This is not to suggest that the words themselves are not meaningful, but rather that the full meaning of the statement transcends the words that it contains.

Although most semanticists capture this two-way distinction, they do so in different ways. In popular usage, the distinction between grammatical and pragmatic meaning has been captured by, respectively, the notions of denotation and connotation. Denotation relates to the dictionary sense of a word, connotation the associations a word evokes. Thus, at the level of denotation, a *politician* is an individual elected to public office (at least in one sense of the word). However, increasingly the word has developed negative connotations so that for many people, a politician is somebody who, for instance, is not to be trusted and will say anything to anyone to get elected. Lyons (1977: 50–6) argues for three types of meaning: descriptive, social, and expressive. Descriptive meaning is related to grammatical meaning; social and expressive meaning are two subtypes of pragmatic meaning. Social meaning "serves to establish and maintain social relations" (Lyons 1977: 51). Expressive meaning is more particular to the individual and characterizes the particular meaning that individuals add to language when they speak.

Descriptive meaning, Lyons (1977: 51) asserts, "has been of central concern in philosophical semantics." For this reason, it will be the primary focus of this chapter. And while many linguists and philosophers may, as Lyons does, subcategorize pragmatic meaning, it is a separate type of meaning deserving of separate treatment, as was shown in Chapter 3.

The morpheme

All words are composed of one or more morphemes. A morpheme is considered the smallest unit of meaning. For instance, the word *dogs* contains two units that are meaningful: *dog*, which specifies a particular kind of animal, and *-s*, which indicates the notion of plurality. Although all morphemes are units of meaning, there are various kinds of morphemes.

Free and bound morphemes

Morphemes can be free or bound. If a morpheme is free, it can stand on its own; if it is bound, it must be attached to a free morpheme. In the word *walking*, the morpheme *walk* is free because it can stand alone as a word. However, *-ing* is bound because it has to be attached to a lexical verb, in this case *walk*. In the examples below, the free morphemes are in italics and the bound morphemes in boldface:

force-**ful**	**dis**-*like*
miss-**ed**	**pre**-*judge*
un-*like*-**li**-**est**	**mis**-*inform*-**ation**

As the above examples illustrate, a word will typically consist of a single free morpheme, sometimes referred to as the **base**. The base, as Plag (2003: 11) states, is "The part of a word which an affix is attached to." However, some words may contain more than one base, and some bases are (arguably) a bound rather than a free morpheme.

Compound words will always contain two bases. The word *upon* is composed of two prepositions: *up* and *on*. The word *bookshelf* contains two nouns: *book* and *shelf*. Many words of Latin origin have a base that is no longer a free morpheme. Consider the words *perceive, receive,* and *conceive.* Each of these words was borrowed whole into English from Anglo-French. However, the words themselves contain the root *-ceive,* which has its origins in Latin *capere* meaning 'to take.' Thus, *perceive* means literally *per* 'thoroughly' + *capere* 'to take.' Does this mean that *perceive* and the other words above should be analyzed as containing two bound morphemes? Certainly, *per-* is more recognizable as an independent morpheme in other English words such as *perennial,* which means 'throughout the year.' But for the average speaker of English, *perceive, receive,* and *conceive* are interpreted as containing a single free morpheme. Whatever meaning the individual parts of these words once had has been lost over time. Therefore, unless one is interested in analyzing the etymology of the individual parts of these words, they are best analyzed as containing one free morpheme.

There is also the issue of whether words such as *the* or *more* can truly stand alone. Matthews (1991: 11–12) questions the status of words such as these as free morphemes, since they are never used alone: the article *the,* for instance, is always associated with nouns. Nevertheless, unless one is willing to create an intermediate category for words such as these – a category on a continuum between free and bound morphemes – the words are best regarded as free morphemes.

Inflectional and derivational morphemes

Bound morphemes are of two types: inflectional and derivational. Because English has so few inflections, they can simply be listed, as is done in Table 6.1. **Inflections** are one type of **grammatical morpheme**, a morpheme that indicates some kind of grammatical relationship. For

Table 6.1. Inflections in English		
Inflections	Description	Examples
-s	3rd person present tense singular	*He/she likes movies*
	Possessive	*the child's toy*
	Plural	*girl/girls*
-ing	Progressive aspect	*He/she is leaving*
-ed	Past tense/perfective aspect	*He/she talked for an hour*
		He/she has talked for an hour
-er	Comparative form of adjective	*mild/milder*
-est	Superlative form of adjective	*mild/mildest*

instance, the -s morpheme on *likes* marks the tense as present and the subject as singular. The -s on the noun *girls* marks the noun as plural. Some free morphemes are also grammatical. While the -s on *child's* indicates possession, so does the preposition *of* in *the roof of the building* or *some friends of mine*. The comparative and superlative inflections are typically used on adjectives that are one or two syllables long (e.g. *happy*, *happier*, *happiest*). However, lengthier adjectives require *more* and *most* (e.g. *beautiful*, *more beautiful*, *most beautiful*). Other free grammatical morphemes include the articles (*a*, *an*, *the*), auxiliary verbs (*be*, *have*), and coordinating conjunctions (*and*, *or*, *but*).

While inflectional morphemes form a small class in English, derivational morphemes are a much larger class. Merriam-Webster's *A Dictionary of Prefixes, Suffixes, and Combining Forms*, for instance, devotes nearly sixty pages to a description of the various derivational morphemes found on English words. Derivational morphemes exhibit other differences from inflectional morphemes as well. Derivational morphemes can be either prefixes or suffixes, whereas inflectional morphemes can be only suffixes. Unlike inflectional morphemes, derivational morphemes can change the meaning of a word or its part of speech: adding *dis-* to the base *like* results in a word – *dislike* – with a completely opposite meaning; adding *-able* to *like* changes *like* from a verb to an adjective: *likeable*. Adding *-ed* to a verb such as *walk* changes neither the meaning of *walk* nor its part of speech.

A word can contain many derivational affixes, but only one inflectional affix; and if a word contains an inflectional suffix and one or more derivational suffixes, the derivational suffixes will always precede the inflectional suffixes. In the examples below, the inflectional affixes are in boldface and the derivational affixes in italics:

declassified: *de* + class + *ify* + **ed**
unlikeliest: *un* + like + *ly* + **est**
disempowering: *dis* + *em* + power +**ing**
reformulations: *re* + formula +*ate* + *ation* + **s**

As these words indicate, when affixes are combined in a word, the spelling of an individual affix will often differ from its spelling in the word in which it is included. As a later section will show, because English words can contain many different derivational affixes, **affixation** – the process of adding derivational morphemes to a word – is a major source of new words in English.

Origins of derivational affixes. Most derivational affixes were borrowed into English from either Greek or Latin. In Modern English, relatively few affixes of Germanic origin can be found. For instance, many negative prefixes, such as *il-*, *im-*, *in-*, and *non-*, were borrowed from Latin into English (the definitions and etymologies given in the lists below are based on those listed in Merriam-Webster's *Third New International Dictionary*):

illegal, illicit, improbable, immoral, incapable, incomplete, nonexistent, nonlethal

Many medical terms in English contain derivational morphemes of Greek origin:

ortho- 'straight' *orthodontics, orthopedics*
epi- 'on' *epidermis, epidural*
hyper- 'excessive' *hypertension, hyperanxiety*
-sis 'disease' *psychosis, neurosis*
peri- 'around' *periodontist, perimacular*
schizo- 'split' *schizophrenia*

Of course, not all of these affixes are restricted to medical terms: they can occur on words with less restricted uses, such as *episode, perimeter,* and *hyperactive.* Moreover, while the affixes in the words above are all of Greek origin, they are not restricted to occurring with bases of Greek origin. For instance, in *hyperactive,* the base, *active,* is of Latin origin (*activus*). Hybrid forms such as this occur in other English words as well, in many cases with bases of Germanic origin:

automobile: auto- (Greek 'same' or 'self') + *mobile* (Latin 'moveable')
bioscience: bio- (Greek 'life') + *science* (Latin *sciens* 'possessing knowledge')
dislike: dis- (Latin 'opposite of') + *like* (Old English *līcian* 'have some
    affection for')
preown: pre- (Latin *prae-* 'before') + *own* (Old English *āgan* 'possess')

Far fewer derivational affixes of Germanic origin can be found on current English words, largely because, as Hogg (2003: 107) notes, "By quite early in the Middle English period many of the original Germanic affixes were lost ... and quickly replaced by new affixes from Latin and French." Some examples of derivational affixes of Germanic origin include *-ard* in words such as *drunkard* or *laggard*; *-dom* in words such as *freedom* or *wisdom*; and *a-* in words such as *asleep* or *asunder.*

The meanings of derivational affixes. In their discussion of affixes in English, Stockwell and Minkova (2001: 89–94) categorize affixes according to the meanings that they express. For instance, a number of affixes, they note, "in some way quantify the root" (p. 89). The prefix *a-* indicates that something is "lacking" (e.g. *amoral, atonal*). The prefixes *mono-, bi-,* and *tri-* number the words to which they are affixed (e.g. *monosyllable, bifocal, triangle*). Many prefixes "say something about place or direction" (p. 90). The prefix *en-* points inward (e.g. *encapsulate, enclose, encircle*); *intra-* locates something within (e.g. *intracity, introvert*); and *retro-* points to the past (e.g. *retrogression, retrograde*).

Unlike most prefixes, suffixes can also change the part of speech of a word, and to varying degrees the meaning of the resultant word as well. As Stockwell and Minkova (2001: 89) observe, the amount of new meaning a suffix adds to a word will vary considerably: the suffix *-ly,* they claim, does little more than change an adjective into an adverb (e.g. *hearty→ heartily*). However, other suffixes create more significant changes in meaning.

Many suffixes, such as -*ation*, -*ness*, and -*ment*, convert verbs or adjectives into abstract nouns known as nominalizations:

verb to noun: *creation, production, realization, establishment, resentment, development*
adjective to noun: *goodness, happiness, likeliness, tastiness, fitness, heartiness*

The suffixes -*ant*, -*er*, and -*ist* convert verbs or nouns into "agentive nouns" (p. 94): nouns with the meaning 'someone who does something':

Verb to noun: *participant* (one who 'participates'), *attendant, driver, rider, owner, fighter, singer*
Noun to noun: *socialist* (a practitioner of 'socialism'), *dentist, linguist, chemist, hypnotist*

The suffix -*ize* converts nouns or adjectives into verbs:

noun to verb: *fantasize* (from the noun 'fantasy'), *idolize, demonize*
adjective to verb: *finalize* (from the adjective 'final'), *criticize, commercialize*

Productivity.   A key difference between inflectional and derivational affixes is centered on the notion of **productivity**. An inflection such as -*ing* can occur on the base form of any verb, regardless of whether it is regular or irregular: *talking, hating, speaking, coming, going, liking.* Therefore, inflections are highly productive because they can be regularly placed on any eligible base: verb inflections on verbs; -*er* and -*est* on adjectives and adverbs; and plural and possessive -*s* on nouns. Of course, -*ed* does not occur on irregular verbs (e.g. *bought, went, sang*) nor -*s* on nouns with irregular plurals (e.g. *geese, oxen, children*). Polysyllabic adjectives and adverbs such as *interesting* and *rapidly* take *more* and *most* rather than -*er* and -*est*: *more/most interesting* (but not **interestinglier* or **interestingliest*), *more/most rapidly* (**rapidlier* or **rapidliest*). Possessive -*s* is more likely to occur on animate rather than inanimate nouns: *my friend's car, his sister's business* but not **the house's roof* or **the desk's top.* But if a noun or verb, for instance, is regular, it will in all cases be able to take a verb or noun inflection.

Derivational affixes, on the other hand, are much less productive: they cannot uniformly be attached to a potentially eligible base, varying considerably in number of bases to which they can be affixed. Matthews (1991: 70) notes that the suffix -*able*, used to convert a verb into an adjective, is highly productive and can be affixed to just about any verb (e.g. *catchable, walkable, hittable, touchable, sellable*). In contrast, he continues, the suffix -*th* can be used on only a very small number of adjectives or verbs to create a noun: *warmth, truth,* or *growth* but not **coolth, *niceth,* or **smallth.* Other derivational affixes will fall between these two extremes in terms of their productivity. A derivational prefix such as *un*- can be used as a marker of negation on many adjectives (*unhappy, unwise,* and *unnecessary*) but certainly not every adjective (**unfine, *uncareful, *unpretty*). The same is true with the derivational suffix -*ly*, an affix that can convert an adjective to an adverb (e.g. *happily, easily, nicely*) but that has limitations on the number of adjectives that can undergo this kind of conversion (**negotiably, *smally, *dirtily*).

Lexical semantics

As the previous section demonstrated, it is possible to study the structure of words in terms of their morphology: the individual units of meaning, called morphemes, of which words are composed. It is also possible, however, to focus more on the meaning of these units. This kind of study is conducted in an area of semantics known as lexical semantics. Although it may seem straightforward to investigate the meanings of words, in actuality, lexical semantics has proven to be one of the more challenging areas of semantics to study. As was noted in Chapter 3, it is often difficult to draw a clear boundary between grammar and pragmatics: between meaning inherent in the words themselves and meaning derived from the social context in which the words are uttered. In addition, while linguists may disagree about exactly what elements should be included in a verb phrase, for instance, it is far easier to define those elements than to define a simple word such as the noun *chair*, a word that the *Oxford English Dictionary (OED)* assigns sixteens different meanings. Consider one of these sixteen meanings as defined in the OED and two other dictionaries:

Oxford English Dictionary (OED): A seat for one person (always implying more or less of comfort and ease); now the common name for the movable four-legged seat with a rest for the back, which constitutes, in many forms of rudeness or elegance, an ordinary article of household furniture, and is also used in gardens or wherever it is usual to sit.

Merriam-Webster's Collegiate Dictionary (11th edn.) *(MW)*: a seat typically having four legs and a back for one person

American Heritage Dictionary of the English Language (AHD): A piece of furniture consisting of a seat, legs, back, and often arms, designed to accommodate one person.

The three dictionaries agree on two characteristics of a chair: that it seats one person and has a back. While the *OED* and *MW* specify that a chair has four legs, the *AHD* states simply that it has legs. The *AHD* also notes that a chair "often [has] arms," suggesting that arms are optional. The other two dictionaries say nothing about arms. The *OED* entry is much more detailed than the other entries, noting that chairs exhibit "comfort" and "ease," are "movable," and are regarded as "household furniture." Although the definitions in the three dictionaries are similar, there are enough differences to illustrate the complexity inherent in defining even the simplest notions.

For most people, word meanings are most closely associated with dictionaries, a general reference guide for meaning and other matters, such as spelling, that people consult from their earliest years in school through adulthood. Within linguistics, however, dictionaries have a somewhat suspect reputation. As Kay (2000: 53–4) observes, many semanticists view lexicography as "largely and lamentably untheorised, uneasily poised between the academic and commercial worlds." In other words, while lexicographers may have developed a methodology for creating dictionaries, their ultimate goal is to sell dictionaries, and their methodologies have drawn little upon modern theories of lexical semantics.

This attitude, Kay (2000: 54) continues, has a historical explanation: the creation of dictionaries is "an ancient craft," one that pre-dates work in semantics by centuries. As a result, the methodology for creating dictionaries has developed quite independently of any direct influences from linguistics. In addition, because dictionaries are reader-based, they have design considerations about which semanticists need not be concerned. Landau (2001: 153–4) characterizes lexicography as "not a theoretical exercise to increase the sum of human knowledge but practical work to put together text that people can understand." But despite having different goals, semanticists and lexicographers have been conducting research in recent years that is more mutually beneficial, particularly in the areas of cognitive linguistics and corpus linguistics. Kay (2000: 57–62), for instance, describes how the cognitive notion of prototype helped in the classification of words and meanings in the *Historical Corpus of English*. Most modern dictionaries use large corpora as sources for definitions and citations. The Oxford English Corpus is a two-billion-word corpus (as of spring 2006) containing various kinds of written texts (e.g. fiction, news, blogs) from which information has been drawn that will assist in the creation of dictionaries by Oxford University Press (www.askoxford.com/oec/?view=uk, accessed September 7, 2007).

Because both lexicographers and semanticists have been concerned with the study of lexical semantics, this section will focus on the various ways that they have studied lexical meaning. The section opens with a description of the practice of lexicography as it has been applied in the creation of English-language dictionaries, with a particular emphasis on how lexicographers determine word meaning from citation slips. It concludes with an overview of the various approaches that semanticists have taken in developing theories for explaining lexical meaning and describing the ways that new words are added to English.

English language dictionaries

There are many different kinds of dictionaries:

Monolingual dictionaries: Monolingual dictionaries are intended for native speakers and as a consequence focus on a single language (e.g. English, German, French). Some of the more well-known monolingual English dictionaries include the *Oxford English Dictionary, Webster's Third New International Dictionary*, and the *American Heritage Dictionary of the English Language*. For non-native speakers, there are specialized monolingual dictionaries known as learner dictionaries. For instance, the *Cambridge Advanced Learner's Dictionary* and the *Collins COBUILD Advanced Learner's English Dictionary* are written specifically for non-native speakers of English, and thus contain simpler definitions than would be found in a typical monolingual dictionary and a greater emphasis on vocabulary, such as idioms or phrasal verbs, that give individuals learning English as an additional language considerable difficulty.

Bilingual dictionaries: Bilingual dictionaries focus on two languages and are designed for individuals who are native speakers of a particular language learning another language as an additional language. For English speakers, there are English/Spanish dictionaries, English/Italian dictionaries, and so forth.

Unabridged/abridged dictionaries: The major dictionary makers will periodically release large unabridged dictionaries from which they will produce smaller, abridged dictionaries that contain a subset of the words in the unabridged dictionary as well as newer words that have entered the language since the publication of the unabridged version. For instance, *Webster's Third New International*, an unabridged dictionary produced by the G & C Merriam Company in Springfield, MA, was released in 1961. Since the publication of this dictionary, Merriam-Webster has published eleven collegiate dictionaries – dictionaries that contain fewer entries than *Webster's Third* but that at the same time have been updated so that they contain newer words than the unabridged version. Because the Webster name is so closely associated with the nineteenth-century American lexicographer Noah Webster, many dictionaries have been published under the Webster name. However, the G & C Merriam Company is the only publisher of a Webster dictionary having any connection to Noah Webster's 1828 dictionary, *American Dictionary of the English Language*.

Thesauruses: These are dictionaries that specialize in providing synonyms for the main entries that they contain. One of the more famous English Thesauruses is *Roget's Thesaurus*, published in 1852 and written by Peter Roget. Because the name of this dictionary was never copyrighted, many thesauruses contain the name Roget, even though they are not derivative of the original thesaurus.

Specialized dictionaries: Many dictionaries focus on vocabulary specific to a particular occupation or area of interest. Physicians and lawyers, for instance, can make use of dictionaries that define medical and legal terms, such as *Tabler's Cyclopedic Medical Dictionary* or *Black's Law Dictionary*. Musicians can consult dictionaries of musical terms, such as the *Grove Dictionary of Music and Musicians*. Scrabble players have dictionaries containing words permissible in Scrabble games. Since the range of interests is large, so are the number of dictionaries catering to these interests.

Even though many different kinds of dictionaries exist, most individuals are probably most familiar with abridged or unabridged monolingual dictionaries: the primary focus of discussion in this section. The creation of a monolingual dictionary is essentially a two-stage process: determining the meaning of words by studying their use in context, and then crafting definitions of the words that will be appropriate for the readership of the particular dictionary being created.

Determining the meaning of words.   Because a monolingual dictionary needs to be comprehensive, lexicographers have developed a methodology for discovering word meanings that is based heavily on collecting words from primarily written sources and then recording the meaning of the words (as well as additional information) on a citation slip, literally a slip of paper for earlier dictionaries but now a computerized file containing such information as the sentence in which the word was used as well as a bibliographic entry of the source from which the word was taken. Lexicographers rely heavily on citation slips because they determine the meanings of words from the contexts in which they occur. The creation of the *OED* provides a good illustration of how this process works.

The *OED* was an extremely ambitious project. As articulated in the (1859) statement "Proposal for the Publication of a New English Dictionary by the Philological Society," the dictionary was to include every word in the English language from 1250 to 1858. Words to be included in the dictionary would be based on vocabulary found in printed matter written during these years. These goals resulted in "the only English dictionary ever created wholly on the basis of citations" (Landau 2001: 191). The heavily empirical nature of the *OED* placed a great burden on its creators to find individuals willing to read books and create citation slips. To find volunteers, both the 1859 "Proposal" and a later (1879) document ("An Appeal to the English-speaking and English-reading public to read books and make extracts for the Philological Society's *New English Dictionary*"), written after James A. H. Murray became editor, actively solicited readers.

Because the *OED* was intended to be a historical dictionary, it was decided that it should include vocabulary taken from texts written during three time periods: 1250–1526, 1526–1674, and 1674–1858. These three time frames were chosen because they delineate periods "into which our language may, for philological purposes, be most conveniently divided" (from *Proposal for the Publication of A New English Dictionary by the Philological Society*, Philological Society, 1859, p. 5). The year 1526, for instance, marked the publication of the first printed edition of the New Testament in English, 1674 the death of Milton. While these are certainly important historical events, they hardly correspond to the major periods in the development of English, especially since the *OED* is based exclusively on written texts, ignoring speech completely. Moreover, as Landau (2001: 207) notes, "the core of citation files tend to be those of the educated and upper classes," hardly making them representative of the language as a whole. But since there was really no feasible way (or desire, for that matter) to collect spoken data during this period, it was unavoidable that the data be biased in favor of written English.

The first edition of the *OED*, published in 1928, was based on four million citation slips supplied by approximately 2,000 readers (Francis 1992: 21). These individuals, as Gilliver (2000: 232) notes, either provided specific examples of words, or collected them from sources they were asked to read. Gilliver (2000) provides brief descriptions of the contributions that some of these individuals made. For instance, one of the early editors of the *OED*, Frederick James Furnivall, supplied 30,000 quotations taken from newspapers and magazines (p. 238). Harwig Richard Helwich, a Viennese philologist, supplied 50,000 quotations, many from a medieval poem entitled *Cursor Mundi*, "the most frequently cited work in the dictionary"

(p. 239). The physician Charles Gray contributed 29,000 quotations, many providing examples of function words taken from texts written in the eighteenth century (p. 238).

Specific instructions were given to readers telling them how they should collect words for inclusion on citation slips:

Make a quotation for *every* word that strikes you as rare, obsolete, old-fashioned, new, peculiar, or used in a peculiar way.

Take special note of passages which show or imply that a word is either new and tentative, or needing explanation as obsolete or archaic, and which thus help to fix the date of its introduction or disuse.

Make as *many* quotations *as you can* for ordinary words, especially when they are used significantly, and tend by the context to explain or suggest their own meaning.

(from the Historical Introduction of the original *OED*, reprinted in Murray 1971: vi)

After a word was selected, it needed to be included on a citation slip, which had a specific format, illustrated in Figure 6.1. The word appeared in the upper left-hand corner of the slip, and was followed below by complete bibliographical information of the source from which the word was taken. The quotation itself was placed at the bottom of the slip. The slips were then sent to Oxford, where they were placed in one of the 1,029 pigeon-holes in a *Scriptorium* constructed by the main editor of the *OED*, James A. H. Murray. Murray and his assistants used the citation slips as the basis for entries and illustrative quotations in the *OED*.

Britisher

1883 <u>Freeman</u> <u>Impressions U.S.</u> iv. 29

I always told my American friends that I had rather be called a Britisher than an Englishman, if by calling me an Englishman they meant to imply that they were not Englishmen themselves

---

FIGURE 6.1
Citation slip from *OED*.

Because lexicographers rely so heavily on context for meaning, they must base their dictionaries on citation slips taken from very large sources of text. This is because the frequency of vocabulary in a given text is determined by Zipf's Law, a formula for calculating word frequency developed by George Kingsley Zipf (see Zipf 1932 for details). Essentially, Zipf's Law predicts that in any text, a small number of words will occur very frequently and a large number of words will occur quite rarely. To illustrate this point, consider the distribution of vocabulary in an earlier paragraph in this section that contained a total of 119 words.

Table 6.2. Most frequent words in sample paragraph	
Word	Number of occurrences
the	10
a	7
of	6
word(s)	6
as	5
from	3
on	3
which	3
Total	43

Table 6.2 lists the words in the paragraph occurring three or more times. These eight words (including the combined frequencies of singular and plural forms of *word*) constituted 36% (43 of 119) of the words occurring in the paragraph. Of the remaining words in the paragraph, 12 words (20%) occurred twice (24 of 119), and 52 words (44%) occurred once (52 of 119). As Table 6.2 shows, the most frequent words were function words: the articles *the* and *a* and prepositions like *of* and *on*. The least frequent words in the paragraph were content words – words such as *methodology*, *monolingual*, and *discovering* that occurred only once. What these distributions mean for lexicographers is that they must collect examples from very large databases or they will not capture all the words occurring in a language or all the meanings that they have, since the words that are of primary concern to lexicographers – content words – are the words that occur least frequently.

For this reason, modern lexicographers have abandoned handwritten citation slips created by thousands of individuals and have turned instead to collecting examples automatically from very large corpora. For instance, the publisher Harper-Collins created the *Collins Word Web* (www.collins.co.uk/books.aspx?group=180, accessed September 10, 2007) as the source for citation files used to create a number of dictionaries that they have published, including *The Collins English Dictionary* (2007). The *Collins Word Web* is currently 2.5 billion words in length and contains various kinds of spoken and written English. It is constantly being updated so that new words entering the language can be detected and included in upcoming editions of dictionaries.

Advances in software development have also aided in the creation of citation slips. A concordancing program can be used on any computerized text to very quickly create a KWIK (keyword in context) concordance. Figure 6.2 contains a KWIK concordance window based on a sampling of occurrences of the word *chair* in the Cambridge International Corpus, a word whose meaning was discussed earlier in the chapter. As this figure illustrates, all instances of *chair* are vertically aligned so that their use in

```
1993                           e.g., chair, cushion, table, rug, bed, bath
1994 age " in his gown, sitting in a chair' ' (4.3.27.s.d.).
1994 val in the final moments " in a chair' ' (5.2.282.s.d.) then serves as a vi
1994 limactic link between the royal chair and potential diseases to come.
1993 ainless, and to Gordon Stewart, chair of the Department of History, who tol
1993 could climb onto it): Open that chair.
1993 ascinating Miss Fleming," and a chair upon which she props up the muddy ski
1994  " Enter the Friar sitting in a chair' ' and notes (p. 57): " q' s in his s
1993                 The back of the chair on which Gennaio is sitting is carved
1995 in an elaborately carved wooden chair.
1993 n "the man standing behind that chair" or "the man with the white beard" ca
1995 ohn B. Watson left his academic chair at The Johns Hopkins University for a
1993 ich some Peeress might take the chair at a drawing-room meeting," Philip, e
1995 heney, for instance, the former chair of the National Endowment for the Hum
1993                             A chair consists of four legs, a seat, and a
1993 d "the man standing behind that chair" are referentially interchangeable in
1993 elief, the "floor" on which the chair and the feet of the female figure res
1992 ifted her obesity on the Viking chair and pressed her massive gut to the ta
1994  property would more resemble a chair of state than a stretcher.
1993 ptor wished to be sure that the chair was correctly placed in the mass of s
1994                       The chair here recalls the various chairs of 2.
1993 ich are the four corners of the chair.
1993 buried alive in the back of his chair" (OMF i, 2), cultivates a nonentity b
2004 e toddler starts rocking in his chair and repeatedly touching his forehead,
```

FIGURE 6.2
Concordance view of the word *chair*.

context can be easily examined. Although only sentence fragments in which *chair* occurs can be seen, often only a limited context is needed to determine the meaning of a word. If a larger context is desired, most concordancing programs allow for the entire sentence or surrounding sentences to be viewed.

While lexicographers will need to examine many uses of a word to determine its meaning(s), the twenty-four instances of *chair* in Figure 6.2 begin to reveal its meaning. Three of the examples point to a chair as a place to sit:

... in his gown, sitting in a chair ...
Enter the friar, sitting in a chair ...
The back of the chair on which Gennaio is sitting ...

One example actually provides a definition of a chair:

A chair consists of four legs, a seat, ...

Another contains a few words, "carved wooden chair," specifying what a chair is made of.

Other examples indicate that *chair* is **polysemous**; that is, that it has more than one meaning. A chair is not simply a concrete object used for sitting, but an abstract noun designating someone who is the head of something, or who holds some highly esteemed position at a university:

... Gordon Stewart, **chair** of the Department of History, ...
... B. Watson left his academic **chair** at The Johns Hopkins University ...

Of course, more examples beyond those in Figure 6.2 would be needed to verify this meaning of *chair*. But as lexicographers begin isolating multiple meanings of words, they can search for other examples to determine how widespread the meanings are.

Deciding whether a given word has one or more meanings is often difficult to determine. For instance, the last example in Figure 6.2 associates the notion of movement with a chair. In this example, it is not clear whether the child referred to is rocking in a regular chair, or sitting in a rocking chair. A "rocking chair" differs from other chairs because it does not have four legs but two curved legs that are shaped in a way that permits the chair to move forwards and backwards. A "computer chair" also moves but typically has four legs with wheels. A "beanbag chair" has no legs or arms but a flexible area for sitting.

All of these types of chairs are little more than variations on the traditional notion of "chair." For this reason, no lexicographer is likely to list them in a dictionary in a separate entry. Other cases, however, are less straightforward. In his now classic study of the meaning of the word *cup*, Labov (1973) found considerable variation in the types of objects that people judge as "cups" rather than some other drinking vessel, such as a "mug." To elicit judgments of the meaning of *cup*, Labov (1973: 354) presented people with pictures of various objects. Each of the objects contained a handle, but varied in width, depth, and shape. Figure 6.3 presents four objects that varied in width but not depth, ranging from a width/depth ratio of 1.2 (object 1) up to a ratio of 1.9 to 1 (object 4). Other objects (not included in the figure) had differing width/depth ratios and also differing shapes.

FIGURE 6.3
Cups and the notion of width (adapted from Labov 1973: 354).

Labov (1973: 355) asked subjects to name the objects in four different contexts. For instance, one context was labeled "neutral": subjects were simply asked to supply a name for the object; another context was labeled "food" because subjects were asked what they would call the object if it contained mashed potatoes and was placed on a dinner table. Labov (1973: 356) found that size was a greater influence in the food context than the neutral context. For instance, in the neutral context, all subjects called object 1 a cup. However, in the food context, roughly 75 percent of the subjects called the object a cup, and 25 percent a bowl. In the neutral context, 25 percent named object 4 a cup, with 75 percent calling it a bowl. In the food context, all subjects called object 4 a bowl. Labov (1973: 357) found similar influences in the other contexts he tested, leading him to conclude that "the consistency profiles for any given term are radically shifted as the subjects conceive of the objects in different functional settings."

Lexicographers handle such variability in meaning, Labov (1973: 350) notes, by including in their definitions "qualifying words like *chiefly*, *commonly*, or *the like*, etc." (italics represent underlining in original). For instance, *Merriam-Webster's Collegiate Dictionary* (11th edn.) uses the qualifying word *usually* to define a cup: "an open usually bowl-shaped drinking vessel." While such impressionistic language might be objectionable to semanticists, Labov (1973: 351) argues that such language quite effectively captures the "scalar" nature of meaning: the idea that the difference in meaning between words is not absolute, but on a scale, with one meaning grading into another. Such language is also desirable for lexicographers because it enables them to present word definitions to their readership more concisely – one of many considerations, as the next section will demonstrate, that guide lexicographers in the wording of their definitions.

Creating word definitions. Dictionaries contain a wealth of information about words: their meaning(s), spelling, pronunciation, and etymology. However, questionnaires surveying what people actually use dictionaries for have revealed that dictionaries are consulted "mostly to find out the meanings of words, particularly rare words" (Béjoint 2000: 152). Because dictionaries are, as noted earlier, user-oriented, lexicographers have developed a methodology for defining words that presents meaning to their readership concisely and clearly.

There are various philosophies among lexicographers for defining words. Landau (2001: 153) notes that the traditional Aristotelian notion of definition "demand[s] that the word defined (called in Latin the *definiendum*) be identified by *genus* and *differentia*" (italics in original). Thus, in *Merriam-Webster*'s above definition, *cup* is a member of the class of *drinking vessels* (genus) but differs from other drinking vessels because of its size and shape (differentia). But *Merriam-Webster* also employs encyclopedic definitions: "definitions [that] are often long paragraphs that seem to aim at giving a 'complete' description of the referents rather than extracting what is essential for the comprehension of the concept" (Béjoint 2000: 51). For instance, *Webster's Third New International Dictionary* opens its definition of the word *window* with a basic definition of the word:

1 a (1) : an opening in a wall of a building or a side of a vehicle to admit light usually through a transparent or translucent material (as glass), usually to permit vision through the wall or side, and often to admit air.

However, this basic definition is followed by a discussion of different types of windows: windows through which transactions at banks are conducted or tickets are sold, or which enable people to view items on display for sale in a store.

Dictionary definitions are based on headwords. Headwords consist typically of the base of a particular word. Thus, a dictionary will define the word *cup* but not its plural form *cups*. Likewise, the verb *run* will be defined but not *ran* or *running*. However, dictionaries will often contain entries for words with affixes having a different meaning from the base forms from which they are derived. For instance, the *OED* contains a definition of the noun *help* as well as two forms with related but slightly different meanings that are derived from *help*: *helpful* and *unhelpful*. Recent dictionaries have challenged the notion that definitions should be based on only single headwords. Under the direction of John Sinclair, the first edition of the *Collins Cobuild English Language Dictionary* began the practice of paying attention to collocations in definitions: multi-word combinations that frequently co-occur and have a systematic meaning. Moon (2007: 168) notes that corpus-based work done on the *Collins Cobuild Dictionary* revealed that "semantically independent meanings of *take* such as 'remove, move, steal, escort' are less common than its use in structures such as *take a step*, *take part*, *take a long time*." The *Collins Cobuild Dictionary* therefore makes note of collocations such these in its definitions and in the illustrative examples that it includes.

Because dictionaries use words to define words, lexicographers have to make sure that their readership fully understands the words that are used in definitions. In learner dictionaries, this is in part controlled by the number of words upon which definitions are based. The *Collins Cobuild Dictionary*, a learner dictionary, bases its definitions on 2,500–3,000 words (Moon 2007: 171), largely because the audience for such a dictionary (non-native speakers) requires a more restricted vocabulary than native speakers. But clarity of definition is equally important for dictionaries in general. Landau (2001: 160) argues that "readers [of monolingual dictionaries] have a right to expect that if they do not know the meaning of a word used in the definition, they can look that word up and find it defined." But fulfilling this criterion can be difficult, especially for technical vocabulary, which appears not just in specialized dictionaries but general-purpose dictionaries as well. *Webster's Third New International* defines the computer term *byte* as:

a unit of computer information or data-storage capacity that consists of a group of eight bits and that is used especially to represent an alphanumeric character.

For the technological novice, this definition contains words – *bits*, *alphanumeric character* – that will be unfamiliar. Of course, these individual words themselves could be looked up elsewhere in the dictionary, but the willingness to do this will vary considerably from user to user.

Lexicographers follow other conventions in their definitions. The form of definitions for different parts of speech will vary: nouns will be defined in noun phrases, adjectives in set phrases (e.g. *able to*, *exhibiting*, *of*, *denoting*), and verbs in *to*- infinitive clauses (Landau 2001: 171–7). Thus, according to the *OED*, The noun *cup* is a "drinking vessel"; the adjective *small* refers to something/someone "Of relatively little girth or circumference"; the verb *talk* involves verbal utterances whose purpose is "To convey or exchange ideas, thoughts, information, etc. by means of speech." Some learner dictionaries depart from this practice by defining all words in complete sentences. The adjective *fair* in the *Collins Cobuild Dictionary* is defined in the sentence "when it is **fair**, the weather is pleasant, dry and fine" (quoted in Moon 2007: 170).

Because most modern dictionaries are now based on corpora, many of these dictionaries order definitions of words by frequency, with the most frequent definitions first followed by progressively less frequent definitions. This practice has resulted in changes in the ordering of definitions from earlier dictionaries. For instance, Moon (2007: 163–5) demonstrates that earlier dictionaries tended to include the more concrete definition of *impact* ('the force of something hitting something else') before the more abstract meaning ('the effect that something has on something else'). However, in terms of frequency, the abstract meaning is more common than the concrete meaning. Thus, by ordering meanings by frequency, dictionaries give users a more accurate depiction of which definition predominates.

Corpora have also enabled lexicographers to include illustrative quotations that are not invented but taken from real sources. Of course, this practice can be found as early as Samuel Johnson's 1755 *A Dictionary of the English Language* and was a key characteristic of the *OED*. But in these dictionaries, quotations had to be collected by hand, whereas with corpora, they can be automatically extracted. Illustrative quotations are important because they provide dictionary users with an example of how a word is used in a real context.

Lexicographers follow other principles in defining words. They attempt to keep definitions brief. They avoid circularity in their definitions so that if, for instance, "a *lynx* is defined as 'a bobcat', a *bobcat* is not defined as 'a lynx'" (Landau 2001: 158). Some lexicographers strive for substitutability in their definitions: the idea that the definition for a given word should be able to substitute for the word itself. If a dog is defined as a four-legged canine, then one ought to be able to say either *I have a new dog* or *I have a new four-legged canine*. Of course, as most lexicographers will acknowledge, not all words (particularly function words like *a* or *by*) can be defined in a manner that satisfies this principle.

But whichever principle of definition a lexicographer follows, the goal is to present definitions to users of dictionaries that provide clear definitions of previously unknown words.

Componential analysis

While dictionaries use groupings of words to define single words (or collocations), semanticists engaged in componential analysis (sometimes referred to as **lexical decomposition**) attempt to define words in terms of a set of abstract semantic primitives that break down a word into its essential components. For instance, Leech (1981: 90) proposes the features below to define the words *man, woman, boy,* and *girl*:

man: +human, +adult, +male
woman: +human, +adult, −male
boy: +human, −adult, +male
girl: +human, −adult, −male

In interpreting semantic features, it is important to note that features such as +human or −adult bear no relation to the words *human* or *adult*. Instead, these features designate the abstract notions of "humanness" and "adultness." Therefore, the word *boy*, for instance, has an inherent mean-ing based on the notion of "humanness" but lacking the notion of "adult-ness." In addition, it is often difficult to determine precisely which fea-tures are necessary to define a given word. In the above list, Leech (1981) chooses to mark gender differences between the words with the features +/−male. He could just as easily have chosen the features +/−female, or +male and +female. These latter two terms have the undesirable effect of adding one additional feature (+female) to the inventory of features need-ed to define the words. But the features +male and +female do more accurately define the words, since the feature −male defines "femaleness" in terms of the absence of "maleness," an unfortunate consequence to say the least. As will be demonstrated later in this section, the choice of fea-tures becomes even more problematic when abstract vocabulary (e.g. *free-dom*) is considered.

Leech (1981: 90) notes that the words in the list above stand in binary opposition to one another: they differ in meaning in terms of the pres-ence or absence of certain features (e.g. +adult vs. −adult). However, with other groups of words, Leech argues, different types of features are neces-sary. The words *mother* and *daughter*, for instance, share the feature +female. However, the feature +/−adult is not relevant with *daughter*, since an individual can be someone's daughter at any age. Arguably, this feature is also not relevant with *mother* either, since someone could be a mother at a very young age before reaching adulthood. But there is a dif-ferent relationship between the two words, what Leech (1981: 102–3) describes as a relation of opposition that "involves a contrast of direction": if I am your mother, you are my daughter; if you are my daughter, I am your mother. To express this kind of relationship, Leech (1981: 103) uses a left or right arrow with the feature 'parent':

mother: +female →parent
daughter: +female ←parent

The right arrow means 'parent of'; the left arrow 'child of.'

Other relationships involve what Leech (1981: 101) terms polar opposi-tions: words "best envisaged in terms of a scale running between two poles or extremes." Because the words *hot/warm/cool/cold* describe tempera-tures at varying points on a scale, Leech proposes that words such as these have features marked with up or down arrows of varying heights. The arrows below illustrate the varying degrees of temperature that the four words above express:

hot: temperature ↑
warm: temperature ↑
cool: temperature ↓
cold: temperature ↓

Of course, there are other kinds of relationships that exist between words, but once one looks beyond basic vocabulary, such as kinship terms, to the whole of the English lexicon, it becomes increasingly difficult to decide what semantic features are necessary to define words with less easily identifiable meanings. While the words *freedom* and *slavery* stand in opposition to one another, it is not entirely clear exactly what features should be posited to distinguish the words. Abstract words in particular are not amenable to componential analysis. What features define *livelihood*, for instance, or *fear*, *anger*, and *happiness*?

The inability of componential analysis to describe the meaning of words such as these has led many linguists to abandon this approach as a viable means of theorizing about the meanings of words. However, there are ways to simplify the number of semantic features needed to describe and distinguish words. For instance, Cruse (2004: 244) describes an approach in which semantic features are associated with a word through a series of "lexical contrasts." In the group of words below, he assigns features to the word *chair* by contrasting it with words that move progressively closer in meaning to *chair*:

chair vs. *thought* [CONCRETE]
      vs. *cat* [INANIMATE]
      vs. *trumpet* [FURNITURE]
      vs. *table* [FOR SITTING]
      vs. *sofa* [FOR ONE]
      vs. *stool* [WITH BACK]

The words *chair* and *thought* have very little in common because while *chair* has the feature [CONCRETE], *thought* does not. The word *cat* is slightly closer in meaning to *chair*: it does have the feature [CONCRETE] but not the feature [INANIMATE]. Both *sofa* and *stool* are quite close to *chair*, except that *sofa* lacks the feature [FORONE] and *stool* the feature [WITHBACK]. The obvious advantage to this approach is that it does not attempt to assign every word a series of features that definitively define the word. Instead, words are assigned general features based on comparisons with other words.

Another variation on componential analysis focuses not on the assignment of features to individual words in a language but rather on the development of features that specify what kinds of semantic features are universal to all languages. Wierzbicka (1996 and 2006) has developed a series of what she terms semantic primes: abstract semantic features that, at least in theory, occur in all languages. The most current version of the theory contains "some sixty universal conceptual primes" (Wierzbicka 2006: 17), which are classified into sixteen general categories. For instance, within the category of "Descriptors" are the primes BIG and SMALL. Like the features used to conduct componential analysis, these primes do not refer to the words *big* and *small* but rather to the notion of size existing at two ends of a continuum. How these primes are realized within a given language will vary. For instance, the category "Determiners" includes the primes THIS, THE SAME, and OTHER/ELSE. English will realize notions of definiteness with determiners (or determinatives, as they have been termed in this book) such as *the*, *this*, or *that*. Languages lacking determiners (e.g. Russian and Japanese) will use other linguistic means to express the notion of definiteness.

Some of the other categories and primes Wierzbicka has developed include:

Evaluators: GOOD, BAD
Actions, events, movement: DO, HAPPEN, MOVE
Existence and possession: THERE IS/EXIST, HAVE
Time: WHEN/TIME, NOW, BEFORE, AFTER, A LONG TIME, A SHORT TIME, FOR SOME TIME, MOMENT
Space: WHERE/PLACE, BE (SOMEWHERE), HERE, ABOVE, BELOW, FAR, NEAR, SIDE, INSIDE, TOUCHING

(Wierzbicka 2006: 18)

As will be shown in a later section, two of these categories – time and space – are deictics that play a key role in anchoring speakers/writers temporally and spatially.

Semantic relations

Although the goal of componential analysis is to develop semantic features that define an individual word, the features also serve to distinguish words from one another. For instance, as we saw above, Cruse (2004) proposed a system which compared words such as *chair* with a series of words that differed from *chair* by a single feature. More traditionally, semanticists have compared words in terms of a group of more general semantic relations that describe various degrees of similarities and differences that words exhibit. In her survey of the literature on semantic relations, Sparck Jones (1986: 42–7) identifies twelve different relations that have been proposed, including the three below:

Synonymy: words having the same meaning (e.g. *help/assist, common/ ubiquitous, hard/difficult*)
Antonymy: words having opposite meanings (e.g. *light/dark, heavy/light, open/closed*)
Hyponymy: words whose meanings are included in the meaning of a more general word (e.g. *daisy, rose, tulip → flowers*; *desk, table, sofa → furniture*; *sparrow, robin, crow → birds*)

Even though the above relations do not exhaust the number of relations that exist, they are very common and, additionally, play an important role in human cognition. We perceive the world in terms of similarities, differences, oppositions, and class inclusion – general perceptual categories that also apply to our views of the relationships existing between words in a language.

Synonymy.   Synonymy is a semantic relation that has been extensively studied. The true test of synonymy is substitutability: the ability of two words to be substituted for one another without a change in meaning. For instance, the example below contains the verb *assist*.

The research assistant was available to **assist** patients completing the survey.

(CIC)

If *help* is a synonym of *assist*, then it should be able to be substituted for *assist* in the above example without a change in meaning:

The research assistant was available to **help** patients completing the survey.

Because the two sentences are identical in meaning, *help* and *assist* can be considered, at least in the above contexts, as absolute synonyms.

However, absolute synonymy is a controversial notion. Bolinger (1977: ix–x) proposed the non-synonymy principle because he believed that absolute synonymy does not exist. For him, every linguistic form has one (and only one) meaning. Therefore, even though two words may be close in meaning, they will never be identical in meaning. Edmonds and Hirst (2002: 107) argue that "Absolute synonymy, if it exists at all, is quite rare" because if words were truly synonymous they would need to "be able to be substituted one for the other in any context in which their common sense is denoted with no change to truth value, communicative effect, or 'meaning' (however 'meaning' is defined)." It is easy to find examples illustrating the difficulty of the notion of absolute synonymy.

Most dictionaries will list *hard* as a synonym of *difficult*. In the two examples below, both *hard* and *difficult* can be interchanged with little difference in meaning:

He finds it **difficult [hard]** to describe his feelings

(BNC A06 838)

I do not deal with the equally **hard [difficult]** problem of the patient who is admitted unconscious to hospital after a suicide attempt

(BNC ASK 1523)

In the next two examples, substituting *hard* for *difficult* produces constructions that are not entirely idiomatic:

Charles also found himself in a **difficult [?hard]** position.

(BNC AOF 140)

Thus Frits Staal distinguishes between "the **difficult [?hard]** ways of contemplation" and "the easy way of drugs" by means of ...

(CIC)

While *stupid* and *unintelligent* both mean 'lacking intelligence,' the substitution of one for the other produces very different results. The example below is taken from an academic book in which the author wishes to counter the common assumption that people who are illiterate lack intelligence. Because the word *stupid* has such negative connotations, using it in this context would negate the intended meaning of the author.

Freire believed that peasant adults, though often illiterate, are not **unintelligent [stupid]** and can reflect on their own experience, make connections, and cooperate to achieve agreed objectives.

(CIC)

In contrast, the short excerpt below was taken from a casual conversation in which the speaker wishes to directly convey that the person being discussed is indeed not very smart. Using *unintelligent* would reduce the emphasis that the speaker wishes to achieve.

He's just so **stupid [unintelligent]**.

(CIC)

Part of the force of *stupid* is that it has become, as the *OED* notes, "a term of disparagement or abuse." Thus, this more recent meaning of *stupid* may cloud other meanings just as describing someone as being *gay* is more likely to lead to the interpretation that the individual is homosexual rather than happy.

Other differences are more subtle, as in the case of *buy* and *purchase*. There are certainly cases where the two words can be interchanged:

The family **bought [purchased]** a house in Park Street, London, and another converted Tudor farmhouse near Esher.

(ICE-GB W2F-017 082)

Sangster recently **purchased [bought]** a 10-acre property in the South of France, apparently to concentrate on his golf.

(BNC A4B 342)

However, forms of the two verbs occur in very different contexts. In the BNC, *bought* and *purchased* have very different distributions across registers. In spontaneous conversations, *bought* occurs at a frequency of 348 occurrences per million words; *purchased*, in contrast, did not occur at all. Of all the registers in the BNC, commerce had more instances of *purchased* (67 occurrences per million words) than any other register. The reason for this distribution is that unlike *bought*, *purchased* is associated with some kind of formal commercial transaction. Thus, *bought* sounds somewhat awkward in the first example below, since what is being offered for sale is a commercial product in a formal business context:

The serving machines are available in a selection of sizes and can be leased or **purchased [?bought]**.

(BNC A0C 1147)

In the examples below, *purchase[d]* sounds awkward because the transactions are quite inconsequential, and the contexts highly informal:

I had a long layover in Memphis and I went and **bought [?purchased]** this magazine just cuz it sounded like it was going to be fun and it was

(MICASE LES565SU137)

Can I **buy [?purchase]** you a cognac?

(BNC CEC 829)

Because word pairs such as *difficult/hard*, *unintelligent/stupid*, and *buy/purchase* cannot always be substituted for one another, they are regarded as near synonyms, which many linguists argue are more common in natural language than absolute synonyms.

Antonymy. While synonyms have similar meanings, antonyms have opposite meanings. For Lyons (1977: 279) and Murphy (2003: 170), antonymy is a type of contrast; for Cruse (2004: 162), it is a type of oppositeness. But while these and other theorists acknowledge some kind of difference between word pairs that are antonyms, exactly which pairs are actually considered antonyms is subject to some disagreement.

More narrowly focused definitions of antonymy restrict the class of antonyms to adjectives that are gradable. According to this view, adjectives such as *old* and *new* would be antonyms because they depict two extremes on the scale of age:

old   new

There are various linguistic devices that can be used to mark points between these two extremes. First, both these adjectives have comparative and superlative forms: *older/oldest* and *newer/newest*. Thus, one can say that X is newer or older than Y, or that X is the oldest and Y is the newest. Second, both adjectives can be preceded by degree adverbs, such as *very* and *somewhat*, indicating differing points on the scale of oldness and newness:

very old   old   somewhat old   somewhat new   new   very new

With *old* and *new*, two distinct words are antonyms. But in English, it is also possible to create an antonym simply by adding a negative prefix, such as *un-*, to an adjective. Table 6.3 contains examples of both types of gradable antonyms.

Table 6.3. Examples of gradable antonyms	
Separate words	Prefixing with *un-/in-/im-*
young/old	intelligent/unintelligent
hot/cold	decent/indecent
beautiful/ugly	attractive/unattractive
tall/short	likable/unlikable
fat/thin	comfortable/uncomfortable
heavy/light	probable/improbable
high/low	forgettable/unforgettable
wide/narrow	civilized/uncivilized
happy/sad	happy/unhappy

But while many words that contrast are gradable adjectives, others are not. For instance, *dead* and *alive* are words that are clearly opposite in meaning. However, they do not exist on a scale: something or someone is either dead or alive, and there is no point on a scale between these two extremes, as evidenced by the fact that it is impossible to describe a person, for instance, as being *very dead*. It is possible to find intensification of such adjectives, as when Fidel Castro was described in 2006 as being "very alive and very alert" following surgery. But such expressions are more figurative than literal. Because *dead* and *alive* are binary opposites, Lyons (1977) does not characterize the relationship between them as antonymy but instead opposition. Others, however, take a more expansive view of antonymy. Jones (2002: 1), for instance, argues that because word pairs such as *dead* and *alive* are "intuitively recognized as 'opposites'," they should be included within the class of antonyms proper. And, indeed, empirical studies of antonymous word pairs provide many convincing examples of antonyms having a range of different forms.

In their analysis of word pairs marked as antonyms in the *Collins Cobuild Advanced Learner's English Dictionary* (4th edn.), Paradis and Willners (2006) found that while the majority of antonyms were adjectives (59%), other form classes were represented as well: nouns (19%), verbs (13%), and other (9%). In an empirical study of antonyms in a 280-million-word corpus of articles from *The Independent*, Jones (2002: 31) chose to focus on 112 antonym pairs from four different word classes:

Adjectives: *active/passive, bad/good, illegal/legal, long/short, feminine/ masculine, rural/urban, gay/straight*
Nouns: *advantage/disadvantage, boom/recession, guilt/innocence, optimism/ pessimism*
Verbs: *agree/disagree, confirm/deny, disprove/prove, fail/succeed, lose/win*
Adverbs: *directly/indirectly, explicitly/implicitly, officially/unofficially, quickly/slowly*

Jones' decision to include the nouns *optimism/pessimism*, for instance, is quite justified because these nouns are very close in meaning to the gradable adjectives *optimistic/pessimistic*. It would thus be quite arbitrary to exclude *optimism/pessimism* from the class of antonyms simply because they are nouns.

But despite the fact that nouns, verbs, and adverbs can be antonyms, antonymy is still, as Paradis and Willners' (2006) frequencies demonstrate, primarily a relation between adjectives. In addition, of the five most frequent antonyms occurring in the corpus that Jones (2002: 33) examined, which totaled 25 percent of the pairs he discovered, four were adjectives: *new/old, private/public, bad/good, hate/love*, and *poor/rich*.

Hyponymy.   Hyponymy is a relation in which the meaning of a word is included in the meaning of a more general word: *poodle* is a hyponym of *dog* because the meaning of *poodle* is included within the more general meaning of *dog*. In the relation of hyponymy, the more specific word is known as a **hyponym** and the more general word a **hypernym**. Words such as *poodle, basset hound*, and *golden retriever* are considered **co-hyponyms** because their meanings are all included within the meaning of *dog*, and each of these words is of equal specificity: they are all "types of" dogs. Because *dog* is more general than *poodle* or *basset hound*, it would be considered a hypernym of these words.

While *poodle* is a hyponym of *dog*, it can potentially be a hypernym as well if it is considered in relation to a more specific word, such as *toy poodle*, which would be a hyponym of *poodle*. Thus, whether a word is a hyponym or hypernym depends upon where it is positioned relative to other words to which it is related. In this sense, hyponymy is very much a hierarchical relationship: it "imposes a hierarchical structure upon the vocabulary and upon the fields within the vocabulary" (Lyons 1977: 295). As an illustration of this point, consider the words in Figure 6.4.

toy poodle

miniature poodle

standard poodle

large poodle

    poodle

      dog

        domestic animal

          animal

            organism

              living thing

                whole, unit (an assemblage of parts that is regarded as a single entity)

                  object, physical object (a tangible and visible entity; an entity that can cast a shadow)

                    physical entity (an entity that has physical existence)

                      entity (that which is perceived or known or inferred to have its own distinct existence (living or nonliving))

FIGURE 6.4
Hyponym chain for *poodle* (adapted from http://wordnet. princeton.edu).

The information in this figure was taken from Wordnet (wordnet.princeton.edu), a large on-line lexical database (Fellbaum 1998). WordNet contains entries for content words – nouns, verbs, adjectives, and adverbs – that are grouped into synsets: a series of words that are synonymous. For each individual synset, it is possible to retrieve a chain of hyponyms and hypernyms. In Figure 6.4, hypernyms are displayed as one progresses vertically downward. Thus, *animal* is a hypernym of *domestic animal* but a hyponym of *organism*. At any point on the chain, various co-hyponyms could be added. For instance, a separate search of *organism* yielded numerous co-hyponyms in addition to *animal*, including *person*, *plant*, *plankton*, *parasite*, *clone*, and *fungus*. A search for co-hyponyms of *person* turned up so many matches that the search limit for WordNet was exceeded. Below are just some of the co-hyponyms that were listed:

self, adult, capitalist, captor, contestant, coward, creator, entertainer, individualist, intellectual, nonworker, traveler, unskilled person, worker, acquaintance, actor, adoptee, amateur, bullfighter

Because WordNet was "manually constructed" (Fellbaum 1998: 4), it obviously does not contain an exhaustive list of hyponyms for a given word, especially for a word as general as *person*.

Although hyponymy is a relation "far more frequently found among nouns," it is also possible to find examples with verbs and adjectives (Croft and Cruse 2004: 142). The verbs *whisper*, *mumble*, and *yell* are co-hyponyms of *speak*; the verbs *jog*, *trot*, and *sprint* are co-hyponyms of *run*. Cruse (1986: 89) includes the adjective *scarlet* as a hyponym of *red*. Comparable examples with other colors are possible too, for instance *navy blue* as a hyponym of *blue*. But the concept of hyponymy is more problematic with adjectives, as evidenced by the fact that hyponyms in WordNet are restricted to the class of nouns and verbs.

Among any group of co-hyponyms, certain words will be more prototypical than others. The notion of **prototype** is very important in cognitively based theories of language and is based on the notion that:

Not all the members of a category have the same status within the category. People have intuitions that some category members are better examples of the category than others. Members that are judged to be best examples of the category can be considered to be the most central in the category.

(Croft and Cruse 2004: 77)

With co-hyponyms, this notion is especially salient. In each of the word groups below, the hypernym is given first and is followed by a group of co-hyponyms. The least prototypical hyponyms are in boldface:

drinking vessel: glass, cup, mug, **goblet**, **stein**
furniture: desk, chair, couch, table, **waterbed**, **ottoman**
book: textbook, workbook, novel, cookbook, **catechism**, **popup book**
food: leftovers, produce, turkey, **polenta**, **partridge**

Although *goblet* is not prototypical for most speakers of English, some of the other words will vary by speaker and by cultural context. If an individual has young children, then a *popup book* might be highly prototypical, since such books are quite popular with young children.

Creating new vocabulary

The discussion thus far has dealt with the meaning of existent words in English. Sometimes, however, a different situation arises: some new phenomenon is introduced into human experience for which some new word needs to be created. While it is possible to identify a series of general processes by which new words are formed, it is difficult to determine precisely when a new word was first used, and why all speakers of a language ultimately agreed to use it. For instance, the computer term *memory* was created through the process of meaning extension: the meaning of *memory* as it applies to the human mind was extended to cover the inner workings of a computer. In the *OED*, the earliest citation containing a use of *memory* with this meaning (taken from CIC) dates back to 1945:

The memory elements of the machine may be divided into two groups – the "internal memory" and the "external memory."

(OED Online)

While *memory*, as it is used in this example, is undoubtedly a new usage, the usage did not originate in this example. Dictionaries can therefore provide only general information about the origins of words, and they certainly cannot explain why a given word ultimately gains universal acceptance. However, there is one new word in English – *9/11* – that can provide an interesting perspective on the process of word creation, and that can also be used to describe the various word formation processes that serve to provide general templates for the introduction of new words into English.

9/11: A case study in word formation. The word *9/11* not only dates the attacks on the World Trade Center in New York City and the Pentagon in Washington, DC on September 11, 2001 but has come to symbolize an event that ushered in an entirely new threat: global terrorism. The word is uniquely American because in the US, numerical representations of dates have the order month/day/year (9/11/2001). Outside the US, the order is day/month/year (11/9/2001). Because the word dates the event it describes, it is easy to find citations containing very early uses of the word, and to view the processes at work that gave rise to the word. Meyer (2003) lists examples of *9/11* in newspapers occurring as early as September 12, 2001:

You want a defining national moment for your lifetime? No? You don't have a choice in the matter. If Dec. 7, 1941, lives in infamy, then Tuesday is going to endure as the day that evil ambushed America. Sept. 11, 2001. The ninth month and 11th day. **9–11**. 9-1-1. Apocalypse. Now.
(*The Times Union*, September 12, 2001)

Headline: "America's Emergency Line: **9/11**"
(*NY Times*, September 12, 2001)

America opens at 9, which is to say 9-ish, which has become our saddest hour. 9:02, for example. Or 8:45, or 9:04. Or 9:11, six minutes after the second jet hit the second tower, and the mind started connecting dots in a panic. At some point we may have stopped to consider the date, **9/11**, which reads as 9-1-1, which is keypad-speak for: Oh God no, help, please.
(*Washington Post*, September 13, 2001)

Shoreline resident Michael Rush carries a personal memorial to the victims of Tuesday's terrorist attacks on his walk yesterday from Shoreline to Seattle Center along Highway 99. On his flag, the twin towers of the World Trade Center stand in for the "11" in "**9-11**," the date of the tragedy and the call for emergency help.
(*Seattle Times*, September 15, 2001)

In each of the examples, there is a level of iconicity in the word: the date 9/11 is identical with the telephone number 911, which is an emergency telephone number in all regions of the US. In addition, the two number 1s are symbolic of the two towers of the World Trade Center.

At this level, *9/11* is similar to *memory* in that it results from extending the meaning of the date on which the attacks occurred as a way of describing the event itself. Meaning extension is a very common process in English, and often the new word is a metaphor of the word on which it is based. For instance, just about every part of the human body has become a metaphor:

the **head** of an organization
the **heart** of the problem
at **arm's** length
the **foot** of the mountain
won by a **nose**
I'm all **ears**

But meaning extension is not restricted to creating a metaphor based on an existing word: just about any word, if it is around long enough, will have its meaning extended at some time during its life. For instance, the *OED* lists many meanings for the word *family*. One of the more common meanings centers on the notion of a group of people who are related and who live together. Citations illustrating this meaning date back to 1667. However, this meaning of *family* has been extended to designate a group of people engaged in organized crime. Thus, *family* in *the Gambino family* refers not to parents, children, and other relatives having the surname *Gambino* but rather to a group of people involved in organized crime headed by individuals with this surname. The earliest citation of this meaning in the *OED* is 1954.

But while the iconic appeal of *9/11* may be one reason for its existence, there are other reasons too. National disasters in the US have typically been named after the locations in which they occurred: *Pearl Harbor, Oklahoma City, Three Mile Island*. Creating new words from proper nouns has precedent in English: *Marxism* (Karl Marx), *quixotic* (Don Quixote), *sadism* (Marquis de Sade), *sandwich* (Earl of Sandwich), *boycott* (Charles Boycott). These words will vary in the extent to which speakers will recognize them as having their origins in proper nouns. Because *Marxism* is capitalized, it will be more easily recognized as a proper noun than *boycott*, a word based on Charles Boycott's surname. During his tenure as a land agent in Ireland in the nineteenth century, the British-born Charles Boycott was subjected to a rebellion by his tenants over his unfair treatment of them. But naming the attacks that occurred on September 11 after the locations in which they occurred was not possible, "because the events of the day happened in several different places – giving the date is more compact than saying 'The terrorist attacks on the World Trade Center and the Pentagon and in a plane over Pennsylvania'" (Nunberg 2004: 156).

Initially, *9/11* competed with *September 11* as the official word for the attacks, but in current usage, *9/11* is the preferred term. Will *9/11* survive as a viable word in English well beyond the current time, or will it suffer the fate of *Bushlips* ('insincere political rhetoric'), a word that was selected as word of the year by the American Dialect Society in 1990 (www.americandialect.org/index.php/amerdial/1990_words_of_the_year, accessed April 5, 2008) and that has no current relevancy? Given the importance of the events that *9/11* describes, it stands a very good chance of becoming a permanent addition to the lexicon of English.

Other word formation processes.   There are many other word formation processes beyond those already discussed. Some of these processes are very common; others are quite rare and have not over time contributed many new words to the English language.

Compounding, according to Plag (2003: 132), is "the most productive type of word-formation process in English." Historically, it has a long tradition in English: two-thirds of the words in the Old English poem *Beowulf*, for instance, are compounds. Compounding involves combining two base morphemes to create a word with a new meaning that is not necessarily a sum of the meanings of the individual words. For instance, *hot* and *house* have individual meanings, and a *hothouse* is certainly a building kept at a high temperature. But it is not simply any kind of "overheated" building but one in which plants requiring very high temperatures are grown.

Orthographically, compounds can be spelled as a single word (e.g. *policeman*), as a hyphenated word (e.g. *word-formation*), or as two separate words (e.g. *police officer*). But practice will vary. In this section, *word formation* is spelled as two words, whereas in the quote above, it is spelled with a hyphen. On the one hand, these differences may simply reflect a greater preference for hyphenation of compounds in British English than American English (Quirk *et al.* 1985: 1569). On the other hand, the differences indicate how semantically integrated the two units are: *policeman* has been in the language much longer than *police officer*, which is much newer. Over time, it is quite possible that *police officer* will be spelled as a single word.

In speech, compound words have a specific pattern of stress. One syllable in the first element will receive **primary stress**, and one syllable in the second element **secondary stress**. Consider the examples below:

whíte hóuse ('a house colored white')
Whítehòuse ('the house in Washington, DC where the president of the United States lives')

In the first pair of words, the adjective *white* merely modifies *house*. Thus, both words would receive relatively equal stress. In the second pair of words, however, the first element, *White*, would receive much greater stress than *house*. This is the typical pattern of stress found in compounds.

Compounds are formed through various combinations of parts of speech:

noun + noun: *letter carrier, birthmark, life raft, clergyman, talk radio, fire fighter, streetlight, salesperson, deathwatch, human shield, spacewalk, sandcastle, senior moment, podcast*
adjective + noun: *close call, small talk, blacklist, blackberry, heavyweight, bigwig*
preposition + preposition: *upon, within, unto, into, onto*
verb + noun: *chokehold, playroom, treadmill, call box, punch card, hitman*
verb + preposition: *breakdown, walkup, teach-in, playoff, takeout, startup, walkthrough, drawdown*

These categories do not exhaust the types of compounds that are possible in English, but do demonstrate that it is a highly productive type of word formation process.

Affixation and lexical borrowing are very common too. Because English contains so many different prefixes and suffixes, **affixation** has always, as an earlier section demonstrated, played an important role in forming new vocabulary. Some more recent words formed through affixation that have appeared on the American Dialect Society's Words of the Year lists include *texter* (an individual who sends text messages), *subprime* (a risky loan made to people seeking home mortgages), *boomeritis* (diseases affecting baby boomers as they age), and *flexitarian* (someone who claims to be a vegetarian but sometimes eats meat).

Borrowing is a process by which a language receives a word directly from another language, usually as a result of contact with the language. Although English has borrowed heavily from Latin, Greek, and French, other languages have contributed vocabulary as well:

Old Norse (many words beginning with the sounds /sk/): *skirt, sky, skin, scrape*
German: *blitz, kindergarten, hamburger, strudel, dachshund*
Arabic: *coffee, alcohol, jar, jihad, albatross, giraffe, hashish*
Yiddish: *bagel, schlep, schmooze, schmaltz, chutzpah*
Chinese: *chow mein, chopstick, ginseng, tycoon, tai chi, kung fu*
Spanish: *avocado, barrio, taco, mosquito, mesa, adobe*

Many languages resist borrowing vocabulary from other languages. However, English has historically been very receptive to borrowing.

The remaining word formation processes have contributed relatively few words to English. Functional shift involves changing the part of speech of a word rather than its form. Thus, *bottle* in the sentence *The woman bottles her own beer* results from changing *bottle* from a noun to a verb. Other examples of nouns being converted to verbs include *man* and *impact*:

The sessions are being **manned** by a team

(CIC)

The article was a review of process developments over the years and the way changing technology has **impacted** on fuel design.

(BNC HPB 207)

The search engine *Google* has seen its name converted into a verb so that now one sees examples such as *I googled myself on the Internet*.

The search engine name *Google* is based on the word *googol*, a word with a very interesting history. In its entry for this word, *Webster's Third New International Dictionary, Unabridged* notes that *googol* was "coined by Milton Sirotta, nine-year-old nephew of Dr. Edward Kasner" and designates 10^{100} (unabridged.merriam-webster.com, accessed April 13, 2008). Because *googol* is an invented word – one with no prior linguistic history – it is known as a root creation. Root creations can be "echoic," as McArthur (1992: 876) notes, and include words such as *cuckoo, zap,* and *splash*. They can also be trade names with generic uses. While *Kleenex* can be used to describe any kind of soft paper tissue, the word itself is the name of a specific brand of tissues. Other trade names that have developed generic meanings include *Dacron* and *nylon* (types of fabric), *Tylenol* (a brand name for the painkiller aceta-minophen), *coke*, *Xerox*, and *band-aid*. Trade names still associated with companies will be capitalized, and companies wanting to prevent their products from being used generically have sometimes resorted to lawsuits to protect the distinctiveness of the names of their products.

Two processes involve either the shortening of single words or the fusion of two words into one. Clippings are words that have been shortened: *flu* is a clipped form of *influenza*; *phone* is a shortened form of *telephone*. Additional examples include *doc(tor)*, *sec(ond)*, *taxi(meter) cab(riole)*, *(omni)bus*, *auto(mobile)*, *gas(oline)*, and *(inter)net*. Blends result from parts of two words being combined to create a single word. The word *brunch* is a combination of *breakfast+lunch*. Other examples include:

stagflation (stagnation + inflation)
chortle (chuckle + snort)
smog (smoke + fog)
infomercial (information + commercial)
snizzle (snow + drizzle)
blog (web + log)
Docudrama (documentary + drama)
Podcast (ipod + broadcast)

Acronyms and abbreviations are formed using the first letters of two or more words to form a single word. The difference between the two processes is that while acronyms can be pronounced as a single word, abbreviations have to be spelled out. Thus, *AIDS* is an acronym because it can be pronounced as a single word, while *CIA* is an abbreviation because the individual letters have to be pronounced. Acronyms and abbreviations are very common in English. Examples abound:

Abbreviations
LSD (lysergic acid diethylamide)
DVD (digital video disc)
CPA (certified public accountant)
IED (improvised explosive device)
ID (identification)
lol (laughing out loud)
WMD (weapons of mass destruction)
MP (member of parliament, or military police)

Acronyms
yuppie (young urban professional)
MADD (mothers against drunk drivers)
NATO (North Atlantic Treaty Organization)
RAM (random access memory)
NIMBY (not in my backyard)
radar (radio detection and ranging)
sonar (sound navigation and ranging)
laser (light amplification by the stimulated emission of radiation)

Typically, an abbreviation or acronym is spelled entirely with capital letters. However, *lol* is entirely in lower case because it comes from a medium – instant messaging – in which lower-case letters are generally preferred. Words such as *radar* or *sonar* are lower case because these words are not perceived to be acronyms: they are regarded as words themselves, not letters derived from a series of words.

Back formations are words that are created through a reverse process of affixation. For instance, the noun *television* is not a nominalization derived from the verb *televise*. Instead, the reverse process occurred: *televise* resulted from removing the *-ion* from *television*. The words below were all derived through the removal of an affix:

enthuse (from *enthusiastic*)
attrit (*attrition*)
liaise (*liaison*)
burgle (*burglar*)
edit (*editor*)
euthanize (*euthanasia*)
advert (*advertising*)
laze (*lazy*)
pea (*pease*)

The last word in the list, *pea*, has an alternative analysis. This word is derived from the Middle English word *pease*, which was a collective noun (like *family* or *team*), not a plural form. However, the *-se* ending (pronounced as /z/) was reanalyzed as a plural marker. This reanalysis led to the formation of *pea* as a singular form of plural *peas*. This process is known as folk etymology. It typically occurs with borrowings into English that have forms that are reinterpreted in terms of English vocabulary or grammar. The word *chaise lounge* is a good example. This word, borrowed from French, literally means 'long chair.' But since attributive adjectives in English come before not after the head noun, French *longue* is reanalyzed as English *lounge* (as in a place to relax). The expression *humble pie*, according to the *OED*, is based upon a specific kind of pie, *umble pie*, made from *umbles* (the intestines of an animal, such as a deer). *Umbles* became associated with *humble*. Hence, the expression *Eat your humble pie* (i.e. accept the humility you deserve for some act you've committed).

Deixis

In addition to having meaning, words also have a pointing function commonly referred to as **deixis**. As an illustration of the pointing function of language, consider the two utterances below:

Ray Magliozzi: Don't drive like my brother
Tom Magliozzi: Don't drive like my brother

These statements occurred at the end of a call-in show on car repairs broadcast on National Public Radio in the United States. They were uttered by the two hosts of the show, who are brothers. Although the two utterances contain exactly the same words, they are not redundant because while the phrase *my brother* has the same meaning in both utterances, it has two different referents: two different individuals in the external world to which the phrase refers, or points. The ability of words to refer is known as referential deixis. Two other types of deixis – spatial and temporal deixis – specify how words can situate language in space and time.

Referential deixis

According to Halliday and Hasan (1976: 33), there are two types of referential deixis: **exophora** and **endophora**. The two instances of *my brother* in the previous example are exophoric because they refer outside the text to the particular situational context in which they were uttered. In other words, to fully understand the reference of *my brother*, one needs to be listening to the actual radio show to know that the two people uttering the exchange are brothers and that they are referring to each other. The excerpt below, taken from a conversation between two people discussing real estate listings, contains a number of instances of exophoric reference, all highlighted in boldface:

Speaker A: **I**'m hungry. Ooh look at **that**. Six bedrooms. Jesus. It's quite cheap for six bedrooms isn't it seventy thou. Not that **we** could afford it anyway. Is that the one **you** were on about?

Speaker B: Don't know.

(CIC)

The personal pronouns *I*, *we*, and *you* are each exophoric because they refer to the individuals engaged in the conversation – individuals who will only be known by those people directly engaged in the conversation. The pronoun *I* refers to the speaker, *we* to both the speaker and the person being addressed, and *you* to the addressee. The pronoun *that* is also exophoric because this pronoun refers to a particular description in a written text that the two speakers are reading together. This use of *that* is also spatial, a point that will be discussed in greater detail in the next section.

Because exophoric reference is so context-dependent, it predominates in spoken texts – texts created in contexts where speakers and addressees are physically present and have access to the surroundings in which they are speaking. First and second person pronouns can certainly occur in writing, where they refer to the writer and reader, respectively, but such usages are generally confined to informal rather than formal writing. Writing therefore consists primarily of reference that is endophoric, or textual. That is, words refer to other words present in the text itself. This type of reference was discussed in Chapter 4 because it helps create cohesive ties in a text. In the example below, the proper noun *Sophie Green* is introduced as new information. This individual is subsequently referred to as *she*. Towards the end of the excerpt, *them* refers back to *both men and women*:

Later, and in recognition of her own achievements, **Sophie Green** was awarded a scholarship to attend a summer course at Bryn Mawr College, Pennsylvania in 1928 and in the following year **she** became a co-opted member of the Kettering Education Committee. Because **she** lacked academic qualifications, Miss Green never conducted a Tutorial Class, but **she** revelled in her Terminal and, less frequently, One-Year courses. Nevertheless, she was unequivocally ambitious for **her** students, **both men and women**, and unfailingly encouraged **them** to proceed

(BNC AL8 119)

Reference back to an antecedent noun phrase is known as **anaphoric reference**. Less common is **cataphoric reference**: reference that points forward in a text. In the above excerpt, the pronoun *she* in *Because she lacked academic qualifications, Miss Green* ... not only refers back to the initial mention of *Sophie Green* but anticipates a repetition of this individual in the noun phrase *Miss Green*. Cataphoric reference is mainly restricted to occurring in a subordinate clause beginning a sentence that is followed by a main clause:

Although **he** was tired, **the man** tried to stay awake.
When **they** were young, **the students** were best friends.

In other syntactic environments, a pronoun preceding a noun will not be interpreted as co-referential with the noun. In the example below, *he* is co-referential with *the man* because the reference is anaphoric:

The man said that **he** was leaving soon.

However, if the two noun phrases are reversed, as in the next example, *he* cannot be co-referential with *the man* but has an entirely different referent:

He said **the man** was leaving soon.

In all of the examples of endophoric reference discussed thus far, a third person pronoun has referred to a specific noun phrase. However, it is also possible for third person pronouns to refer to larger structures, that is, to have broad reference. In the example below, *that* refers not to a single noun phrase but to the entire idea that the community as a group attends the high school play:

so everyone in the community goes to the high school play **that**'s very interesting

(MICASE OFC115SU060)

In the next exchange, *this* in Speaker B's turn refers back to everything that Speaker A uttered in the first turn:

Speaker A: And then it just went into a scab and then sort of crumbled and went into another scab. And then I mean like when I wash my hair it softens. And when I put the it softens. And it's it's not a very stable scab. But er and I've got these lumps as well on my neck.
Speaker B: Yes. Oh dear **this** sounds awful.

(CIC)

Because the reference of *that* and *this* is so expansive in the preceding examples, broad reference tends to predominate in informal speech.

In instances of exophoric or endophoric reference, the referents can be either **generic** or **specific**. If a noun phrase has generic reference, it will refer to all members of a class rather than to specific members of the class. In the example below, the noun phrase *students* refers to the class of all students entering a university, not to a specific group of students at a specific university:

Even when **students** arrive at university and grab gratefully at the nearest approximation which they can find to a state-of-the-pre-Reformation Church essay question, their responses tend to reflect the same general ethos.

(CIC)

Likewise, in the next example, the noun phrases *dinosaurs* and *mammals* refer to the class of these types of animals, not to specific instances of the animals:

The idea that **dinosaurs** simply radiated into the ecological niches that had already been vacated, and that **mammals** 130 million or so years later did the same thing after the dinosaurs had departed, has profound philosophical implications.

(BNC B7K 494)

In contrast, specific reference involves reference to an actual entity. In the example below, both *students* and *the students* have specific reference because they refer to actual groups of students:

SUSPECTED Sikh terrorists yesterday shot dead 19 **students** and seriously wounded several others in Patiala, Punjab, raising fears of a fresh extremist offensive in the north Indian state before this month's parliamentary polls. **The students**, all Hindus from colleges of the neighbouring states of Uttar Pradesh and Haryana, had come to Patiala for a students' festival and were sleeping in a dormitory when they were attacked yesterday. The assailants, armed with automatic rifles, burst into the dormitory.

(BNC A87 438)

Noun phrases with specific reference can be indefinite or definite. Indefinite noun phrases can be either plural (without an article) or singular (with an indefinite article). The first noun phrase above, *students*, is indefinite because it lacks an article. If this noun phrase were singular, it would have been preceded by an indefinite article (e.g. *Sikh terrorists yesterday shot a student dead*). The second noun phrase, *the students*, is definite because it is preceded by the definite article *the*. Typically in a text, information that is new information will have indefinite reference, and information that is old will have definite reference.

In the next example, the reference is indefinite not only because the noun phrase is new information but because the speaker and hearer do not share knowledge of the actual student being referred to:

I have **a student** ... who is very talented in programming.

(CIC)

If the speaker and hearer had shared knowledge of the student, the speaker might have said something like "Remember the student I told you about who was a good programmer?"

Spatial deixis

In addition to having referring capabilities, *this* and *that*, along with their plural counterparts *these* and *those*, can be used to situate the speaker/writer spatially with respect to what these expressions are referring to. This kind of deixis, known as spatial or space deixis, is also associated with the adverbs *here* and *there* and some uses of prepositions such as *in* or *on* (e.g. *in the room, on the roof*).

The adverbs *here* and *there* as well as the demonstratives *this/that* and *these/those* have **proximal** and **distal** interpretations. Proximal uses of these constructions locate something close to the speaker. In the example below, *this* locates the computer relatively close to the speaker:

Spent a lot of time on **this** computer this weekend. Watch what happens. Boo. "Non system disk or disk error." Oh. "Replace and press any key…"

(CIC)

In the next example, the two instances of *these* locate the chairs and tables close to the speaker:

You know you can, you can take few of **these** chairs, and, **these** chairs and tables here, in the evening, whenever you want to read there, you can do that.

(BNC KCV 941)

Distal uses of demonstratives locate referents farther away from the speaker. In the example below, the use of *that* locates the individual farther away from the speakers than *this* would:

that guy's talking pretty loud

(MICASE OFC115SU060)

this guy's talking pretty loud

In the exchange below, Speaker A uses *these* to refer to plants close to her, while Speaker B uses *those* in reference to begonias that are farther away.

A: Well, **these** damn plants have shot up in price so much of the last year or two
B: Yes, **those** few begonias were a pound.

(ICE-GB S1A-007–21-22)

In all of the examples thus far, the demonstratives have been used to point to specific items that are either close to or more distant from the speaker. However, as Huddleston and Pullum (2002: 1505) note, physical distance from the speaker is not always a consideration in the choice of one demonstrative over the other; moreover, they continue, the demonstratives can also refer "to properties of such objects or to actions taking place or other abstract features of the situation of utterance." Thus, in the excerpt below, the two instances of *that* point to some statement made previously by the speaker. Using *this* rather than *that* would not necessarily place the statement closer to the speaker.

Oh I don't remember what it was. Right forget **that**. Scrap **that** point.

(CIC)

Other kinds of spatial adverbials locate items in various positions relative to the speaker. In the example below, the speaker is looking for something that is missing and cannot determine whether it is close to him – *here* – farther away – *there* – or somewhere else altogether: *upstairs*.

Is it **here**, or is it **there**? I think it's I've got it **upstairs**.

(BNC KC4 1844)

The various spatial adverbials in the two examples below likewise specify locations relative to the speakers of the utterances:

Well I stayed **there in the room**.

(CIC)

And I live **on the same floor** as his bloody girlfriend **a few doors away**.

(ICE-GB S1A-090–234)

Temporal deixis

Historically in English and other languages, spatial prepositions, such as *in* and *on* in the two previous examples, developed temporal meanings over time, a reflection of the general trend for notions of space to develop into notions of time. Thus, prepositions such as *in*, *on*, *at*, and *by* in the phrases *in the morning*, *on time*, *at noon*, and *by the evening* can now be markers of temporal, or time, deixis: the use of language to anchor the speaker/writer in time.

Temporal deixis in English is marked linguistically by both temporal adverbials (e.g. *yesterday*, *tomorrow*, *in the morning*) and tense markers (present and past) on verbs. Although aspect markers on verbs are not strictly speaking deictic (a point that will be clarified later in this section), the past tense, for instance, can be used in place of certain perfective verb forms, and tense works with aspect to delineate certain temporal sequences.

When considering the particular time frames that temporal deictics mark, it is important to realize that "The principal reference point for temporal deixis is the present, the contextual time at which the utterance occurs" (Frawley 1992: 282). Thus, if someone says *I walked to school yesterday*, he or she is speaking in the present about an event that happened in the past.

As was noted earlier in this chapter, English has two tenses that are morphologically marked on verbs: the present and past. However, English has no future tense – that is, an inflection that is placed on a verb to mark an event taking place in the future. Instead, English uses the modal verbs *shall* or *will* –

I **shall** speak to him on his return

(ICE-GB W16-01B-098)

The woman **will** be employed by a charity or public body and will be resident with the people being cared for.

(BNC G2N 373)

the phrasal modal *be going to*:

People **are going to** start getting anxious now aren't they.

(CIC)

I **am going to** leave this job.

(BNC A6V 1397)

or a verb in the present tense occurring with a temporal adverbial indicating future time:

Meanwhile I **go** to pick up my results **tomorrow**.

(ICE-GB W1B-007–069)

I **return** to town **next week** – for the 18th.

(CIC)

The modal *shall* tends to be used mainly in British English with first-person subjects; American English prefers *will*. With present tense verbs, a temporal adverbial marking future time is necessary for the sentence to have a future time interpretation. However, temporal adverbials can also be used with *will*, *shall*, or *be going to* as a redundant marker of future time:

Good well I'**ll** see you **tomorrow morning** then alright

(MICASE ADV700JU023)

The markers of future time in several of the sentences above are plotted on Figure 6.5 at points (a)–(c), points in time beyond the present at which the event taking place will happen.

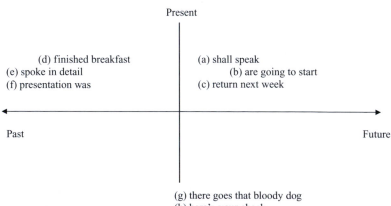

FIGURE 6.5
Tense in English.

The past tense points to an event that occurred at a specific time in the past. In the examples below, the verbs *finished*, *spoke*, and *was* point to times in the past when the events they describe occurred, events that have been completed:

We **finished** our breakfast.

(BNC A0F 2871)

The fourth issue which we **spoke** in detail about during our last presentation **was** how can generations determine the needs and assets of the children

(MICASE STP560JG118)

The events described by these verbs are located at points (d)–(f) in Figure 6.5.

The present tense is more complicated. As Quirk *et al.* (1985: 180) observe, one use of the present tense is to mark a period of time that ends immediately after a statement is uttered, a tense they term "the instantaneous present." In both of the examples below, the events are over once each sentence is spoken:

There **goes** that bloody dog.

(BNC KE6 8942)

And here's [here is] your check.

(CIC)

The events that these verbs mark would be located at points (g) and (h) on Figure 6.5.

However, Quirk *et al.* (1985: 179) also note that the present tense can mark (1) statements that are in effect timeless, "the state present":

Well she also **speaks** English

(ICE-GB S1A-069-116)

Although she **lives** in Brazil, Ms Bueno **remains** active in tennis through regular personal appearances in several countries.

(BNC AOV 939)

or (2) events that occur on a regular basis, "the habitual present":

She **stays** up till about half past five **gets** up at nine every day.

(CIC)

What's interesting though about the epidemiology of diaries is that they **appear** regularly among different ethnic minorities

(MICASE COL605MX039)

That the present tense marker in English can mark time frames other than the immediate present has led many grammarians, including Quirk *et al.* (1985), to argue that semantically English does not have a present tense per se but rather a past tense and a non-past tense. Moreover, the present tense verb marker in a sentence such as *The man works every day* is more an indicator of aspect than tense; that is, it does not mark a point in time but a habitual action. As was noted in the last chapter, the notion of aspect relates to the "temporal flow" of an event. For this reason, aspect is not deictic. Unlike tense, it does not point to a specific point in time but rather views time as, for instance, continuous or habitual. However, the distinction between tense and aspect in English has become blurred in many instances: the past tense can sometimes substitute for the past perfect, and in some instances, there is little temporal difference between the past and the present perfect.

Morphologically, English has two aspects: the perfective and the progressive. These two aspects work together with tense to yield various temporal sequences. The perfective is formed with either a present or past tense form of the auxiliary *have* in conjunction with an *-ed* participle. The present perfect is used to indicate an event that started at some time in the past but continues to the present (and possibly into the future). In the example below, the verb phrase *have made* indicates that the progress defined in the sentence began in the early fifties and has continued until the present.

In many ways, then, we **have made** progress since the early fifties.

(BNC C9S 63)

In the next example, the verb phrase *has produced* indicates that from its inception until the present, vaccine research has not resulted in many useful vaccines.

Vaccine research **has produced** few hopeful candidates, and although millions of dollars are poured into research, an effective vaccine is years away.

(CIC)

The events in these two sentences would begin at points (a) and (b) on Figure 6.6 and continue until the present.

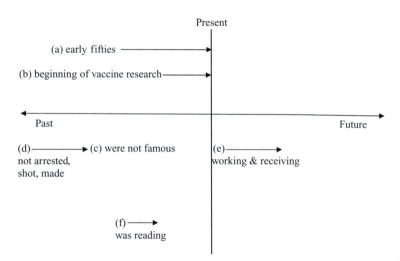

FIGURE 6.6
Aspect in English.

The past perfect is also used to describe an event that occurred in the past, but the event ended prior to beginning of some other event. The example below contains a past tense verb (*were*) in the first clause followed by three instances of the past perfect. In the first clause, the women are described as having not been famous at one particular time in the past. The three past perfect verbs in the second clause describe activities (e.g. making pornographic movies) that had not happened during a period ending with the assertion of the women not being famous.

The women were not particularly famous, and none **had been** arrested for subversive activities, or [**had**] **been** shot for spying, or **had made** pornographic movies, or anything.

(ICE-GB W2F-009-139)

The events in this sentence are located in Figure 6.6 at point (c), when the women were famous, and during the periods of time beginning at (d): a period during which the women had not been shot or arrested, or made pornographic movies.

In Contemporary English, the past perfect is being replaced by the simple past. For instance, in the example below, the act of arriving concluded prior to the start of the conversation. However, instead of *had arrived* being used in the first clause, the simple past tense form *arrived* is used instead.

Shortly after I arrived, there arose a new topic for conversation.

(BNC A0F 774)

The reason that the past perfective verb form is unnecessary is that the temporal sequence is conveyed by the adverbial *Shortly after*.

In other cases, there simply is not a real difference between the present perfect and the past. In the example below, there would be little difference in meaning between the simple past tense verb *left* and the present perfect *has left*:

Uh, ya know everybody just **left** the room.

(CIC)

... everybody **has** just **left** the room.

Again, the time sequence is conveyed by the adverbial *just*, making the verb form redundant.

The progressive aspect is formed with a present or past tense form of the verb *be* followed by an *-ing* participle. This aspect describes an ongoing event that began in either the past or the present. The example below contains two present progressive verb forms that indicate that the working and receiving described in the two sentences are ongoing activities in the present.

Doug **is working** on a graphic display of housing sales. He **is receiving** a considerable amount of help from Terry.

(CIC)

These activities are located at point (e) in Figure 6.6. In the next example, the act of reading is similarly an ongoing activity. However, while this activity was ongoing when it occurred, it is now over.

That's funny cos I **was reading** somewhere that historically if you said someone has left his coat you could mean male or female

(ICE-GB S1A-006-217)

This activity began at point (f) in Figure 6.6.

The perfective and progressive aspects are not mutually exclusive. They can be combined to produce varying time frames. In the example below, the act of listening began in the past, lasted for three days, and is over (the perfective interpretation). However, the use of the progressive aspect on *listening* emphasizes the ongoing nature of the listening.

I **have been listening** to 'Shepherd Moons' for three days straight

(BNC ED7 1769)

Had only the perfective been used, as in the example below, the ongoing nature of the listening would not have been as apparent.

I **have listened** to 'Shepherd Moons' for three days straight

However, the difference in meaning between the perfective/progressive and perfective versions of the sentence is subtle.

Summary

Words in English have a particular structure: all have a base to which various kinds of prefixes and suffixes can be attached. English has many derivational prefixes and suffixes. These affixes can change the meaning of a word (e.g. *happy*/**un**happy*) or its part of speech (e.g. *happy* [adjective]/*happiness* [noun]). English also has a small number of inflections: *-ed* to mark the past tense on regular verbs, for instance, or *-est* to create the superlative form of an adjective. Unlike derivational affixes, inflections do not change the meaning or part of speech of a word, but instead mark various grammatical relations.

There are various ways to study the meaning of words. Both lexicographers and semanticists have done extensive work in the area of lexical semantics. Lexicographers have developed a methodology for determining the meaning of words for purposes of creating dictionaries. Semanticists have developed various theories designed to study the meaning of words.

Self-study activities

1. What are TWO key differences between inflectional and derivational morphemes in English?
2. In the words below, identify all bound, free, derivational, and inflectional morphemes:
   nonconformist, decontextualized, repeating, upon, scariest, untested, carelessly
3. Is *fight* a member of a closed class of words or an open class?
4. What is lexical decomposition, and why is it difficult to decompose words like *love* and *hatred* into semantic features?
5. What semantic features do the English words *bull* and *man* have in common? What features distinguish the words?
6. Is it possible for two words to be completely synonymous? Explain, using examples to develop your response.

7. Match the word groups in the left-hand column with the semantic relation in the right-hand column with which each group would be associated.

   (1) bee/mosquito
   (2) hot/cold
   (3) help/assist
   (4) anthropology/sociology
   (5) guilty/innocent
   (6) warm/tepid

   a. synonyms
   b. co-hyponyms
   c. antonyms

8. Match the word in the left-hand column with the word formation process in the right-hand column with which the word is associated.

   (1) caveman
   (2) unhelpful
   (3) Xerox
   (4) attrit
   (5) RAM
   (6) Fahrenheit
   (7) hand (e.g. "give me a hand")
   (8) DOA
   (9) bottle (used as verb)
   (10) toilet
   (11) pea
   (12) smog
   (13) gas

   a. affixation
   b. compounding
   c. root creations
   d. clippings
   e. back formations
   f. abbreviations
   g. acronyms
   h. proper nouns
   i. folk etymologies
   j. borrowings
   k. functional shift
   l. meaning extension
   m. blends

Further reading

General overviews of semantics can be found in J. Lyons, *Semantics*, Vols. I and II (Cambridge: Cambridge University Press, 1977) and W. Frawley, *Linguistic Semantics* (Hillsdale, NJ: Lawrence Erlbaum, 1992). P. Matthews' *Morphology* (2nd edn., Cambridge: Cambridge University Press, 1991) describes English morphology. J. M. Sinclair's *Corpus, Concordance, Collocation* (Oxford: Oxford University Press, 1991) discusses how collocations can be studied in linguistic corpora.

A lexicographical perspective on lexical semantics is presented in S. Landau, *Dictionaries: The Art and Craft of Lexicography* (2nd edn., Cambridge: Cambridge University Press, 2001); linguistic treatments of the topic are covered in D. A. Cruse, *Lexical Semantics* (Cambridge: Cambridge University Press, 1986) and M. L. Murphy, *Semantic Relations and the Lexicon* (Cambridge: Cambridge University Press, 2003). The WordNet database is discussed in C. Fellbaum (ed.), *WordNet: An Electronic Lexical Database* (Cambridge, MA: MIT Press, 1998).

A cross-linguistic description of semantic primitives is outlined in A. Wierzbicka, *Semantics: Primes and Universals* (Oxford: Oxford University Press, 1996). Word formation processes in English are described in both L. Bauer, *English Word-Formation* (Cambridge: Cambridge University Press, 1983) and I. Plag, *Word-Formation in English* (Cambridge: Cambridge University Press, 2003).

7 The sounds of English

CHAPTER PREVIEW

This chapter provides an overview of the sound system of English. It begins with a discussion of the smallest unit of sound, the **phoneme**, and continues with a description of the **phonetic alphabet** and how it differs from the English alphabet. The phonetic symbols for English consonants and vowels are then presented and classified according to three criteria: **voicing** (whether the vocal cords vibrate or not), **place of articulation** (where in the mouth the sound is produced), and **manner of articulation** (how the airstream flows in the mouth during the articulation).

KEY TERMS

Allomorphs

Allophones

Articulators

Consonants

Intonation

Manner of articulation

Phoneme

Phonetic alphabet

Place of articulation

Sentence stress

Tone unit

Voicing

Vowels

Word stress

Introduction

The study of speech sounds can involve either **segments** or **suprasegmentals**. Analyses of speech segments are focused on the individual sounds in a given word. For instance, the word *hat* has three segments: two consonants beginning and ending the word and a single vowel between the two consonants. To describe these sounds, linguists use a set of symbols from the phonetic alphabet, an alphabet in which each symbol corresponds to one (and only one) sound. Thus, the word *hat* would be transcribed as /hæt/. A phonetic alphabet is necessary because in the English alphabet, for instance, a single symbol can represent more than one sound: the pronunciation of orthographic *a* in *hat* is different from its pronunciation in *talk*.

The study of suprasegmentals moves the analysis beyond individual speech sounds to syllables within a given word or to intonational patterns across words, phrases, and clauses. In a word such as *recording*, for instance, one can say that the primary stress is on the second syllable: re.'cor.ding. The sentence *When we arrived at the party, everyone was having fun* can be analyzed into two tone units. In each of the two tone units, the pitch will rise, peak on one syllable, and then fall. The syllable with the highest pitch will receive the greatest stress (indicated by the capital letters below) of any syllable in the tone unit:

when we arrived at the PARty

everyone was having FUN

Of course, the stress could be placed elsewhere in each of the tone units if some kind of emphasis is desired. For instance, in the second unit, the first syllable of *everyone* could receive the primary stress if the speaker wished to emphasize that all people at the party were having fun:

EVeryone was having fun

But the point when studying suprasegmentals is that sound can be examined beyond individual speech segments.

This chapter explores in detail how speech segments and suprasegmentals are studied. It opens with a discussion of segments – how they are identified, transcribed, and classified – and concludes with an overview of how stress is placed on syllables in English words and how pitch and stress are assigned in tone units.

Speech segments

Speech segments can be either **phonemes** or **allophones**. Phonemes are distinctive speech sounds; that is, they create meaningful differences in words. One way to determine whether a speech sound is distinctive is to examine **minimal pairs**: words that differ by only a single phoneme in the same position in a word. For instance, the words *bat* and *cat* differ by only

one sound: the second and third segments are the same vowel and consonant – /æ/ and /t/, respectively – but the two initial sounds are different:
bat begins with /b/ and *cat* with /k/. That *bat* and *cat* are different words
provides evidence that the sounds /b/ and /k/ in English are phonemes.
Indeed, considering other minimal pairs with these sounds points to their
status as phonemes:

ta**ck**/ta**b**
cake/**b**ake
kind/**b**ind

Phonemes are abstract representations of speech segments.
Consequently, the words *pot* and *spot* both contain the phoneme /p/.
However, if the actual pronunciation of these words is considered, it turns
out that the phoneme /p/ is pronounced differently in the two words.
When /p/ occurs at the start of a syllable, as in *pot*, it is **aspirated**: a puff
of air accompanies the pronunciation of this sound. In contrast, when /p/
occurs in the middle of a syllable, as in *spot*, or at the end of a syllable, as
in *top*, it is unaspirated. It is possible to actually feel the presence or
absence of air by placing your hand in front of your mouth while pronouncing each of these three words. But while aspirated and unaspirated
/p/ are different sounds, they are not phonemes (at least in English)
because they are not distinctive. It is not possible to create minimal pairs
with these two sounds: no way to create two separate words in English
that differ only by aspirated and unaspirated /p/. These two sounds are
therefore considered allophones: predictable variations in pronunciation
of a phoneme. The phoneme /p/ is aspirated initially in a syllable and
unaspirated elsewhere. A later section will consider in greater detail other
types of allophonic variation in English.

Languages vary in terms of the inventory of phonemes that they contain. While aspirated and unaspirated /p/ are not distinctive in English, in
Hindi they are. English has the phoneme /ð/ at the beginning of a word
such as *the*. German, a language that is very closely related to English,
lacks this phoneme, using /d/ to begin words for the definite article: *die*,
der, and *das*. English distinguishes /ɹ/ and /l/ in words such as *right* and
light; many Asian languages, such as Japanese, do not. There is tremendous variation in the number of phonemes across languages, with the
"range in size from around a dozen phonemes to nearer a hundred
depending upon the language" (*Handbook of the International Phonetics
Association*, p. 27).

The phonetic alphabet

To study phonemes, it is important to use a system of symbols that represent one and only one sound. To see why such a system is necessary, it is
useful to compare the English alphabet with a phonetic alphabet. In
alphabetic writing systems, there is a (loose) association between letters of
the alphabet, or **graphemes**, and sounds. In English, the graphemes c-a-t
in the word *cat* correspond to the three phonemes in this word: /k/, /æ/,

and /t/. But as is the case in most alphabetic writing systems, there is not a one-to-one correspondence between sound and grapheme – graphemes can have more than one pronunciation. This is why the grapheme *a* in *cat* can be associated with many different sounds: /eɪ/ in *broadway*, /ɪ/ in *substance*, and /ə/ in *addiction*.

There are a number of reasons why over time English graphemes have deviated from English pronunciation. First of all, English uses the Roman alphabet, an alphabet originally designed to spell Latin. Because Latin and English have different sounds, the Roman alphabet had to be adapted to spell certain English sounds. For instance, Latin lacks the phonemes /ð/ and /θ/ found at the beginning of English words such as *the* and *thin*, respectively. To spell these sounds in English, the digraph *th* had to be created. Writing is also more conservative than speech. As a result, changes in pronunciation are not reflected in spelling. The word *knight* has six graphemes but only three phonemes: /n/, /ai/, and /t/. However, during Chaucer's time, the word had a pronunciation that more closely reflected its spelling: /kənixt/. The spelling of *knight* therefore reflects the history of the word: additional phonemes that are no longer pronounced, and one phoneme, /x/, spelled with the digraph *gh*, that no longer exists in English (and is roughly equivalent to the final sound in *Bach*).

To advance the study of speech, the International Phonetic Association was founded in 1886 with the goal of developing a phonetic alphabet known as the International Phonetic Alphabet (or IPA). This alphabet went through several revisions, with the most recent version established in 2005 (see www.arts.gla.ac.uk/ipa/ipachart.html, accessed April 30, 2008). In this alphabet, each symbol corresponds to a single sound, making it possible to describe the sounds of any language in the world. The IPA allows for two types of transcription: a **broad transcription** or a **narrow transcription**. A broad transcription is focused on individual phonemes. For instance, the words *pat* and *spat* would be transcribed, respectively, as /pæt/ and /spæt/. A narrow transcription, in contrast, would capture the phonetic differences between the sounds in these words, specifically that in *pat* the /p/ is aspirated, as indicated by a superscript *h* following /p/: [pʰæt]. There are two conventions for transcribing phonemes and allophones. Transcriptions of phonemes are placed within slashes: //. Transcriptions of allophones of a phoneme are included within brackets: [].

To provide a more detailed description of the IPA, the next two sections describe the symbols used in the IPA as they apply to consonants and vowels in the English language. For all consonant and vowel sounds described in these sections, simple English words containing the sounds will be provided to aid in matching symbols with the sounds that they describe.

English consonants

English consonants are classified along three parameters: voicing, place of articulation, and manner of articulation. To introduce these notions, one type of consonant – **plosives** – will be described before the entire range of consonants in English is presented.

Plosives.   Table 7.1 lists all of the consonant phonemes in English. Across the top of the table are the places of articulation: the parts of the mouth involved in the articulation of each phoneme. The left-hand column classifies the consonants according to their manner of articulation: where the air flows in the mouth while each consonant is articulated, and the degree to which the air flows freely or is subject to varying degrees of constriction.

Table 7.1. Consonants in English

	bilabial	labiodental	dental	alveolar	postalveolar	palatal	velar	glottal
plosives	p b			t d			k g	
nasals	m			n			ŋ	
fricatives		f v	θ ð	s z	ʃ ʒ			h
affricates						tʃ dʒ		
central approximants	(w)			ɹ		j	w	
lateral approximants				l				

English has six plosives, which are found at the start of each word in the list below:

/p/ pat   /t/ tack   /k/ kite
/b/ bat   /d/ dark   /g/ get

Three of the plosives are voiceless (or unvoiced): /p/, /t/, and /k/. Three are voiced: /b/, /d/, and /g/. Voicing is a property of the vocal folds, which are located in Figure 7.1 at the bottom of the vocal tract. When the vocal folds vibrate during the articulation of a consonant, the consonant is voiced; if the vocal folds do not vibrate, the consonant is voiceless. Thus, /p/ and /b/ contrast because the latter is voiced but the former is not. It is easy to recognize the absence or presence of voicing in these sounds by feeling the larynx when pronouncing syllables such as *pa* and *ba*: *pa* will produce much less vibration than *ba*.

     While these two consonants differ in voicing, they are identical in terms of their place of articulation. Both sounds are bilabial because their articulation involves the lips, which move together as /p/ and /b/ are produced. The remaining four plosives have different places of articulation. The consonants /t/ and /d/ are alveolar because when they are articulated, the tip or blade of the tongue touches the alveolar ridge in the mouth (again, see Figure 7.1 for these and other places of articulation). The remaining two stops, /k/ and /g/, are velar because during their articulation,

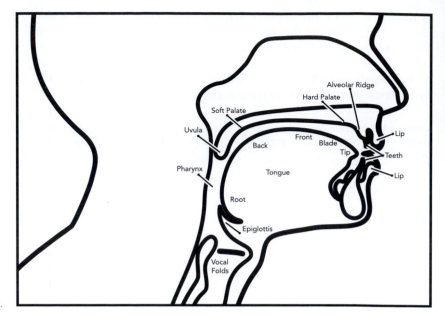

FIGURE 7.1
Places of articulation.

the back of the tongue touches the soft palate (also known as the velum). All six consonants are considered plosives because of their manner of articulation. That is, when these sounds are made, the flow of air in the mouth is initially blocked and then subsequently released. When /p/ and /b/ are articulated, for instance, the lips will initially be pursed, causing blockage of air in the oral cavity. The lips are then opened, allowing the air to flow outside the mouth. With the alveolar and velar stops, a similar effect is achieved with the tongue, which first touches the alveolar ridge or soft palate, blocking the flow of air. The tongue then pulls away, allowing the air to flow outside the mouth.

Nasals.   English has three **nasal** consonants, each of which is voiced:

/m/ make
/n/ nice
/ŋ/ long

These sounds have the same place of articulation as the six plosives in English. The manner of articulation is likewise identical, except that the air flows through the nasal cavity rather than the oral cavity. With the exception of the nasals, all consonants in English are oral: the soft palate moves back in the mouth and touches the pharynx, preventing air from flowing through the nasal cavity and forcing it instead through the oral cavity. With nasal consonants, however, there is no such movement of the soft palate. Consequently, the air is allowed to flow through the nasal cavity.

Fricatives.   English has nine **fricatives**, each of which, except for voiceless /h/, has a voiceless and voiced counterpart. The fricatives in the top row are voiceless; those in the bottom row are voiced:

/f/ five	/θ/ thin	/s/ sip	/ʃ/ ship	/h/ hip
/v/ vice	/ð/ this	/z/ zip	/ʒ/ measure	

The phonemes /f/ and /v/ are labiodental. When they are articulated, the upper teeth touch the lower lip. The phonemes /θ/ and /ð/ are dental. To produce these sounds, the tip or blade of the tongue touches the upper teeth. The phonemes /s/ and /z/ are alveolar. The phonemes /ʃ/ and /ʒ/ are postalveolar: the articulation of these sounds involves the tip or blade of the tongue touching the back of the alveolar ridge. The phoneme /h/ is glottal. Because this sound originates at the glottis, its articulation is independent of the other articulators (e.g. the tongue or lips). Instead, it is produced "by bringing the vocal folds close enough to produce a hissy sound" (Hewlett and Beck 2006: 36).

With fricatives, there is some constriction of the airflow in the oral cavity. For instance, when /θ/ and /ð/ are articulated, the tongue does not completely block the flow of air as it touches the upper teeth. Instead, it creates a narrow opening through which the air flows, resulting in turbulence in the oral cavity. In fact, with some fricatives, such as /s/ and /z/, one can even hear a hissing sound as the sound is produced.

Affricates.   English has two **affricates**, one voiceless and the other voiced:

/tʃ/ church
/dʒ/ judge

Both of these sounds are palatal. Their articulation involves the front of the tongue touching the hard palate. As the IPA symbols for these sounds suggest, an affricate is the combination of a stop and a fricative. That is, when these sounds are produced, the tongue causes complete blockage of air. However, after the air is released, the tongue creates enough obstruction of the flow of air to create the kind of turbulence associated with a fricative.

Approximants.   There are two types of **approximants**: central and lateral. English has three central approximants:

/ɹ/ ripe
/j/ yet
/w/ wet

and one lateral approximant:

/l/ like

All four approximants are voiced. The phonemes /ɹ/ and /l/ are alveolar, while /j/ is palatal. The phoneme /w/ is different from the other approximants in that its articulation is bilabial/velar. That is, as this sound is articulated, the lips narrow and the back of the tongue touches the soft palate. Thus, the production of this sound involves two places of articulation. In some dialects of English, it is possible to find a voiceless equivalent of /w/, which is transcribed as /ʍ/ and is typically found in words beginning with the orthographic characters *wh*. For speakers who make the distinction, the word *witch* would begin with /w/ and *which* with /ʍ/. While common in earlier periods of English, the distinction between /w/ and /ʍ/ is currently maintained by relatively few speakers of English. With all four approximants, there is relatively little obstruction of the air in the oral cavity – certainly much less than is found with fricatives. For this reason, the approximants are sometimes regarded as semi-vowels, since the articulation of vowels involves very little obstruction of the flow of air.

Vowels in English

While the number of consonants across dialects of English is relatively constant, with vowels there is considerably more dialectal variation. For this reason, the discussion in this section will be restricted to the vowels found in the standard varieties of American and British English. These varieties are sometimes referred to, respectively, as General American (GA) and Received Pronunciation (RP) or BBC English. It must be emphasized, however, that while these varieties have a certain amount of prestige in the United States and Great Britain, they are not spoken by everyone in these countries, and variations from these standards do not necessarily result in non-standard pronunciation. In the United States, people residing in Nashville, Tennessee, for instance, do not desire to speak like people in Chicago, Illinois. Each part of the United States has its own regional standard of pronunciation, which may or may not resemble GA. The same situation holds true in Great Britain, where only a small fraction of individuals (10 percent of population) actually speaks RP.

Table 7.2 lists the vowels found in General American and RP. As this table illustrates, vowels are classified according to the relative position of

Table 7.2. Vowels in English (adapted from Ladefoged 2005: 28–30)					
	Front	near-front	central	near-back	back
Close	i				u
Near-close		ɪ		ʊ	
Close-mid	eɪ				oʊ (GA) əʊ (RP)
Mid			ə		
Open-mid	ɛ			ʌ	ɔ
Near-open		æ			
Open				ɑ (GA) ɒ (RP)	

the tongue in the mouth: how high or low the tongue is positioned (the vertical axis on the left) and the degree to which the tongue is placed in the front or back of the mouth (the horizontal axis on top). The vowel /i/ is considered a close front vowel because when this vowel is articulated, the front of the tongue is at a very high position in the very front of the mouth. The vowel /u/ is a close back vowel because like /i/ the tongue is high in the mouth. However, rather than the tongue being positioned in the front of the mouth, the back of the tongue is high in the back of the mouth. The vowel /ɑ/ is also a back vowel but it is open because unlike /u/ the back of the tongue is low in the mouth. The vowel /ə/, known as the **schwa**, is pronounced with the tongue at a height mid-way between the top and bottom of the mouth and positioned in the center of the mouth. The vowel /ɛ/ is pronounced with the tongue positioned slightly lower in the mouth than the schwa but not as close to the front of the mouth as /i/. The remaining vowels exhibit varying degrees of height and frontness and backness.

It is important to realize that the system of vowel classification illustrated in Table 7.2 is somewhat of an idealization. Ladefoged (2001: 71) characterizes notions such as height and frontness and backness as "labels that describe how vowels sound in relation to one another. They are not absolute descriptions of the position of the body of the tongue." Unlike consonants, he continues, "there are no distinct boundaries between one type of vowel and another." But while the categories in Table 7.2 may indeed be merely "labels," they are a convenient way for linguists to describe and compare vowels.

Vowel differences between GA and RP. To illustrate how vowels differ between GA and RP, it is first of all necessary to see how each vowel in Table 7.2 is pronounced in actual words:

/i/ feet	/ɪ/ fit
/eɪ/ fate	/ɛ/ pet
/u/ suit	/æ/ sack
/oʊ/ soak (GA)	/ʊ/ book
/əʊ/ soak (RP)	
/ɔ/ fought	/ə/ arrive [vowel in first syllable]
/ɑ/ cot (GA)	/ʌ/ fun
park (RP)	
/ɒ/ cot (RP)	

Although many of the words in the list are pronounced similarly, there are some notable differences. The vowels in *boat* and *cot*, for instance, are pronounced differently in GA and RP. Within the United States itself, many speakers would not pronounce *cot* with /ɑ/ but with /ɔ/ because the vowels /ɑ/ and /ɔ/ are merging, with /ɔ/ replacing /ɑ/ in many words. But the most notable difference between GA and RP is the pronunciation of the word *park*, a word that would be pronounced as /pɑɹk/ in GA but /pɑk/ in RP. GA is **rhotic** because /ɹ/ occurs following vowels within a syllable. RP is **non-rhotic** because /ɹ/ does not occur following vowels in the same context.

Because RP is non-rhotic, it has many more **diphthongs** than GA. All of the vowels discussed thus far have been **monophthongs**: vowels whose "quality remains relatively constant" during their articulation (Ashby and Maidment 2005: 75). If, however, a vowel occurs within a syllable and its quality changes during its articulation, the vowel becomes a diphthong. GA and RP share three diphthongs:

/aɪ/ fight
/aʊ/ house
/ɔɪ/ boy

In each of the diphthongs above, the tongue changes position as each part of the diphthong is articulated. In the case of /ɔɪ/, for instance, the tongue is initially positioned in the lower back part of the mouth and then "glides" to the upper front of the mouth. This feature of diphthongs explains why in the American tradition of transcription, the three diphthongs above are transcribed, respectively, as /ay/, /aw/, and /ɔy/. The sounds /y/ and /w/, sometimes referred to as glides (or semi-vowels), are used to reflect the gradual transition between vowels inherent in diphthongs.

   While GA and RP share three diphthongs, RP has four additional diphthongs occurring in syllables where GA would have a vowel + /ɹ/ sequence, a sequence leading to an /ɹ/-colored vowel (Ladefoged 2005: 30). Thus, the four words below would have different pronunciations in GA and RP:

	GA	RP
fear	/fɪɹ/	/fɪə/
fair	/fɛɹ/	/feə/
tire	/taɪɝ/	/taə/
four	/foʊɹ/	/fʊə/

In GA, any time a vowel occurs before an /ɹ/ in a single syllable, the /ɹ/ "colors" the vowel, creating in a sense a single sound. In RP, in contrast, no such sequences of vowel + /ɹ/ exist, resulting instead in a diphthong.

Other classifications of vowels.   Vowels have additional classifications. In Table 7.2, all of the vowels outside the rectangular box are considered tense, those within the box lax. In English, tense vowels tend to be long, while lax vowels are short. For instance, the tense vowel /i/ in a word such as *feet* has a longer duration than the lax vowel /ɪ/ in *fit*. But tense and lax vowels have other differences too. While tense vowels can occur in both **open** and **closed** syllables, lax vowels are restricted to closed syllables. A closed syllable is a syllable ending with a consonant. In such syllables, one finds either tense or lax vowels:

Tense vowels: *read* /rid/, *suit* /sut/, *hate* /heɪt/, *talk* /tɔk/
Lax vowels: *fit* /fɪt /, *sat* /sæt/, *help* /hɛlp/, *took* /tʊk/

Open syllables, in contrast, end in a vowel. Only tense vowels can occur in such syllables:

bee /bi/, *sue* /su/, *pay* /peɪ/, *law* /lɔ/

Tense and lax vowels also have different distributions on the vowel chart in Table 7.2, with tense vowels on the "periphery" and lax vowels (enclosed in the square box) "in the central regions" (Hammond 1999: 6).

Vowels can also be rounded or spread. Most vowels in English are spread; that is, when a vowel such as /i/ is articulated, the lips are spread apart. In contrast, when /u/ is pronounced, the lips are rounded. The rounded vowels in English are the back vowels /u/, /ʊ/, /oʊ/, /əʊ/, and /ɔ/. All other vowels are spread.

Allophones and allomorphs

The discussion thus far has focused on phonemes: the distinctive sounds (consonants and vowels) that exist in the English language. As was noted earlier, however, phonemes have different pronunciations in specific contexts. For instance, the phoneme /p/ is aspirated initially in a syllable but unaspirated medially or finally. Thus, the phoneme /p/ has two allophones that are in complementary distribution: aspirated [pʰ] in one context and unaspirated [p⁻] in another. Similar kinds of variation occur with morphemes. The plural marker -s has three different pronunciations that are in complementary distribution: [s], [z], and [əz]. The specific environments in which each pronunciation occurs will be described later in this section. But because these variations in pronunciation involve morphemes, they are considered allomorphs of the plural morpheme in English.

This section contains a description of some examples of allophonic and allomorphic variation in English, with an emphasis on one more general process, **assimilation**, as well as several other processes. Because the focus is on allophones and allomorphs rather than phonemes, a narrow system of transcription, enclosed in brackets [ ], will be used.

Assimilation. Assimilation is a general process whereby adjacent sounds with differing properties become more similar in terms of their voicing, place of articulation, or manner of articulation:

Nasal plosion
In a word such as *flatten* [flætⁿn̩], the alveolar plosive /t/ undergoes nasal plosion. First of all, /t/ occurs at the end of a syllable before the alveolar nasal /n/. Both of these consonants are therefore homorganic: they share the same place of articulation. Second, /n/ is syllabic: it occupies a single syllable with no accompanying vowel and is thus transcribed narrowly as [n̩]. In this environment, when the plosive is released, the air flows through the nasal cavity rather than the oral cavity in anticipation of the articulation of the nasal consonant /n/. In this environment, the plosive is transcribed narrowly with a superscript *n*: [tⁿ]. Other words in which this process occurs include *hidden* [hɪdⁿn̩] and *written* [ɹɪtⁿn̩]. The process also applies, as Yavas (2005: 59) notes, before /n/ occurring at the beginning of either a subsequent syllable, as in *madness* [mædⁿnɛs], or a subsequent word, as in *sad news* [sædⁿnuz].

Other assimilatory processes involving nasals
When the bilabial nasal /m/ and alveolar nasal /n/ occur before the labiodental fricatives /f/ and /v/, the nasals become labiodentals [ɱ]. Thus, *comfort*

would be pronounced [kʌɱfɝt] or [kʌɱfət] and *convince* as [kʌɱvɪns]. When /n/ occurs before a dental consonant such as /θ/, its articulation becomes more dental [n̪]. Words such as *tenth* would therefore be pronounced as [tɛn̪θ]. Vowels occurring before nasal consonants will themselves be nasalized: ran [ɹæ̃n], room [ɹũm], ring [ɹĩŋ].

Devoicing of consonants

When plosives, fricatives, and affricates occur before unvoiced consonants, they will be devoiced. For instance, in isolation, *his* ends with the voiced fricative /z/: /hɪz/. However, if *his* is followed by a word beginning with a voiceless consonant, the /z/ becomes devoiced [z̥]. Thus, *his fist* would be pronounced as [hɪz̥ fist]. Other examples include:

had to [hæd̥ tu]
with sympathy [wɪð̥ sɪmpəθi]
yours truly [jɝz̥ tɹuli]

Voicing assimilation with English -s:

The inflection *-s* in English occurs in three contexts: as a third person singular present tense verb form (*takes*), as a plural marker on nouns (*dishes*), and as a marker of possession (*man's*). But while each inflection is spelled as *-s* or *-es*, the inflections have three different pronunciations.

   Two of the pronunciations, [s] and [z], are the result of voicing assimilation between the consonant ending the base to which these inflections are attached and the inflections themselves. If the base ends with a voiced consonant or a vowel (all vowels in English are voiced), then the inflection will be voiced [z]:

hose [hoʊz] or [həʊz]
feels [fiəlz]
child's [tʃaɪldz]
doors [doʊɹz] or [dʊəz]
gangs [gæŋz]

If the stem ends with a voiceless consonant, the inflection will be voiceless:

walks [wɔks]
fights [faɪts]
fifths [fɪfθs]
lips [lɪps]
huffs [hʌfs]

With stems ending with the consonants /s/, /z/, /ʃ/, /ʒ/, /tʃ/, and /dʒ/, neither [s] nor [z] is possible, since a consonant cluster such as [ss] or [dʒz] is not possible in English. As a result, it is necessary to insert an [ɪ] or [ə] between the consonant ending the stem and the inflection [z]:

hisses [hɪsɪz] or [hɪsəz]
fizzes [fɪzɪz]

washes [wɔʃɪz]
George's [dʒɔʊɹdʒɪz]
churches [tʃɝtʃɪz]

Place of articulation assimilation with negative prefixes

The negative prefixes *im-*, *in-*, *il-*, and *ir-* all mean 'not' in words such as *impertinent* or *illegal*. Exactly which of these three prefixes is used depends upon the place of articulation of the consonant beginning the base to which they are affixed. If the base begins with a bilabial sound, then [ɪm] will be used:

immodest [ɪmmɑdɪst]
imperfect [ɪmpɝfɛkt]
immobile [ɪmmoʊbəl]
implausible [ɪmplɔzəbəl]

If, on the other hand, the stem begins with an alveolar or velar consonant, then [ɪn] or [ɪŋ] will be used:

intangible [ɪntændʒəbəl]
incomplete [ɪŋkʌmplit]
inauspicious [ɪnɔspɪʃəs]
indefensible [ɪndifɛnsəbəl]

If the stem begins with [l] or [ɹ], the prefixes [ɪl] and [ɪɹ] are used, respectively:

illegal [ɪlligəl]
illicit [ɪllɪsɪt]
irrelevant [ɪɹɹɛləvənt]
irredeemable [ɪɹɹədiməbəl]

Miscellaneous processes.   Other processes occur in English as well:

Alveolar flapping

In American English, the words *writer* and *rider* can be homophones because the alveolar plosives /t/ and /d/ can undergo a process known as alveolar flapping, resulting in both words being pronounced as [ɹaɪɾɝ]. For this process to apply, /t/ or /d/ must occur between vowels, and the primary stress needs to be placed on the syllable preceding /t/ or /d/. Both of these conditions apply in *writer* and *rider*, as both /t/ and /d/ occur between vowels, and the primary stress occurs on the syllables preceding both consonants. Other words in which this process can apply include *butter* [bʌɾɝ], *literature* [lɪɾɝətʃɝ], and *fatter* [fæɾɝ].

Lengthening of vowels

Vowels will differ in length depending upon whether they occur before a voiced or unvoiced consonant. In the list below, the vowels in the second column are lengthier because they occur before voiced consonants. The vowels are shorter in the first column because they occur before voiceless consonants:

bit [bɪt]   bid [bɪːd]
feet [fit]   feed [fiːd]
hiss [hɪs]   his [hɪːz]
leaf [lif]   leave [liːv]

Intrusive /ɹ/

Some speakers of English will insert an /ɹ/ in contexts where one is not ordinarily found. In the 1960s, the former US President John F. Kennedy made famous the pronunciation of *Cuba* as [kjubɝ] rather than [kjubə]. This process occurs when a word ends in a schwa [ə] and precedes either a pause or a word beginning with a vowel. Therefore, President Kennedy would have said *Cuba* [kjubɝ] *is a threat* but *Cuba* [kjubə] *threatens us*. Other words in which intrusive /ɹ/ can occur include *idea*, *Toyota*, and *Rebecca*.

Suprasegmentals

The study of suprasegmentals extends the focus of inquiry to units that are larger than individual segments – syllables, words, phrases, and clauses – and to the features of sound that describe these units, specifically stress and intonation. Of key importance to both stress and intonation is the notion of the syllable.

Syllables

A syllable consists of three parts: an onset, a nucleus, and a coda. The nucleus typically consists of a vowel that is preceded by the onset and followed by the coda. In a simple word such as *hat*, the nucleus would be the vowel /æ/, the onset /h/, and the coda /t/. While the nucleus is usually a vowel, it is also possible, as suggested earlier, for the nasal consonants /m̩/ and /n̩/ to be syllabic in words such as *bottom* and *button* and for the approximant /l/ to be syllabic in words such as *bottle* /batl̩/ and *little* /lɪtl̩/.

Most people have an intuitive sense of what a syllable is. For instance, if presented with a word such as *happiness*, even a non-linguist would recognize this word as containing three syllables (separated by periods) with the primary stress (marked by ') falling on the first syllable: /ˈhæ.pi.nɛs/. More formally, Ashby and Maidment (2005: 7) define a syllable as:

one pulse of speech. It always contains one loud or prominent part (almost always a vowel sound), and may optionally have consonant sounds preceding or following the vowel.

Because many words in English have alternate pronunciations, differing pronunciations will sometimes lead to varying numbers of syllables. The word *smile* can be pronounced with one syllable /smaɪl/ or two syllables /smaɪ.yəl/. Syllable boundaries can also vary. In the word *ketchup*, it is possible to place the syllable boundary in two places, depending upon how the word is pronounced: /kɛtʃ.ʌp/ or /kɛ.tʃʌp/.

Exactly which consonants can occur in the onset and coda is determined by a series of **phonotactic constraints**. The assignment of the primary stress to a particular syllable in a word is dictated by a fairly complex set of rules for stress assignment in English.

Phonotactics.   English has a series of constraints, known as phonotactics, that specify the permissible sequences of consonants in the onset and coda. For instance, /p/ can occur singly in the onset /pæt/ or the coda /tæp/. It can also follow /s/ in the onset /spæt/. However, it cannot precede /s/ in the onset (e.g. */psæt/). The other consonants in English have similar constraints: other consonants before or after which they can or cannot occur. In total, English allows up to three consonants in the onset and three consonants in the coda, with different sequences of consonants permissible in each.

With the exception of /ŋ/, all consonants in English can occur singly in the onset. The velar nasal /ŋ/ is somewhat exceptional in that it is usually found only singly in the coda in words such as *ring* /ɹɪŋ/ and *sing* /sɪŋ/. It can also occur before /θ/ in one-syllable words such as *strength* /stɹɛŋθ/. However, in this and other similar words (e.g. *length*), some speakers of English will substitute /n/ for /ŋ/ (e.g. /lɛnθ/) and use /ŋ/ only singly in the coda.

As consonants are added to the onset, more restrictions are placed on the possible combinations that are permitted. For instance, if the onset contains two consonants, all plosives and voiceless fricatives can occur prior to the approximant /ɹ/ in words such as *pray* /pɹ/, *trip* /tɹ/, *crime* /kɹ/, *bring* /bɹ/, *drink* /dɹ/, *greed* /gɹ/, *free* /fɹ/, *through* /θɹ/, and *shrill* /ʃɹ/. Many (though not all) of these same consonants can precede /l/: *play* /pl/, *clasp* /kl/, *blank* /bl/, *glad* /gl/, and *slap* /sl/. The approximants /j/ and /w/ permit a wide range of consonants to precede them in many syllables. Some examples with /j/ include the first syllables in words such as *puny* /pj/, *furious* /fj/, and *humid* /hj/. Some syllables can contain an optional /j/. For instance, the first syllable in *coupon* can be pronounced as either /kju/ or /ku/. Some examples with /w/ include *twice* /tw/, *quick* /kw/, and the first syllable of *dwindle* /dw/. If the onset contains three consonants, the options are very limited. Some examples include *spring* /spɹ/, *splash* /spl/, *strike* /stɹ/, and *scratch* /skɹ/.

In the coda, all consonants are permitted singly with the exception of the fricative /h/ and the approximants /j/ and /w/. Whether /ɹ/ is allowed, as in *harm* /hɑɹm/ or in the second syllable of *never* /nɛvɹ̩/, depends upon whether the speaker's dialect is rhotic or non-rhotic. In codas with two consonants, the approximants /l/ and (in rhotic dialects) /ɹ/ can precede many different consonants, as in, for instance, *help* /lp/, *bold* /ld/, *self* /lf/, *elm* /lm/, *harsh* /ɹʃ/, and *church* /ɹtʃ/. The three nasals too can precede a range of different consonants, as in *lamp* /mp/, *hand* /nd/, and *link* /ŋk/, as can the plosives /k/ and /p/ in words such as *sixth* /ksθ/, *ax* /ks/, and *taps* /ps/. Sometimes, whether a coda can be said to contain two or three consonants depends upon whether the speaker actually articulates all of the consonants possible. For instance, all speakers would articulate a word such as *unkempt* as containing three consonants in the coda: /mpt/. However, in other cases, such as *twelfth*, some speakers might include three consonants in the coda /lfθ/, while others might pronounce only two /lθ/.

Stress.   All English words will contain one syllable that has primary stress: a syllable that is more prominent than the other syllables in the word. In the word *happy*, for instance, the primary stress falls on the first syllable because of the two syllables in this word, the first syllable is more prominent than the second syllable: ˈha.ppy. Some words contain syllables with varying degrees of stress. As was noted in the last chapter, compound words in English are marked by a specific stress pattern: primary stress on the first element and secondary stress on the second element, as in ˈhead. ˌlight. However, the extent to which English words consistently exhibit varying degrees of stress is a controversial notion. As a result, most discussions of word stress in English focus mainly on primary stress.

Because English is a language with variable stress rather than fixed stress, determining which syllable in a word receives the primary stress can be a very complicated process. A language such as French exhibits fixed stress because the primary stress falls most frequently on the last syllable of a word, and less frequently on the second to last syllable. English, however, has variable stress. A survey of words in English reveals that the primary stress falls on many different syllables. In the examples below, the primary stress falls on three different syllables:

ˈcon.cert (penultimate [i.e. second to last] syllable)
re.ˈplace.a.ble (antepenultimate [i.e. third to last] syllable)
re.ˈceive (ultimate [i.e. last] syllable)

The variability of stress placement in these and other words in English is on one level a consequence of the history of the language, specifically the fact that English vocabulary is a mixture of words of Germanic and non-Germanic origin. And two of the languages from which English has borrowed extensively – Latin and French – have different conventions than English for the assignment of primary stress.

Words of Germanic origin in English are subject to the Germanic stress rule, which stipulates that primary stress is placed on the first syllable of the base of a word, as in the examples below:

ˈba.by	ˈbel.ly
ˈhun.gry	ˈfa.ther
ˈmo.ther	ˈpre.tty
ˈfriend.ly	ˈha.ppy

Even if derivational affixes are added to words of Germanic origin, the primary stress remains on the first syllable of the base:

ˈbel.ly.ful	ˈfa.ther.less
ˈmo.ther.less	ˈpre.tti.ness
un.ˈfriend.ly	un.ˈha.ppiness

During the Middle English period, however, English received an extensive number of borrowings, particularly from French and Latin. As Italic (or Romance) languages, French and Latin had, as Fournier (2007) comments, very different systems of stress. In Germanic languages, as demonstrated above, primary stress is on the initial syllable of the base. If a single prefix is added, as in the case of *unfriendly*, the stress moves rightward to the first syllable of the base. In contrast, Italic languages such as Latin and French "share a feature which is the exact opposite of the stress systems of Germanic languages: stress is determined from the end of words (or tone units) rather than from their beginning" (Fournier 2007: 228). In the word *de.'vout*, a French borrowing into Middle English, the stress is on the final (ultimate) syllable, a common stress pattern for disyllabic words in Romance languages. When a suffix is added, as in *de.'vo.tion*, the primary stress moves leftward to the penultimate syllable.

As a result, during the Middle English period, two very different systems of stress placement co-existed. One consequence, as Dresher and Lahiri (2005: 78) note, were "doublets," words with two different patterns of stress: one Germanic, the other Latinate or French. Commenting on the list of words below, Dresher and Lahiri (2005) remark that while Chaucer would have employed the French system of stress, the Germanic system would have existed in English as well:

French Stress	Germanic Stress	Modern English Gloss
ci.'tee	'ci.tee	'city'
com.'fort	'com.fort	'comfort'
di.'vers	'di.vers	'diverse'
ge.'aunt	'ge.aunt	'giant'
Pla.'to	'Pla.to	'Plato'
pre.'sent	'pre.sent	'present'

Early (pre-1500) disyllabic borrowings such as these have almost entirely been assimilated into the Germanic system of stress. In a survey of 200 disyllabic French loanwords from this period in Wells' (2000) *Longman Pronunciation Dictionary*, Svensson and Hering (2005: 123–4) found that only six words in Modern English had stress on the final syllable (as in *di.'verse*). However, later borrowings (post-1700) revealed a greater mixture of the Germanic and French systems, and also some notable differences between Modern British and American English. For instance, while words such as *'bro.chure* and *'ca.fe* carry primary stress on the first syllable in British English, in American English the primary stress is on the second syllable (*bro.'chure* and *ca.'fe*).

Later borrowings had an additional effect on stress placement in English: they introduced into the language words and affixes that resulted in polysyllabic words that were often three syllables in length or longer. The resultant words brought about significant changes in the assignment of primary stress, so that in Modern English, assignment of primary stress is dependent upon (1) the type of affix added, (2) the number of syllables a word contains, and (3) which syllables in the word are

light (incapable of taking primary stress) or **heavy** (capable of taking primary stress).

The word pairs below illustrate how word stress is affected by what Stockwell and Minkova (2001: 169–71) term stress-neutral and stress-demanding suffixes.

'hope.ful	'hope.ful.ness
'pro.fit	pro.fi.'teer

The words *hopeful* and *hopefulness* contain suffixes, *-ful* and *-ness*, that are stress-neutral: their addition to *hope* has no effect on the placement of primary stress, which remains on *hope*. However, in the words *profit* and *profiteer*, the suffix *-eer* is stress-demanding: its addition to *profit* causes the stress to shift to the end of the word. Other suffixes that Stockwell and Minkova (2001) classify as stress-neutral include *-ess* (e.g. 'host., 'hos.tess), *-man* (e.g. po.'lice, po.'lice.man), and *-ist* (e.g. 'fet.ish, 'fet.ish.ist); those they classify as stress-demanding include *-naire* (e.g. 'ques.tion, ques.tion.'naire), *-esce* (e.g. in.can.'des.cent, in.cand.'esce), and *-tee* (e.g. 'am.pu.tate, am.pu.'tee).

The word pairs below illustrate the effects of the number of syllables in a word on stress placement as well as whether a potential syllable for stress is light or heavy:

'mul.ti.ply	mul.ti.pli.'ca.tion
'mys.ti.fy	mys.ti.fi.'ca.tion

In each of the pairs above, the second examples are derived from the first examples through the process of affixation, a process that in each example adds additional syllables and shifts the placement of primary stress. In 'mult.i.ply, the primary stress is on the antepenultimate (third to last) syllable, whereas in mul.ti.pli.'ca.tion, the primary stress is on the penultimate (second to last) syllable. The difference in stress placement in these words is directly attributable to the kind of syllable occurring in the penultimate position.

In mul.ti.pli.'ca.tion, the penultimate syllable (spelled *ca* but pronounced /keɪ/) is heavy: it contains a tense vowel. If the penultimate syllable is heavy, it will carry the primary stress (heavy syllables can also contain any vowel, tense or lax, followed by a consonant, which is why a word such as con.'tent.ment has primary stress on the penultimate syllable, even though the vowel in *tent*, /ɛ/, is not tense but lax). In contrast, in 'mul.ti.ply, the penultimate syllable is light: it contains only a lax vowel (spelled *i* but pronounced as /ə/). With light syllables in the penultimate position, stress is moved to the antepenultimate syllable.

Additional examples are given below, with heavy syllables in the first column and light syllables in the second column:

Penultimate stress	*Antepenultimate stress*
res.ti.'tu.tion	mul.ti.'fac.e.ted
dis.con.'tent.ment	rep.re.'hens.i.ble
ad.jec.'ti.val	de.'riv.a.tive
fun.da.'men.tal	pre.'var.i.cate

While derivational affixes affect stress placement, inflectional affixes do not. In all of the word pairs below, even though the addition of a suffix adds an additional syllable to each word, the placement of stress does not change:

pre.'var.i.cate   pre.'var.i.ca.ted
es.'tab.lish   es.'tab.lish.ing
fa.'mil.iar.ize   fa.'mil.iar.iz.es

Of course, there are exceptions to many of the patterns of stress discussed thus far. Words such as *ex.'pa.tri.ate* and *'con.cen.trate* have primary stress on the antepenultimate syllables, even though the penultimate syllables in these words are heavy and should therefore carry the primary stress. Just the opposite is true as well: words such as *re.'vi.sion, fru.'i.tion,* and *con.'fe.ssion* in which the penultimate syllable is stressed despite the fact that it is light. The noun and verb forms of certain words are distinguished simply by changes in stress. When the stress is on the first syllable, as in *'cont.ract,* the word is a noun. When the stress is on the second syllable, the word is a verb: *con.'tract.* Other examples include *'re.cord/re.'cord, 'con.vict/con.'vict,* and *'im.port/im.'port.* And as noted earlier, there are a number of disyllabic words in English (e.g. *ga.'rage*) that contain primary stress on the final rather than the first syllable, contrary to the more common patterns of stress assignment in English. These and other exceptions indicate that stress assignment in English is, at best, only partially predictable.

Intonation

The study of intonation involves the investigation of pitch and stress across groups of words occurring within a tone unit. In a typical (i.e. unmarked) tone unit, the pitch will begin rising at the start of a tone unit, peak on one particular syllable occurring towards the end of the tone, and then fall before rising again at the start of the next tone unit. For instance, the excerpt below contains two tone units:

I couldn't **REAlly** ‖ let my company **DO** this ‖

(London-Lund S.12.6.758-759)

In this excerpt, the tone unit boundaries are indicated by the two vertical lines ‖ and the syllables receiving the highest pitch and the greatest stress are marked with upper-case letters and bold-face type. (To enhance readability, the annotation used above and elsewhere in this section has been changed from the annotation used in the London-Lund Corpus.) In the first tone unit, the pitch rises, peaks on the first syllable of *REAlly,* which receives the greatest stress of any word in the tone unit, and then falls. In the second tone unit, this same pattern is repeated, except that after the pitch peaks on *DO,* the tone unit does not end until after the following word, *this.* To understand why this pattern exists, it is important first of all to distinguish word stress from what is sometimes referred to as **sentence stress,** and to discuss the role that intonation plays in highlighting new information, a point introduced earlier in the section of Chapter 4 dealing with information structure.

In an unmarked tone unit, the pitch will peak on the **tonic syllable**. As the last section demonstrated, in isolation all words will have one syllable carrying primary stress: the preposition *be.'tween* has primary stress on the second syllable, the adverb *'rea.lly* in the above example on the first syllable. However, when words occur together in an unmarked tone unit, one syllable of one word will receive greater stress (called sentence stress) than the other words. This stress will occur on the syllable, called the tonic syllable, carrying primary stress in the last content word of the tone unit. In unmarked tone units, only content words will contain the tonic syllable, not function words. This is why in the second tone unit in the example above, the lexical verb *do* (a content word) contains the tonic syllable rather than the last word in the tone unit, the pronoun *this* (a function word).

The reason that content words rather than function words contain the tonic syllable results from the fact that the goal of intonation in spoken discourse is to highlight new information. And since content words are more meaningful than function words, it is only natural that content words would receive the greatest stress in a tone unit. In fact, function words are often so lightly stressed in rapid speech that the vowels they contain become subject to **vowel reduction**, and the consonants ending function words are sometimes deleted. Vowel reduction occurs when the vowel in a lightly stressed syllable changes to a schwa [ə]. For instance, if carefully articulated, the articles *a* and *the* in English can be pronounced as [eɪ] and [ði], respectively. However, if the articles are lightly stressed, they will be pronounced as [ə] and [ðə]. The conjunction *and* [ænd] can have its vowel reduced too, and one or both of its final consonants deleted, resulting in pronunciations of [ən] or simply [ə].

While function words do not ordinarily contain the tonic syllable, with some kind of contextual motivation, they and potentially any word in a tone unit can contain the tonic syllable. For instance, if the invented tone unit below is unmarked, the tonic syllable will occur on the second syllable of *tomorrow*:

I will call you toMORrow ‖

It is possible, however, to imagine contexts in which just about any word in the above tone unit could contain the tonic syllable, resulting in a marked tone unit, a tone unit in which the tonic syllable occurs somewhere other than in the last content word of the tone unit. For instance, if several people are speaking and one person asks two of the conversants which one will call her, one of the conversants could reply by placing the tonic syllable on *I* to emphasize that she rather than the other person will be doing the calling:

I will call you tomorrow ‖

If one of the conversants is worried that one of the others will not call her tomorrow, the person who will be making the call can place the tonic syllable on *will* to reassure the person being called that she will indeed be called:

I WILL call you tomorrow ‖

One could imagine other contexts in which other words in the tone unit could receive the tonic syllable, but the point to remember is that potentially any word in a tone unit can be heavily stressed for purposes of emphasis and meaning.

In addition to highlighting new or important information, tone units help to segment spoken language into grammatical units. The extent to which tone unit boundaries correspond to major grammatical boundaries depends upon the particular grammatical boundary being considered and also whether the spoken text is planned or spontaneous. In an analysis of a spoken monologue, a more carefully planned type of speech, Altenberg (1990) found that while certain kinds of structures were very commonly associated with tone unit boundaries, others showed a weaker correspondence. For instance, Altenberg (1990: 279) discovered that 150 of 153 (98%) coordinated main clauses were separated by a tone unit boundary, whereas only 19 of 32 (59%) of nominal *that*-clauses were set off by a tone unit boundary. These trends can be observed in the excerpt from a monologue below:

your Provost has **SAID** ‖ that I was going to talk about the **ARTS** ‖ and indeed I had in**TEN**ded ‖ to **TALK** about that ‖ but hearing President **NIX**on ‖ **MOU**thing about the **DEATH** penalty ‖ and about the permissive so**CI**ety ‖ I decided that I would talk in**STEAD** ‖ about something which con**CERNS** me ‖ in the **THE**atre ‖

(London-Lund S.12.7.2–10)

There are two instances of coordinated main clauses separated by a tone unit boundary: the coordinator *and* in the early part of the excerpt (*and indeed I had*) is preceded by a tone unit boundary, as is the coordinator *but* (*but hearing President NIXon*). In contrast, the one instance of a nominal *that*-clause is not set off by a boundary (*I decided that I would talk*).

If, however, a spontaneous dialogue is examined, there is less of a correspondence between grammatical and tone unit boundaries, largely because the spontaneous structure of such speech-types often results in fewer grammatically well-formed structures. In addition, because the speaker is planning what to say as he or she is speaking, there are more hesitations, reformulations, and so forth that interrupt the flow of speech. In the excerpt below from a spontaneous dialogue, one finds boundaries before the two clauses introduced by *so* (*...so I said FINE... so I got a perEMPtory*), but also boundaries not separating major grammatical categories, such as the boundary between the two repetitions of *I'm* (*I'm ‖ I'm just hanging ON*) and between an adjective and noun within a noun phrase (*a perEMPtory ‖ command*).

oh well you **KNOW** I ‖ might get **TERR**ibly ‖ you **KNOW** I`m ‖ I`m just hanging **ON** now ‖ and could take you on **PER**manently ‖ we may need **YOU** ‖ to do some work in the **EVE**ning ‖ so I said FINE ‖ being o**BLI**ging ‖ so I got a per**EMP**tory ‖ co**MMAND** ‖ over the **PHONE** ‖ **RIGHT** ‖

(London-Lund S.1.5.223–234)

There are many other features of intonation that can be described. Speech is filled with pauses, which are distinct from tone unit boundaries. The tone and tempo of speaking is also important: speakers can vary the loudness of what they say, and the tempo (fast, slow) at which they speak. In declarative sentences, the pitch falls after the tonic syllable is reached:

We are LEAVing now

In a *yes/no* question, the pitch rises at the end of the tone unit:

Are we LEAVing now

Rising intonation can also be used to end a declarative sentence, but with differing effects:

We are LEAVing now

The effect of this pattern of intonation is not to simply inquire whether the group is leaving, but rather to express concern or disappointment over the group's departure.

Summary

The study of sound can be focused on either individual segments (phonemes) or suprasegmentals (features such as stress or pitch covering segments larger than phonemes). Like all languages, English has a distinctive set of speech segments called phonemes: consonants and vowels that make up the inventory of sounds in English. It is possible to determine which sounds in English are distinctive by examining minimal pairs: words that differ by a single phoneme. All English phonemes can be described in terms of their place of articulation – where the tongue and lips are positioned when a sound is articulated – and manner of articulation: where the air flows in the oral or nasal cavities and the degree to which the airstream is obstructed or allowed to flow freely. Phonemes can also be voiced or unvoiced, depending upon whether the vocal cords vibrate or not.

The study of sound, however, is also suprasegmental: it extends beyond single phonemes to syllables, words, phrases, and clauses. All words in English contain one or more syllables, and one of these syllables will carry the primary stress. Intonation also serves to segment speech into grammatical structures, though the correspondence between grammar and intonation is closer in more carefully prepared speech than in spontaneous dialogues.

Self-study activities

1. If instead of using the English alphabet for spelling we used a phonetic alphabet, would English spelling be easier?
2. Why are the words *fast* and *feast* evidence that the sounds /æ/ and /i/ are phonemes in English?
3. Identify the number of different phonemes that each word in the list below has. Remember that many words have more graphemes than phonemes. The word *though*, for instance, has six graphemes but only two phonemes.
    (a) toss
    (b) heat

(c) mystic
(d) fastest
(e) five
(f) heavenly
(g) frosty
(h) convention
(i) plasticity
(j) capstone

4. The pairs of phonemes in the left-hand column below differ by one fea-
    ture: voicing, place of articulation, or manner of articulation. For instance,
    the consonants /p/ and /b/ have the same place of articulation (bilabial)
    and manner of articulation (plosives), but differ in voicing: /p/ is
    unvoiced, while /b/ is voiced. Match each pair of phonemes in the left-
    hand column with the one feature in the right-hand column that distin-
    guishes the pair.

    (1) /d/ and /n/   a. voicing
    (2) /θ/ and /ð/   b. place of articulation
    (3) /b/ and /g/   c. manner of articulation
    (4) /s/ and /z/
    (5) /d/ and /ɹ/
    (6) /f/ and /ʃ/

5. English has numerous allophones. For instance, the syllable-initial
    unvoiced plosives /p/, /t/, and /k/ are aspirated; medially and finally in a
    syllable they are not. Vowels are longer before voiced consonants than
    unvoiced consonants. In the list of words below, indicate which stops are
    aspirated, and which vowels are lengthened. Some words may not illus-
    trate either of these processes; other words may illustrate both processes.

    (a) pad
    (b) tram
    (c) grip
    (d) sting
    (e) stink
    (f) play
    (g) crab

6. Indicate which syllable in the words below carries the primary stress.

    (a) recitation
    (b) predominate
    (c) cigarette
    (d) contest
    (e) bureau
    (f) contentment
    (g) dislike
    (h) unconvincing

7. Each of the examples below contains one or more tone units, whose
    boundaries are marked with ‖. Show where the tonic syllable would
    occur if the tone unit is unmarked. Then, suggest other places in the tone
    unit where the tonic syllable could occur if the tone unit were marked.
    Briefly explain how the meaning changes in marked tone units.

    (a) The turtle walked slowly ‖ into the room ‖
    (b) Our teacher helped us ‖ with our homework ‖
    (c) With little or no resistance ‖ the child put his shirt on ‖

Further reading

General introductions to phonetics can be found in M. Ashby and J. Maidment, *Introducing Phonetic Science* (Cambridge: Cambridge University Press, 2005) as well as P. Ladefoged, *A Course in Phonetics* (4th edn., New York: Wadsworth Publishers, 2005). H. J. Giegerich's *English Phonology* (Cambridge: Cambridge University Press, 1992) provides an overview of the systematic nature of the English sound system, with discussions of allophones and word stress. R. Stockwell and D. Minkova, *English Words: History and Structure* (Cambridge: Cambridge University Press, 2001) describe word stress in a series of succinct rules (pp. 168–76). R. Quirk *et al.*, *A Comprehensive Grammar of the English Language* (London: Longman, 1985) provide an overview of tone units and their relationship to grammar (pp. 1355–75). A more general overview of English intonation can be found in P. Tench, *The Intonation Systems of English* (London: Cassell, 1996).

Appendix: Linguistic corpora consulted

The British National Corpus (BNC): 100 million words of different types of speech (10 million words) and writing (90 million words). Examples taken from the BNC that are included in this book contain an identification number specifying the register, particular text, and particular lines within the text from which the example was taken. More information on the registers in the BNC can be found at: http://www.natcorp.ox.ac.uk/XMLedition/URG/codes.html#classcodes (accessed June 19, 2008)

The International Corpus of English (ICE): Examples from three components of ICE are included in this book (see below). For general information on ICE, go to: http://www.ucl.ac.uk/english-usage/ice/index.htm (accessed June 19, 2008)

The British Component of the International Corpus of English (ICE-GB): one million words of various kinds of speech (600,000 words) and writing (400,000 words). Examples taken from ICE-GB that are included in this book contain an identification number indicating whether the example was taken from speech (S) or writing (W) and specifying the particular register, sample number, and line number from which the example was taken. Additional information about ICE-GB can be found at: http://www.ucl.ac.uk/english-usage/projects/ice-gb/ (accessed June 19, 2008)

The New Zealand Component of the International Corpus of English (ICE-NZ): Same kinds of texts as ICE-GB. The same identification numbers used to document examples from ICE-GB are included following examples cited in this book. For details on this component, go to: http://www.victoria.ac.nz/lals/research/corpora/index.aspx#ice (accessed June 19, 2008)

The American Component of the International Corpus of English (ICE-USA): currently under development; will eventually contain the same kinds of texts in ICE-GB and ICE-NZ.

The Cambridge International Corpus (CIC): The CIC is a computer database of contemporary spoken and written English, which currently stands at over one billion words. It includes British English, American English and other varieties of English. It also includes the Cambridge Learner Corpus, developed in collaboration with the University of Cambridge ESOL Examinations. Cambridge University Press has built up the CIC to provide evidence about language use that helps to produce better language teaching materials.

Michigan Corpus of Academic Spoken English (MICASE): 1.8 million words of various kinds of speech found in academic contexts (e.g. class lectures, study groups, advising sessions). Examples from this corpus used in this book contain an identification number listing the particular register, sample, and line number within the sample from which the example was taken. For additional details, go to: http://quod.lib.umich.edu/m/micase/ (accessed June 19, 2008)

Santa Barbara Corpus of Spoken American English (SBCSAE): transcriptions and audio recordings of hundreds of dialogues and some monologues; the transcriptions will eventually become part of ICE-USA. For more information, go to: http://www.linguistics.ucsb.edu/research/sbcorpus.html (accessed June 19, 2008)

The London-Lund Corpus: One million words of various kinds of spoken English representing many different registers, from spontaneous dialogues to scripted monologues. Samples have been prosodically transcribed with annotation marking various features of intonation (e.g. tone unit boundaries). Examples included in this book contain identification numbers similar to those used in ICE-GB. For additional information, go to: http://khnt.hit.uib.no/icame/manuals/londlund/index.htm (accessed June 21, 2008)

Glossary

acceptability:
: Judgments that speakers make concerning what they feel are good vs. bad uses of language. For instance, many people dislike double negatives or the word *ain't*, even though these expressions are perfectly grammatical and are regularly used by many speakers of English. Compare with **grammaticality**.

active voice:
: The form of a verb in a clause such as *The author wrote the book* in which the agent (the doer of the action, in this case *The author*) is the **subject**, and the person or thing affected by the agent (*the book* in the above example) is the **object**. Compare with **passive voice**.

adjacency pair:
: A two-part construction, such as a greeting, in which the first part (e.g. one person saying "hello") elicits the second part (the person being greeted also replying with "hello"). Question/answer sequences are another example of an adjacency pair.

adjective phrase:
: A **phrase** such as *very delicious* whose **head** is an adjective.

adverbials:
: A **clause function** realized by noun phrases, adverb phrases, and prepositional phrases expressing notions such as time, place, and logical connection. The key test for many adverbials is that they can be moved around in a clause: ***Yesterday*** *I was ill* → *I was ill* ***yesterday***.

affixation:
: The process of adding **derivational** suffixes and prefixes to a word (e.g. adding *un-* and *-ness* to *happy* to create *unhappiness*)

affixes:
: Prefixes and suffixes added to words. An affix can be a **derivational** morpheme or an **inflectional** morpheme.

affricate:
: A **manner of articulation** associated with sounds, such as /tʃ/ beginning *church*, whose articulation is the combination of a **plosive** and a **fricative**.

agglutinative:
: Languages such as Turkish that have a very complex internal structure. Words contain many **affixes**.

allomorphs:
: Predictable variations in the pronunciation of **morphemes**. For instance, the plural morpheme in English is /s/ following nouns ending in an **unvoiced** sound (e.g. *cats*) and /z/ following a **voiced** sound (e.g. *dogs*).

allophones:
: Predictable variations in the pronunciation of **phonemes**. For instance, /p/ is **aspirated** at the beginning of a syllable, as in *pot*, but unaspirated elsewhere in a syllable, as in *spot* and *top*.

anaphoric reference:
: **Reference** back in a text. In the sentences ***The toy*** *was broken by* ***the child***. ***He*** *dropped* ***it*** *accidentally*, both *He* and *it* refer back to *the child* and *the toy*, respectively.

antonymy:
: A relation between words such as *happy* and *unhappy* that have opposite meanings.

apparent time:
: The idea that language variation is stratified by age: younger speakers will use newer forms more recently introduced into a language, while older speakers will use older, more established forms that they began using when they were younger.

appropriateness conditions:	Conditions on speech acts that must be adhered to in order for the speech act to be successful. For instance, for an apology (a type of **expressive**) to be successful, the person to whom the apology is directed must ultimately accept the apology.
approximants:	A **manner of articulation** associated with sounds such as /w/ beginning *which* in which the airstream in the oral cavity flows freely.
aspect:	Time viewed on a continuum. English has two aspects. The progressive is marked by the *-ing* **participle** form of a verb (e.g. *be+walking*) and indicates continuous time. The perfective is marked on verbs by the *-ed* participle (e.g. *have+walked*) and indicates a period of time from either the past to the present or the past to some other event in the past.
aspirated/aspiration:	A sound, such as /t/ in *tack*, whose articulation involves a puff of air leaving the mouth.
assertive/ representative:	A type of **speech act** in which the speaker's intention is to make a statement of fact, as in *I walked three miles yesterday* or *Bill Clinton is a former president of the United States.*
assimilation:	Sounds becoming closer in their pronunciation because of their proximity. For instance, when any vowel occurs before a **nasal** consonant, such as /n/ in *man*, the vowel will become nasalized too.
auxiliary verbs:	English has two types of auxiliary verbs that occur before the **lexical verb**: primary auxiliaries (*do*, *be*, and *have*) and modal auxiliaries (such as *can*, *could*, *will*, *would*). Modal auxiliaries always occur before primary auxiliaries, as in *could have helped*.
back channels:	Verbal affirmations, such as *yes* or *right*, that people utter as someone else is speaking. Back channels assure the speaker that the listener is paying attention and being supportive of what is being said.
base:	A **free morpheme** to which **affixes** can be potentially added. In the word *dislikeable*, the base is *like*.
base form of verb:	The form of the verb to which no verb **inflections** have been added and which can be preceded by the infinitive marker *to*: *to walk*, *to hit*, or *to hike*.
borrowings:	Words that have entered a language from another language. English has many words from Greek (e.g. *telephone*) and Latin (e.g. *gymnasium*). Compare with **cognate vocabulary**.
bound morpheme:	A morpheme that cannot stand alone but needs to be attached to a **free morpheme**. The word *premeasured* contains two bound morphemes: *pre-* and *-ed*.
broad reference:	**Reference** to lengthy stretches of text. For instance, if one person utters, *Would you like to have dinner and see a movie*, and another replies *Yes, I'd like that*, the pronoun *that* refers back not to a single noun phrase, but to the entire sequence *to have dinner and see a movie*.
broad transcription:	A phonetic transcription that captures only phonemic contrasts in words. Compare with **narrow transcription**.
case:	Inflections or individual words indicating the grammatical role that a word plays in a clause. In Modern English, pronouns are marked for three cases: nominative (or subjective; e.g. *I*, *he*, *she*, *they*), accusative (or objective; e.g. *me*, *him*, *her*, *them*), and genitive (or possessive; e.g. *my/mine*, *his*, *her/hers*, *their/theirs*). Nouns are marked for only one case, the genitive (e.g. *child's*, *person's*). Other languages have additional cases, such as dative or ablative.

cataphoric reference: **Reference** forwards in a text. In the sentence *Although they were late, the students were able to see the play*, the pronoun *they* refers forward to *the students*. Compare with **anaphoric reference**.

clause: A syntactic unit that can be analysed into **clause functions**. For instance, *The car is old* is a clause because it contains a **subject**, *The car*; a **predicator**, *is*; and a **subject complement**, *old*.

clause function: Functions such as subject, predicator, and object that indicate relationships between elements in a clause. The noun phrase *the car* is subject in *The car is broken* but object in *I drove the car*.

cleft sentence: A sentence containing the sequence *it + be +* NP + **relative clause**, as in *It was the door that I closed*. Cleft sentences are used to emphasize some element in the sentence, such as *the door* in the previous example.

closed class: **Word classes** (e.g. articles, prepositions, auxiliary verbs) to which new members are never added. Compare with **open class**.

closed register: A **register** with a very fixed structure that varies very little. For instance, buying lunch meat in a delicatessen (a service encounter) involves a series of exchanges between the seller and the customer that are highly predictable (e.g. "What can I get you?").

closed syllable: A syllable ending in a consonant, as in *run* and the two syllables in *mis. fit*.

cognate vocabulary: Vocabulary that languages share having a common origin in an ancestral language. For instance, words for *father* in languages such as Spanish (*padre*), French (*père*), and German (*Vater*) are all cognates because they originated in a common ancestral language that Spanish, French, German, and English share: Indo-European. Compare with **borrowings**.

coherence: A text that is meaningful and that makes "sense." The two sentences *It was sunny and warm today. Therefore, I wore a winter coat* do not form a coherent sequence because wearing a winter coat is not a logical consequence of the weather being sunny and warm. A more coherent alternative would be *Therefore, I wore a short-sleeve shirt*. Compare with **cohesion**.

cohesion: Achieved in a text containing explicit markers indicating relationships between various parts of the text. In the sentences *My brother is a doctor. He works at a nearby hospital* the pronoun *He* in the second sentence creates a cohesive link with the first sentence because it refers back to *My brother* in the first sentence.

co-hyponyms: A group of words, such as *chair*, *bed*, *dresser*, and *couch*, that are each **hyponyms** of a more general word, in this case *furniture*.

collocations: Words that commonly occur together. For instance, the sentence *I strongly agree* contains two words, *strongly* and *agree*, that commonly co-occur in this context. Other words could certainly follow *strongly*, but are much less likely to do so than *agree* and other words, such as *disagree* or *dislike*, expressing opinions.

commissive: A speech act that commits one to doing something: *I promise to send you my latest novel* or *I will make dinner at 5:00*.

comparative method: A method for determining what language families particular languages belong to. The method is heavily dependent on comparisons of **cognate vocabulary** as a means of determining whether languages should be grouped in the same or different language families.

competence: The unconscious knowledge of **rules** that all speakers of a language possess that allows them to produce grammatical constructions.

componential analysis: The process of describing the meaning of a word by developing semantic features to define the word. For instance, the word *woman* can be defined with the features +adult and +female.

compounding: Creating a new word by combining two **free morphemes** together: *paper + clip → paper clip*. The meaning of a compound is not simply the sum of the meanings of the two morphemes upon which the compound is based.

conjunction: A type of **cohesion** in which expressions such as *therefore* or *on the other hand* mark relationships between parts of **texts**.

constituency: A syntactic notion that certain groups of words form natural groupings. For instance, the clause *The class met in the lab* can be traditionally divided on one level into two main constituents: the **subject**, *The class*, and the **predicate**, *met in the lab*. However, the preposition *in* and the article *the* form no natural grouping: *in the*. Therefore, these two words are not a constituent.

content word: Nouns, verbs, adjectives, and some adverbs that, unlike **function words** such as *the* or *very*, are fully meaningful.

conversation analysis: The analysis of how conversations are organized and structured, focusing on such features of conversation as **turn-taking**.

conversational implicature: The additional meaning that results when one of Grice's maxims of the **cooperative principle** is violated. If speaker A asks *Do you like my new shirt and tie*, and Speaker B replies *I like the shirt*, Speaker A will infer that Speaker B did not like the tie because Speaker B failed to mention it in his reply. In other words, Speaker B's reply was not informative enough, leading to a conversational implicature.

cooperative principle: The philosopher H. Paul Grice's theory that communication among individuals is cooperative. He proposed various maxims specifying precisely how communication is cooperative. For instance, his maxim of quantity stipulates that what we say should be maximally informative: we should not say too much or too little. If we violate a maxim, a **conversational implicature** results.

coordinating conjunction: The conjunctions *and*, *or*, and *but* that link **phrases** and **clauses**.

copula: The verb *be* used as a **lexical verb** in a **clause**, as in *The building **is** very old*.

count and non-count nouns: Count nouns can be counted: *girl*, *girls*. Non-count nouns cannot be counted and therefore do not have a plural form: *furniture*, **furnitures*. Some words, such as *water*, can be both a count noun ("We'll have two waters at this table") and a non-count noun ("We're out of water").

creole: A **pidgin** that has become a first language. For instance, Jamaican Creole is a first language spoken by the descendants of slaves brought to Jamaica from Africa. It is a mixture of English and the African languages that the ancestors of the original slaves spoke.

declarations: A type of **speech act** that leads to a change in the state of affairs: *I now pronounce you husband and wife* or *I sentence you to 10 years in prison*.

declarative sentence: The most common sentence type in English. Declarative sentences contain, minimally, a **subject** and **predicator**, with the subject typically preceding the predicator, as in *The company went out of business* or *The teacher dismissed class early*.

definite reference:	**Reference** to a noun that is often preceded by the definite article *the*. For instance, if one speaker says to another *The child is happy*, *child* has definite reference because his or her identity is known to both the speaker and hearer.
deixis:	The ability of language to point. Deixis can be **referential**, **temporal**, or **spatial**.
demonstrative pronouns:	The pronouns *this*, *that*, *these*, and *those* when not used as **determinatives**, as in *That is correct* or *This can't be done*.
derivational affix (or morpheme):	A prefix or suffix added to a word that often changes the meaning of the word (e.g. *own* → **dis**own) or its part of speech (e.g. *rapid* [adjective] → *rapidly* [adverb]).
descriptivist:	An individual who is primarily interested in describing objectively the structure of language without interjecting his or her biases about language. Linguists are typically characterized as descriptivists. Compare with **prescriptivists**.
determinatives:	A word class containing words such as *a*, *the*, *this*, *some*, and *every* that occupies the first position in a **noun phrase**: *a tiny ant, that tall building, some people*.
diachronic:	Studying a language from a historical perspective. A diachronic study of English would investigate earlier periods of English, such as Old English or Middle English.
dialect:	A variable form of a **language**. Dialects of a language are considered mutually intelligible. Speakers of Northern American English can understand speakers of Southern American English. However, the notion of mutual intelligibility can be problematic, since the dialects of Chinese (e.g. Mandarin and Cantonese) are not mutually intelligible.
diphthong:	A type of vowel occurring within a single syllable whose quality changes during its articulation. Examples of diphthongs in English include the middle sounds in words such as *house* /haʊs/ and *fight* /faɪt/.
direct object:	A **clause function** realized by noun phrases and certain kinds of clauses. Direct objects generally occur after a **transitive verb**. They can often be made subject of a clause in the **passive voice**: *The car hit **the truck** → **The truck** was hit by the car*.
direct speech act:	A type of **speech act** in which the speaker's intentions are clearly spelled out. For instance, if a speaker says *Clean the house later*, her intention is to get someone to do something, since she uses an **imperative sentence**, a form closely linked with a **directive**. Compare with **indirect speech act**.
directive:	**A type of speech act** in which the intent of the speaker is to get someone to do something: *Please leave* or *Could you get me another cup of coffee?*
discourse marker:	An expression, such as *well* in *Well, I guess you're right*, that really has no clearly defined meaning but that is used primarily in conversation to organize what is said or in the case of *well* to express some hesitation as to whether the speaker really agrees that the individual being addressed is right.
disparates:	Individuals (such as a parent and child) between whom an unequal power relationship exists, with one person having more power than the other.
distal deictic:	A word such as *that* or *those* that locates something away from the speaker. Compare with **proximal deictic**.

ditransitive verb: A verb such as *give* or *loaned* that is capable of taking an **indirect object** and a **direct object**: *The movie gave* **me** *a headache*, *The bank loaned* **me** *some money*.

ellipsis: The omission of some element under identity with some other element. For instance, in the sentence *The burglars were jailed, and their accomplices* [ ] *released*, the second instance of *were* is elided under identity with *were* in the first clause.

embedding: A structure occurring within some other structure. In the phrase *the leader of the company*, *of the company* is a prepositional phrase occurring within a noun phrase. Therefore, the prepositional phrase is embedded in the noun phrase.

end-focus: The tendency in English to put the most important information, which is typically **new information**, towards the end of a clause.

endophora: **Reference** within a text. In the sentence *The woman was late for work because her car broke down*, the pronoun *her* refers back in the text to *The woman*.

equals: Individuals between whom no power imbalance exists.

exclamatory sentence: A sentence, such as *What a lovely day it is*! or *How lovely the weather is*!, that begins with *what* or *how* and that is often used for purposes of emphasis. In writing, exclamatory sentences will typically end with an exclamation mark.

exophora: **Reference** outside a text. In the sentence *I will call you later*, both *I* and *you* refer outside the text to the speaker and hearer, respectively.

explicit speech act: A **speech act** containing a **performative verb**, a verb that names the speech act. For instance, the verb *apologize* in *I apologize for being late* marks this speech act as an **expressive**.

expressive: A type of **speech act** in which the speaker expresses his or her attitude. An apology is a type of expressive.

external influences on language change: Social and cultural forces that cause a language to change. Typically, external influences result from **language contact**: English has so many words of French origin, for instance, because of the Norman Conquest and subsequent contact with speakers of French.

face: The self-image that an individual projects in encounters with others.

face-threatening act (FTA): In politeness theory, an utterance that undermines the **face** of the individual to whom the utterance is directed. For instance, if three people are speaking and one says to another, "You look horrible today," the embarrassment that this utterance causes results in a face-threatening act.

felicity conditions: See **appropriateness conditions**.

finite verb: A verb that is marked for tense (e.g. *walks*, *walked*). Compare with **non-finite verb**.

foreign language: An additional language that has no official status. English is a foreign language in Germany because while it is commonly taught in schools, it is not used in any official capacity (e.g. in government or courts of law).

form: All word classes, phrases, clauses, and sentences have a particular form. Most nouns, for instance, can be pluralized by adding -*s*. Verbs take particular verb endings, such as -*ed* or -*ing*. A **relative clause** is headed by a relative pronoun, such as *who* or *which*. Similar types of descriptions can be given of any linguistic construction.

formal definitions:	Definitions of linguistic constructions that are based on morphology or syntax. Adverbs, for instance, sometimes end with the suffix *-ly* (e.g. *willingly*, *desperately*) and can often be preceded by another adverb (e.g. *somewhat willingly*, *very desperately*).
free morpheme:	A morpheme such as *cat* or *house* that can stand alone. Compare with **bound morpheme**.
fricatives:	A **manner of articulation** associated with consonants such as /s/ in *sip* and /z/ in *zip* in which the airstream is constricted in the oral cavity, leading to a certain degree of turbulence.
function:	See **clause function**.
function word:	Words such as *the*, *very*, *and*, and *of* that have little meaning by themselves, but indicate grammatical relationships. For instance, when *the* is placed before a noun, as in *The office is closed*, *the* marks the noun as **definite** and **specific**.
fusional:	A language containing a number of **inflections** that mark such distinctions as **case**, **number**, and **gender**.
gender:	**Inflections** or word forms indicating whether a word is masculine, feminine, or neuter. Modern English has two genders marked only on pronouns: masculine (e.g. *he*) and feminine (e.g. *she*). Pronouns such as *I* and *they* are not considered neuter, but gender-neutral.
General American (GA):	A variety of spoken American English that does not associate a speaker with a particular region in the United States, social class, or ethnic group.
generic reference:	Reference to the class of something rather than to a specific member of the class. In the sentence *Dogs are good pets*, the noun *Dogs* refers to the class of dogs, not to a specific dog. Compare with **specific reference**.
genetic system of classification:	A system of language classification using the **comparative method**. Languages are grouped into families that have parent and sibling languages. English is a member of the Germanic language family, a family having many sibling languages, including not just English but German, Dutch, and Swedish.
given information:	See **old information**.
grammar:	The study of **rules** of language at various levels of structure, from the individual speech sound up to the level of the sentence. A grammar of English, for instance, would contain all the rules necessary for studying the structure of the English language.
grammatical gender:	A system of **gender** assignment in which gender is arbitrarily assigned. In German, the word for *girl*, *das Mädchen*, is assigned neuter gender rather than feminine gender, the actual gender of the noun. Compare with **natural gender**.
grammatical meaning:	Meaning associated with the particular words and constructions in a particular sentence or utterance. For instance, in the simple sentence *I wrote to my father*, all the words have meaning: *father* means 'male parent,' the pronoun *I* refers to the speaker, and the SVO word order means that the *I* of the sentence did the writing, not the father.
grammatical morpheme:	A morpheme expressing some kind of grammatical relationship. The article *the*, for instance, indicates that the noun it precedes is definite. The *-ed* on *parked* marks this verb as being in the past **tense**.

grammaticality: The notion that an element of a language conforms to linguistic rules for the language. The sentence *We like pie* is grammatical because it conforms to rules of English syntax; the sentence *We likes pies* is ungrammatical because it does not conform to rules of subject–verb agreement in English.

graphemes: Individual orthographic characters used to write a language. The word *happy* contains five graphemes: *h, a, p, p, y*.

head: The part of a phrase that gives the phrase its name and upon which all other members of the phrase are dependent. The construction *the full-time workers who worked for the company* is a noun phrase because all constructions in the phrase – *the*, *full*, *time*, and *who worked ...* – are dependent on the head noun *workers*.

heavy syllable: A syllable containing a **tense vowel** or ending in a consonant.

hierarchical structure: The manner in which linguistic constructions are grouped. The construction *British history teacher* is ambiguous because the constructions in this noun phrase can be grouped two ways. If *British* and *history* are grouped together, the phrase refers to 'a teacher of British history.' If *history* and *teacher* are grouped, the phrase refers to 'a teacher of history who is British.'

honorifics: In English, titles such as *Sir, Doctor, Mrs.,* and *Professor* that show respect towards the individual to whom they are addressed.

hyperanalysis (or hypercorrection): Creating a prescriptively incorrect form in an attempt to be correct. The use of *I* in *between you and I* is a hypercorrection because *I* is thought to be more formal than *me* when it is coordinated with *you*. This assumption has its origins in people being corrected as children to say *You and I are leaving early* rather than *Me and you are leaving early*. However, in *between you and I, me* is prescriptively correct because prepositions such as *between* take object forms, not subject forms.

hypernym: A word whose meaning would include the meaning of a more specific word. For instance, the word *flower* is a hypernym of *tulip* because the meaning of *tulip* is included in the meaning of the more general word *flower*. Compare with **hyponym**.

hyponym: A word whose meaning is included in the meaning of a more general word. Because a *magazine* is a type of *periodical, magazine* would be a hyponym of the more general word *periodical*. Compare with **hypernym**. Also see **co-hyponyms**.

illocutionary act: A **speech act** that conveys speaker intentions. The intent of *I'm sorry I'm late* is to issue an apology (a type of **expressive**) for something the speaker has done wrong.

imperative sentence: A sentence such as *Stop talking* in which the **base form** of the verb is used, and the **subject** is an implied *you*.

implicit speech act: A **speech act** such as *Shut the door* that does not contain a **performative verb**.

indirect object: A **clause function** that occurs before a **direct object**. For instance, in *The woman loaned the man some money, the man* is the indirect object preceding the direct object *some money*. One feature of many indirect objects is that they can be moved after the direct object and preceded by the prepositions *to* or *for: The woman loaned some money to the man*.

indirect speech act: A **speech act** in which the speaker's intentions are not directly conveyed, as in somebody saying *It's cold in here* as a request for the heat to be turned up.

inflections:	In English, a small group of suffixes, such as the plural marker on nouns (-*s*) or various verb endings, such as -*ing* and -*ed*. Inflections mark grammatical relationships, and unlike **derivational morphemes** do not change the meaning of a word or its part of speech.
internal influences on language change:	Changes that all languages undergo that are not influenced by **language contact**. For instance, all languages experience mergers: distinctions that are no longer maintained. For instance, in American English, the vowels /ɔ/ and /ɑ/ are being merged so that many speakers use the vowel /ɔ/ in words such as *cot* and *caught*, whereas others will use /ɑ/ in *cot* but /ɔ/ in *caught*.
interrogative sentence:	A sentence in which a question is asked. There are two types of questions in English: **wh-questions** and **yes/no questions**.
intimates:	Individuals (e.g. spouses, parents, children, close friends) who have a close relationship.
intransitive verb:	A verb that does not take an object. The verb *feel*, for instance, is intransitive because it can only take a **subject complement**, such as *good* in *I feel good*. Compare with **transitive verbs**.
irregular verbs:	Verbs that do not follow the regular pattern of adding inflections to show differences in **tense** or **aspect**. The base of some irregular verbs changes form: *go* (base form) → *went* (past form). Other irregular verbs do not change form at all in some instances: *bet* (base form) → *bet* (past or -*ed* participle form).
isolating:	Languages that tend to express meaning in separate morphemes. Chinese is a heavily isolating language lacking any **inflections**: words tend to be **monosyllabic**. Although English has inflections, it has lost most of its inflections over time and is moving towards being a more isolating language.
language:	English and French are considered languages because they are mutually unintelligible: a speaker of English cannot understand a speaker of French, and vice versa. However, the notion of mutual unintelligibility is somewhat problematic: Swedish and Norwegian are considered languages, yet they are mutually intelligible. Compare with **dialect**.
language contact:	Speakers of different languages coming into contact that leads to changes in one or both languages. English has so many words of French origin because of contact with speakers of French following the Norman Conquest.
language family:	A grouping of languages resulting from application of the **comparative method**. English, German, Greek, Latin, and Spanish have enough linguistic similarities that they are considered Indo-European languages. English and Spanish have some differences too, though, leading English to be further sub-classified as a Germanic language and Spanish an Italic language.
lax vowel:	A vowel such as /ɪ/ in *bit* and /æ/ in *back* that can only occur in a **closed syllable**.
lexical cohesion:	A type of **cohesion** involving, for instance, the repetition of a word or the use of a synonym, as in the two repetitions of *the group* in *The leader of **the group** resigned. He thought **the group** was not supporting him.*
lexical decomposition:	See **componential analysis**.

lexical semantics:	The study of the meaning of individual words in a language.
lexical verb (or full verb):	A verb that can occur alone or after one or more **auxiliaries** in the verb phrase. In the verb phrase *may have left*, *left* is the lexical verb. Because lexical verbs are an **open class**, there are many different lexical verbs in English.
light syllable:	A syllable ending in a **lax vowel**.
linear structure:	How linguistic constructions are ordered relative to one another. For instance, in English adjectives come before the head noun (e.g. *the healthy child*). In contrast, in languages such as French or Spanish, adjectives tend to come after the noun (e.g. French *l'enfant en bonne santé* 'the child healthy'). Compare with **hierarchical structure**.
linguistic context:	The larger body of words in which linguistic constructions occur, often affecting the use of particular constructions. For instance, **old information** is often placed at the beginning of a clause, as is the case with *He* in the second sentence: *The man committed a crime. He was arrested.*
linguistic reconstruction:	Examining existent languages that are known to be related so that an ancestral language having no surviving records can be conjectured. Indo-European, a **proto-language**, has been entirely reconstructed based on evidence from languages for which surviving records do exist (e.g. English, French, German, and other languages in the Indo-European language family).
linking verb:	A verb occurring in the **predicator** of clauses containing a **subject complement**: *I feel good, That tastes fine, She is my mother.*
literal speech act:	Any **speech act** in which the speaker means what he or she says, as in *I like warm weather*. Compare with **non-literal speech act**.
main clause:	A clause that typically contains a subject, predicator (with a **finite verb**), and no markers of subordination. In *Although we arrived on time, the movie had already started*, the second clause is a main clause that contains a subject (*the movie*), a finite verb (*had*), and no marker of subordination. Because the first clause contains a marker of subordination (*although*), it is not a main clause but a **subordinate clause**.
manner of articulation:	How the airstream flows through the mouth, whether it is completely blocked and then released, as is the case with **plosives**, or flows rather freely through the mouth, as in **approximants**.
marked tone unit:	A tone unit in which the **tonic syllable** does not occur on a syllable in the last content word of the **tone unit**. In a marked tone unit, the syllable containing the tonic syllable occurs in a word being emphasized.
markedness:	The extent to which a linguistic item is common or uncommon. In English, SVO word order is common; therefore, this order is unmarked. In contrast, OVS word order is quite uncommon, making this order (at least for English) marked.
minimal pairs:	Words that differ by only one sound in the same position (e.g. *fit* /fɪt/ and *kit* /kɪt/). Minimal pairs are useful for determining which sounds in a language are **phonemes**.
modal auxiliaries:	A closed class of **auxiliary verbs**, including *may, might, can, could, shall, should, will, would*. Modal auxiliaries always occur before **primary auxiliaries** in the verb phrase: *should have gone*.

monophthong: A vowel, such as /i/ in *keep* or /u/ in *boot*, whose pronunciation remains fairly constant in a syllable. Compare with **diphthong**.

monosyllabic: A word, such as *hit* or *ask*, that consists of a single syllable.

monotransitive verb: A verb such as *drive* or *write* that takes a single object: *I drive a Volvo, The author wrote a book*. Compare with **ditransitive verbs**.

morpheme: The smallest meaningful unit in language. See also **bound, free, derivational**, and **inflectional** morphemes.

narrow transcription: A phonetic transcription that captures all the phonetic features involved in the articulation of consonants and vowels. For instance, even though the words *kit* and *skip* contain the phoneme /k/, in *kit*, /k/ is aspirated and would be transcribed narrowly as /kʰ/; in *skip*, /k/ is unaspirated and would be transcribed as /k⁻/. Compare with **broad transcription**.

nasal: A **manner of articulation** associated with consonants, such as /m/ in *moon*, during whose articulation the air flows through the nasal cavity.

native language: A language a person speaks from birth. Compare with **foreign language** and **second language**.

natural gender: A system of gender in which words marked for gender (such as *he* and *she*) reflect the biological gender of the individuals to whom they refer. See also **grammatical gender**.

new information: Information introduced into a text that has not been introduced previously.

nominalization: A noun derived from a verb: *contain* → *containment*; *realize* → *realization*.

non-finite verb: An *-ed* or *-ing* participle that marks **aspect** on a verb and that typically occurs with an **auxiliary** (e.g. *have walked, is walking*), or the base form of a verb following the infinitive marker *to* (e.g. *to walk, to jump*).

non-literal speech act: A **speech act** in which the speaker does not literally mean what he or she says, as in *I'm so hungry I could eat a horse*.

non-rhotic: A variety of speech in which **post-vocalic /r/** is not pronounced. British English is non-rhotic, while most varieties of American English are **rhotic**.

notional definitions: Definitions that attempt to capture the meaning of grammatical constructions: a noun is a person, place, thing, or idea; a verb expresses action or a state of being. Compare with **formal definitions**.

noun phrase: A phrase having a noun as its **head**: *the ugly **duckling**, many small **animals** that were released into the wild*.

number: **Inflections** or word forms indicating whether a word is singular or plural. Pronouns in Modern English have different forms marking number (e.g. *he, she, it, they*); nouns add orthographic *-s* to indicate plurality (e.g. *toy, toys*), except for irregular forms (e.g. *child/children, goose/geese*). A present-tense verb will add *-s* (e.g. *walks*) if the subject with which it occurs is a singular third person pronoun or noun.

object: A **clause function** realized by a **noun phrase** or certain kinds of clauses. In Modern English, pronouns have **objective forms**, but nouns do not. Instead, other criteria are needed to determine whether a noun phrase or clause is functioning as object. In certain cases, objects can be made subject of sentences in the passive voice: *The man called **the woman** → **The woman** was called by the man*. See also **direct object** and **indirect object**.

objective form (accusative case): The form of pronouns (*me, him, her, them*) when they function as objects: *I called **him**, between you and **me**, We wrote to **them***. Nouns no longer have object forms in English.

old information: Information in a text that was introduced previously. For instance, in *The desk is cluttered. It needs to be cleaned up*, the pronoun *It* is old information referring back to *The desk* mentioned in the previous clause.

open class: **Word classes** (nouns, verbs, adjectives, and adverbs) to which new members are constantly being added. Compare with **closed classes**.

open registers: **Registers** that have a fairly flexible structure. For instance, spontaneous conversations often have a very loose overall structure and can consist of little more than conventions for **turn-taking**. Speakers can switch topics if they want to, and there is no set order for who speaks and when. Compare with **closed registers**.

open syllable: A syllable ending in a vowel, as in the words *he* /hi/ and *to* /tu/. Compare with **closed syllable**.

operator: An **auxiliary verb** or form of *do* used to form a question: *He **should** leave* → ***Should** he leave?* or *She jogs every day* → ***Does** she jog every day?*

overlapping speech: Instances of speech involving two or more speakers talking simultaneously.

participles: English has two participles: an *-ing* participle, added to a lexical verb and combined with a form of the **auxiliary verb** *be* (e.g. *is walking*), and an *-ed* participle, used with a form of the auxiliary verb *have* (e.g. *has walked*). See also **aspect**.

passive voice: The form of a verb in a clause such as *The survey was conducted by a research assistant* in which the doer of the action, the agent (*a research assistant*), is object of the preposition *by*, the person or thing affected by the agent (*The survey*) is the subject, and the verb has a specific form: *be* + *-ed* participle (*was conducted*).

perfective aspect: An **aspect** formed in English by combining a form of the auxiliary *have* with the *-ed* participle: *have walked*, *has taken*.

performance: How speakers actually put language to use. For Chomsky, performance includes hesitations, stammers, repetitions, and mistakes. See also **competence**.

performative verb: A verb such as *order* or *promise* that actually names the **speech act** that it represents. Performative verbs are always in the present tense and occur with a first person pronoun, as in *I order you to leave*.

phonemes: An individual speech segment that is distinctive and that contrasts with other speech segments. One way to determine phonemes in a language is to look at **minimal pairs**. The minimal pairs *hat* and *cat* indicate that the segments /h/ and /k/ are phonemes in English.

phonetic alphabet: An alphabet used to study speech sounds in which every symbol corresponds to one and only one sound.

phonotactic constraints: Constraints on permissible sequences of sounds in a given language. For instance, while English allows the sequence /pl/ at the start of a syllable (as in *play*), it does not allow the sequence */pf/.

phrase: A group of words centered around either a noun, verb, preposition, adjective, or adverb. For instance, *very quickly* is an adverb phrase centered on the adverb *quickly*; *in the morning* is a prepositional phrase centered on the preposition *in*. See also **head**.

pidgin: A second language spoken by groups of speakers who speak different languages. For instance, Chinook Jargon was a pidgin spoken in the nineteenth century in the northwestern part of the United States by the indigenous tribes there engaged in trade with Europeans.

place of articulation: How the articulators – the tongue, teeth, lips, and various parts of the mouth – are involved in the articulation of sounds. For instance, the sounds /p/ and /b/ are bilabial sounds because their articulation involves both lips.

plosives: A **manner of articulation** involving consonants such as /t/ and /g/ whose pronunciation involves complete blockage of the airstream in the oral cavity followed by release of the air.

politeness: Cultural conventions in a language governing polite levels of speech.

polysemous/polysemy: Words such as *bank* that have more than one meaning.

Post-vocalic /r/: The consonant /r/ following a vowel in the same syllable, as in the words *hurt* and *park*.

pragmatic meaning: Meaning that is determined by context. For instance, the sentence *It's cold in here* could mean not just that the temperature is low (its **grammatical meaning**) but that the person uttering this sentence requests that the heat be turned up.

pragmatics: The study of **principles** specifying how language is used. Conventions of politeness, for instance, are dictated by cultural norms having nothing to do with **grammaticality** but rather with conventions for how specific forms should be used. In English, a form such as *Could you please help me?* is a polite form for making a request.

pre-closing sequence: The part of a conversation in which one or both speakers signal that they want to end the conversation. For instance, if a person says *Well, it was great talking to you*, he or she is signaling that the conversation is coming to a close.

predicate: The part of the sentence following the **subject**. In the sentence *The librarian shelved books for an hour*, the predicate would be *shelved books for an hour*.

predicator: A **clause function**, such as *ran* in *The dog ran wild*, that consists of a verb phrase.

prescriptive rules: Rules such as "Never end a sentence with a preposition" that tell people how they should use language. Compare with grammatical **rules**.

prescriptivists: People such as teachers, editors, and writers of usage handbooks who tell people how they should use language. See also **prescriptive rules**.

primary auxiliaries: The verbs *do*, *be*, and *have* used as **auxiliary verbs**, as in *I **do** need a new car*, *The child **is** leaving*, and *The school **has** closed for the year*.

primary stress: The most prominent syllable in a word carries the primary stress. In the word *re.'mar.ka.ble*, the primary stress would be on the second syllable.

principles: Guidelines governing how language is used. For instance, whether the command *Hurry up* is polite or impolite depends very much upon the context in which it is uttered. If said to one's child, it probably would not be impolite. However, if said to someone the speaker does not know well, it would most likely be highly impolite. Compare with **rules**.

productivity: The extent to which a morphological process applies regularly and without exception. For instance, the verb **inflection** -*ing* can be applied to the base form of any verb. On the other hand, the **derivational** affix -*ly* can be added to some but not all adjectives to create an adverb.

progressive aspect: An **aspect** associated with -*ing* participles: *was **writing**, were **riding***.

proto-languages: Languages for which no surviving records exist and that have been created through the process of **linguistic reconstruction**.

prototype: The extent to which a linguistic construction is typical of the class to which it belongs. For instance, a poodle and skipper key are both types of dogs. However, because a poodle is a common kind of dog, it is prototypical. A skipper key, however, is a very uncommon type of dog. Hence, it is not prototypical.

proximal deictic: Words such as *this* or *these* which locate something close to the speaker. Compare with **distal deictic**.

pseudo-cleft: A construction having the structure *what + be*, as in **What** *I would like to do* **is** *have you over next week* or **What** *you needed* **was** *a long vacation*. Such constructions are used for purposes of emphasis and tend to occur primarily in informal speech.

recursion: A property of human language whereby linguistic constructions can be endlessly embedded in other constructions. See also **embedding**.

reference: The property of words to refer to other words within or outside a text. In the sentence *The manager spoke with her employees*, the pronoun *her* refers back in the text to *The manager*. The words *manager* and *employees* refer to individuals outside the text in the external world.

referent: What a word refers to. In *Because the car wouldn't run, I took it to be repaired*, the pronoun *it* has as its referent *the car*. See also **reference**.

referential deixis: A type of **deixis** in which expressions refer to something or someone. For instance, in *The computer is broken*, the noun phrase *The computer* refers to a specific computer in the external world.

register: A type of speech or writing that is characterized by a specific hierarchical structure and a set of linguistic constructions. For instance, a lab report would open with an abstract and contain sections discussing the methodology used to conduct the experiment being discussed and the results of the experiment. Such a report would not contain the pronouns *I* or *you*, but would contain **nominalizations** and **passives**.

regular verbs: Verbs that do not change form when verb **inflections** are added to the **base**: *loans, is loaning, loaned, have loaned*. Compare with **irregular verbs**.

relative clause: A clause **embedded** in a **noun phrase** that begins with a relative pronoun such as *who* or *which*: *the client* **who contacted us**, *the book* **which was approved for publication**.

rheme: The closing part of a clause. In the clause *The author promoted her book*, *promoted her book* would be the rheme; *The author* would the **theme**.

rhotic: A variety of speech in which **post-vocalic /r/** is pronounced. Most varieties of American English are rhotic, while British English in **non-rhotic**.

rhotic vowel: See **post-vocalic /r/**.

RP (Received Pronunciation):   A highly prestigious spoken variety of British English.

rules: Statements that provide formal descriptions of how constructions are formed. For instance, English has a rule of subject–verb agreement specifying that if a third person subject is singular and the verb is in the present tense, the verb needs an *-s* ending: *She likes football*. Rules apply to constructions at all levels of structure, from individual speech sounds up to the level of the sentence.

schwa: The sound /ə/ as articulated in the first syllable of *around*.

second language: A language having an official status (i.e. it is used in education, government, and business) that is spoken as a non-native language in a country whose residents speak one or more native languages. English is a second language in many former British colonies (e.g. India, Singapore, and Hong Kong).

secondary stress: A degree of stress on a syllable in a word that is less prominent than the syllable in the word receiving **primary stress**. Secondary stress is typically found on the second word in a compound word: ˈmailˌman.

segments: Individual phonemes. Compare with **suprasegmentals**.

semantics: The study of meaning in language.

sentence: A grammatically well formed unit that has, minimally, a **predicator** and usually a **subject**. There are four types of sentences in English: **declarative**, **interrogative**, **imperative**, and **exclamatory**.

sentence stress: The assignment of stress across **phrases** and **clauses**. In a **tone unit**, usually one syllable of one word (the **tonic syllable**) will receive the greatest stress.

signs: In semiotic theory, a unit consisting of the signifier (form) and the signified (the meaning associated with the form). In speech, the signifier of a word such as *desk* is the series of phonemes /dɛsk/ associated with this word; the signified would be the meaning (a table on which work can be conducted) that these phonemes evoke.

slang: Highly informal language usually associated with younger speakers of a language. It tends to have a short lifespan and falls out of use quickly as the speakers who use it become older. For instance, words such as *groovy* and *far out*, which are associated with the 1960s, are not heard much anymore, and date the people who speak them.

social context: The larger cultural context in which language takes place. A dinner conversation involves not simply linguistic constructions formed by particular linguistic **rules**. Instead, the constructions that are used and how they are formed are determined by the individuals speaking: their relationships with one another; the past experiences they have had speaking with one another; and additional factors, such as their age, gender, social class, and level of education.

social distance: How close a social relationship individuals have. **Intimates** will have very little social distance between them, whereas a teacher and students will have a greater social distance separating them.

social marker: A usage of language (e.g. *ain't*) that associates an individual with a specific social class.

spatial deixis: A type of **deixis** that locates something spatially relative to the speaker in space, as *there* does in the sentence *The book is over there*.

speaker turn: In a conversation, a speaker's individual time speaking. All dialogic speech is divided into speaker turns: one person speaks, then another, then another, and so forth. There are conventions for how speakers take turns speaking. For instance, one speaker can ask another speaker a question, selecting this speaker to be the next speaker.

speaker variables: Variables, such as age, gender, level of education, ethnicity, and social class, that affect how people speak.

specific reference: Reference to an individual entity rather than to the class to which that entity belongs. In the sentence *Please pass me the salt*, the noun phrase *the salt* has specific reference because it refers to a particular instance of salt. Compare with **generic reference**.

speech acts: Statements of speaker intentions. For instance, the sentence *Leave* is a **directive** whose purpose is to get someome to depart. See also **commissive**, **representative/assertive**, **expressive**, and **declaration**.

stance adverb: An adverb such as *frankly* or *truthfully* that expresses the point of view of the speaker or writer.

style shifting: Changing the way one speaks depending on the context. For instance, people speak differently to their parents than to their friends.

subject: A **cause function** realized by a **noun phrase** or clause. First and third person pronouns have **subjective forms**, but nouns do not. Subjects typically occur towards the start of a clause, except in yes/no questions, where they switch positions with the **operator**: *You are leaving* → *Are you leaving?*

subject complement: A **clause function** realized by a **noun phrase** or adjective phrase following a **linking verb** that names or describes the **subject**, as *warm* does in the sentence *The room is warm.*

subjective form (nominative case): In English, a pronoun such as *I*, *he*, or *she* that can occur only as subject of a clause: ***I** walked to work yesterday*, ***She** enjoys movies*, ***He** travels frequently*, ***They** walk daily.*

subordinate: An individual lower on the power hierarchy. Compare with **equals** and **superordinates**.

subordinate clause: A clause that cannot stand alone but must occur with a **main clause**. Often dependent clauses will be headed with a subordinating conjunction such as *when* or *because*.

subordinating conjunction: A word such as *if*, *when*, or *because* that occurs at the beginning of a **subordinate clause**.

substitution: A type of **cohesion** in which one word substitutes for another. In *I'm going to have an apple. You should have one too*, the word *one* substitutes for *an apple* in the prior clause.

superordinate: An individual higher on the power hierarchy. Compare with **equals** and **subordinates**.

suprasegmentals: Sounds, such as pitch and **sentence stress**, occurring in units larger than the individual phoneme.

synchronic: Studying a language in its current form. A synchronic study of English would focus on Contemporary English: English as it is spoken and written in the early twenty-first century.

synonymy: A relationship between words that are equivalent in meaning.

temporal deixis: A type of **deixis** that locates something temporally relative to the speaker. For instance, in the sentence *We should leave tomorrow*, the adverb *tomorrow* locates the act of leaving in the future relative to the time this sentence was uttered.

tense vowel: Vowels, such as /i/ and /u/, that can occur in either an open or closed syllable. Compare with **lax vowel**.

tense: A point in time marked by an inflection on the verb. In English, a time in the past is indicated by a past tense inflection (e.g. *hat**ed***, *look**ed***). In English, present time is only marked on verbs occurring with singular subjects: *He dislike**s** vegetables*, *The chef bake**s** bread daily.*

text: A body of language that is usually lengthier than a sentence. A text has **unity of structure** and **unity of texture**.

theme: The first part of a clause, which often contains old information. In *The hurricane had devastating effects. It flooded the entire city*, both *The hurricane* and *It* are the theme in the clauses in which they occur. *It* is additionally old information. Compare with **rheme**.

to-infinitive clause: A clause such as *to replace the battery* that begins with the infinitive marker *to* followed by the **base form of the verb**. See also **non-finite verb**.

tone unit: A sequence of words containing one syllable whose pitch is more prominent than the other syllables in the tone unit. For instance, in the tone unit *the snow is BEAUtiful*, the most prominent syllable, or **tonic syllable**, would be the first syllable of *beautiful*.

tonic syllable: The syllable in a **tone unit** receiving the greatest stress. The tonic syllable is usually found on a syllable in the last **content word** of the tone unit.

topicalization: A syntactic process whereby some element in a clause, often an **object**, is fronted. In the clause *Food I like*, *Food* is topicalized because it is moved out of its normal position following the verb.

traditional grammar: A grammar based on terminology found in the classical grammars of Greek and Latin. Early English grammars of the eighteenth century borrowed heavily from early classical grammars because the study of Greek and Latin was popular during this period.

transition relevance place (or TRP): The place in a **speaker turn** (e.g. a pause or the end of a grammatical unit) where a new speaker could begin speaking.

transitive verb: A verb requiring an **object**: *The child **spilled** his milk*, *The workers **remodeled** the kitchen*. Compare with **intransitive verb**.

turns: See **speaker turn**.

turn-taking: Conventions that allow for one speaker to give up the floor and for another speaker to begin speaking. For instance, the current speaker could ask another speaker a question, requiring the other speaker to take the floor. Or a speaker not speaking could overlap his or her speech with the current speaker and make an attempt to take the floor.

typological system of classification: A system of classification of languages according to linguistic features that they have in common. In terms of word order, English and Spanish are typologically similar because both languages have SVO as the most common word order.

unity of structure: The hierarchical structure of a text: its beginning, middle, and end. For instance, a conversation can optionally begin with a greeting, followed by a series of **speaker turns** allowing speakers to talk about various topics, and then end with some kind of salutation. Other texts (e.g. an academic paper) will have a more clearly defined hierarchical structure.

unity of texture: The various devices within a text (e.g. markers of **cohesion**, the placement of **new information** at the beginning of a clause and **old information** at the end) that link sections of the text, tying everything together.

universal grammar: Noam Chomsky's notion that there are features of **grammar** common to all languages. For instance, all languages have first and second person pronouns.

unmarked tone unit: A **tone unit** in which the **tonic syllable** falls on one syllable of the last **content word** in the tone unit.

unvoiced: A sound is unvoiced if during its articulation the vocal cords do not vibrate. Sounds such as /p/, /f/, and /s/ are unvoiced.

utterance: A linguistic construction that may not be grammatically well-formed but that nevertheless has meaning and is communicative. For instance, if one person utters *I just won the lottery* and a second person replies *Wow*, the reply has meaning, even though it is not a grammatically formed sentence with a **subject** and **predicator**.

verb phrase: A **phrase** consisting of an obligatory **lexical verb** and optional **auxiliary verbs**.

voiced: A sound is voiced if during its articulation the vocal cords vibrate. Sounds such as /d/, /v/, and /z/ are voiced.

voicing assimilation: A process whereby a **voiced** or **unvoiced** sound will cause a nearby sound to also be, respectively, voiced or unvoiced. In English, if a noun ends in an unvoiced sound (e.g. /t/ in *hat* /hæt/), when a plural marker is added, the marker is also unvoiced (e.g. /s/ at end of /hæts/).

vowel reduction: A process whereby a vowel such as /a/ in a word such as *on* is reduced to a schwa /ə/ when it is unstressed.

wh-question: A question, such as *Who is leaving?* or *Where did they go?*, that is typically formed with a word beginning with *wh-* (*how* is an exception, as in *How are you doing?*).

word classes: The particular designations given to individual worlds. The major word classes are noun, verb, adverb, adjective, and preposition.

word formation processes: Processes such as **affixation** and **compounding** that lead to the creation of new words.

yes/no questions: A type of **interrogative sentence** formed by inverting the **operator** and **subject**. For instance, the **declarative sentence** *We are late* becomes a yes/no question by inverting the operator *are* and subject *We*: *Are we late?*

Answers to self-study activities

1 The study of language

1. 1 b, 2 c, 3 d, 4 a
2. All languages have rules that specify how constructions are formed, and principles that govern how these constructions are actually used. Rules are tied to competence: the abstract underlying knowledge of a language that any speaker will possess. Principles are tied to performance: how we use the structures that rules create. Thus, if you are studying rules of syntax, you are studying linguistic competence: our knowledge of how we put words together to form phrases and clauses, not our knowledge of how we use these structures once they've been formed.
3. In general, linguists prefer descriptive rather than prescriptive approaches to language study. A descriptivist simply describes language structure, laying out the facts about Language X or Language Y in objective and scientific terms. A prescriptivist, on the other hand, is more interested in telling people how to use language, often times in very subjective and emotional language (e.g. double negatives are illogical and reflect sloppy thinking).
4. A sentence is grammatical if it is rule-governed. Although *He don't know nothin'* is non-standard, it is rule-governed and thus grammatical. This sentence illustrates a differing rule for subject–verb agreement than is found in Standard English: *don't*, which is used in Standard English for plural subjects, is used by some speakers with singular subjects such as *he*. The sentence also contains a double negative, a systematic and rule-governed process whereby the negative is copied on the indefinite pronoun (*anything* becomes *nothing*). But while this sentence is grammatical, for many people it is unacceptable because of its association with non-standard English. Acceptability involves people's personal judgments of linguistic forms and can be highly subjective.
5. English or Spanish are considered languages because we can isolate rules for forming, for instance, grammatical sentences in Spanish. In other words, all languages have a grammar. Even though American Sign Language (ASL) is not spoken but gestured, there are rules for how the gestures are structured. As a result, because ASL has a grammar, it would be considered a language. If ASL were simply gestures modeled on English, it would not have the status of a language.
6. In a system of grammatical gender, gender is somewhat arbitrarily assigned. For instance, in German, *das Mädchen* ('girl') is assigned neuter gender, even though a girl is biologically feminine. In a system of natural gender, there is a more direct association between biological gender and the assignment of gender. This is why in Modern English, the pronouns *he* and *she* always refer to males and females, respectively. There are cases of uses of generic *he*, as in *An employee must make sure he arrives on time for work*, in which *he* refers to both males and females. But this usage is dying out in English, and actually sounds a bit archaic to some.

7. The two initial quotes are statements of facts: it is true that most nations contain bilingual (even multilingual) populations, and that multilingualism alone does not necessarily lead to "civil discord." However, the statement becomes much more prescriptive when it states that multilingual speakers should be allowed to speak whatever language they want to "publicly or privately" and "to maintain their native language... and pass it on to their children." These statements illustrate verbal hygiene because they reveal a certain attitude towards language, specifically that all languages should be valued and their speakers given certain rights.

2 The development of English

1. 1 c, 2 a, 3 a, 4 b, 5 c, 6 a, 7 a, 8 c
2. There are obviously many possible answers to this question. For instance, if you clicked the link to Belize, you would have found that English has the status of a "national or official language." Because English is an official language in Belize, by definition, it is a second (not a foreign) language. Belize has a total population of approximately 273,000 people. Although the precise number of speakers of English is not given, approximately 55,000 are listed as speaking Belize Kriol English. Six languages other than English or Belize Kriol English are listed as being spoken, most commonly Spanish (approximately 80,000 speakers). 70 percent of the population is literate, and residents of Belize attend on average slightly fewer than eight years of school.
3. Answers will vary depending upon the place name chosen, but here is information on Milwaukee, Wisconsin, USA. *The Concise Dictionary of World Place Names* notes two possible origins (p. 340) for the name *Milwaukee*, both based on words from two unspecified Native American languages: *Mahn-a-waukee*, meaning 'gathering place by the river', and *Milioke*, meaning 'good earth' or 'good country.' The *Wikipedia* entry for *Milwaukee* (http://en.wikipedia.org/wiki/Milwaukee, accessed June 17, 2008) provides more specific information, citing three different possible origins from three different Native American languages. The entry notes one of the meanings in the Oxford entry 'Gathering place [by the water]' but claims that this meaning derives from the Ojibwe word *ominowakiing*. This contradictory information reveals that etymology is in many cases a guessing game. At the same time, the information notes the importance the Milwaukee River played in the settlement of Milwaukee and also that the area was originally populated by Native American tribes in Wisconsin.
4. Cognate vocabulary has proven instrumental in grouping languages into language families: the so-called comparative (or genetic) method of language classification. We know that German and English are part of the Germanic language family because words for *father*, for instance, in these languages begin with the sound /f/. In languages outside the Germanic language family, words for *father* begin with /p/ (e.g. Latin *pater*). This is one piece of evidence that Germanic is a separate family but part of a larger language family: Indo-European.
5. Typological classifications of languages group individual languages according to the linguistic structures that they have in common. English and Chinese are typologically similar because, for instance, both are isolating languages (i.e. languages with words that are discrete morphemes). Genetic classifications of languages group individual languages into language "families" using, for instance, cognate words to determine how closely related languages are. Genetically, English and Chinese are very distantly related: English is an Indo-European language, Chinese a Sino-Tibetan language.
6. English is a fusional language because it marks number and one case (the genitive or possessive) on nouns, as in *birds, the boy's book*. But this system is far simpler than those found in

languages such as German or Latin, which have a complex system of inflections marking case, number, and gender. English is therefore more of an isolating language because meaning is expressed in separate words. For instance, some instances of possession can now be expressed by the preposition *of*, as in *a friend of John*.

7. External: Borrowings into a language result from contact with speakers of other languages. English has so many words of French and Latin origin because earlier in its history there was contact between speakers of these languages and speakers of English.

8. No: A language undergoes language death when it no longer has any living speakers. As discussed in the chapter, many of the indigenous languages in the Americas have either died or are in the process of dying because speakers of these languages have over time started to speak other languages (e.g. English or Spanish). Although John Simon may think that English is dying, he is really overreacting. Like many reactionary prescriptivists, he thinks that Modern English is so riddled with grammatical errors that it is in the process of dying. But he couldn't be more wrong: English is spoken by more speakers than any language in the history of civilization.

3 The social context of English

1. 1 a, 2 c, 3 d, 4 b, 5 e
2. A discussion of the grammatical meaning of *I wouldn't mind another glass of wine* would focus on the meaning of the words and structures in this statement. For instance, *I* refers to the speaker; *another glass of wine* works together as a unit of meaning specifying an additional serving of a specific type of alcoholic beverage placed in a drinking vessel typically used to hold this beverage; the expression *wouldn't mind* conveys the meaning that the speaker has no objections to drinking more wine. To determine the pragmatic meaning of the statement, it is necessary to place it in some social context, such as a small get-together among friends. In this context, one could imagine the host asking the speaker whether he or she wanted another glass of wine, and the speaker replying with an indirect speech act for reasons of politeness. If the speaker made the statement without any prompting, it would be interpreted as somewhat impolite because he or she is being a bit too insistent.
3. Grammatically well-formed sentences:
   (i)   *I really like chocolate ice cream*
   (ii) *My second favorite flavor is vanilla*
   (iii) *I don't care for vanilla*
   (iv) *I think it has great taste*
   Utterances (i.e. incomplete sentences that are meaningful but lack a subject and predicator):
   (i)   *Me too*
   (ii) *Too tasteless, in my opinion*
   (iii) *Really*
4. (1) Direct: An imperative sentence that is a directive: the speaker directly tells someone to do something.
   (2) Indirect: This is a "hint": a very indirect suggestion that the addressee shut the door to prevent further mosquitoes from getting into the house.
   (3) Direct: A declarative sentence that is a commissive: the speaker is directly committing himself to doing something in the future.
   (4) Indirect: An interrogative sentence that is a directive: the guest is not interested in knowing whether someone at the table is physically able to give her the butter. She's using a conventionalized yes/no question to politely request that someone give her the butter.

5. Hazel has violated the maxim of relation: her sudden discussion of the weather has nothing to do with Fred's gossip about Christine. But Hazel's violation of this maxim is purposeful, and Fred's likely interpretation of her utterance (i.e. the conversational implicature of her violation) is that Hazel is uncomfortable with his gossiping about Christine, or that she is trying to warn him that they should shift topics so that Christine doesn't hear their gossip.

6. The conventions of formal written English first of all stipulate that writers adhere to the maxim of quantity: they must fully develop the topics they introduce, while at the same time not saying too much so they are not perceived as "padding" their papers. Second, writers must follow the maxim of relation: everything they write must be related and relevant to the topic at hand; digression, or going off topic, is not tolerated. Third, writers must observe the maxim of quality: everything they write must be truthful. There are cases where scientists have gotten into serious trouble for fabricating the results of their experiments. Finally, writers must adhere to the maxim of manner: clarity of expression is of utmost importance in formal written English.

7. In the first turn, the library patron is adhering linguistically to the generosity maxim. In his statements, he expresses the efforts he has exerted to return the missing newspapers to the library. However, instead of simply thanking him, the library worker engages in a serious violation of the tact maxim: he does not "maximize benefit" to the library patron, but very indirectly issues a directive in an attempt to get the patron to do the worker's job for him. In the final turn, the library patron arguably violates the tact maxim too, but given the library worker's violation of this maxim, the patron's anger is justified.

8. (a) The father and child are disparates: the father is higher on the power hierarchy than the child.

   (b) Because of this power imbalance, the father has greater license to utter a statement that is very direct and in this context not a violation of the tact maxim. However, some might disagree and argue that parents need to be just as polite with their children as they are with adults.

9. Slang is a type of "in-group" language. For this reason, it is especially prominent among younger speakers, since they are at an age when identification with their peers is very important. And slang marks them as a "member" of their peer group. This is why as people age, the slang that they used as adolescents becomes archaic or obsolescent.

4 The structure of English texts

1. Although email exists in written form, it exhibits many characteristics of spoken language. It contains frequent instances of first and second person pronouns, which are absent from many kinds of writing. Like speech, it is often not heavily edited. It attempts to express emotive features of speech through the use of abbreviations, such as *lol* ('laughing out loud'), and emoticons that express happiness or sadness. Some email writers even dispense with capitalization and do not capitalize proper nouns and even the first person pronoun *I*.

2. Even though an oral contract is legally binding, a written contract is better because it provides a permanent record of what was agreed on, and can be consulted if the parties to the contract have any disputes. In other cases, speech may be preferred over writing if some kind of direct contact is desired between communicants. This is why spontaneous dialogues are the most common type of human communication that exists: humans need personal contact to be able to exploit the full potential of human communication, which includes not just what is said but intonation and gestures as well.

3. Within the register of medical discourse, a conversation between patient and doctor would be a closed rather than an open register: the organization and structure of such a conversation would be fixed and conventionalized. For instance, as a doctor enters the examination room, she would greet her patient, asking how he is feeling. Then, she would look over the patient's file to see if she needed to follow up on any medical issues discussed during previous visits. During the medical examination itself, the doctor would issue a set of directives asking the patient to do specific things to facilitate the examination: "Breathe in and out," "Roll up your sleeve so I can take your blood pressure," and so forth. The patient would also be given the opportunity to ask questions if he had any.

4. Instances of old information:
   (1) *These* and *They* (refer back to *storms* in first sentence)
   (2) *storms* in second sentence (repeats first mention of *storms* in first sentence)

5. Because passive sentences move constituents around, they are very useful for placing old information at the start of a clause, and new information at the end. In the two sentences below, the passive (b) would be preferred by some over the active (a) because in (b), the old information is placed at the start of the clause, whereas in (a), new information appears in this position.

   Yesterday, John Smith was appointed Executive Director of Accounts.
   (a) CEO Juliet Jones promoted him during the company's annual meeting.
   (b) He was promoted by CEO Juliet Jones during the company's annual meeting.

6. Types of cohesion:
   (1) Lexical cohesion: *natural plows*, *the wrigglers* (synonyms for *earthworms*); *forest* (in *forest floor*, which repeats earlier mention in *forest ecosystem*)
   (2) Reference: *they* (both instances refer back to *earthworms*)
   (3) Conjunction: *But*

5 English syntax

1. The construction *the company* is a constituent, a noun phrase, because a pronoun (*it*) can replace the constituent. Substitution with a pronoun is one test for constituency. However, the construction *president of* permits no such substitution, even though it contains a noun (*president*). Therefore, this unit is not a constituent: it does not form a natural grouping.

2. Definitions containing wording such as "something expresses 'action' or 'a state of being'" are notional: they attempt to define a category by the particular meanings that constructions in the category express. A formal definition of a verb would focus on, for instance, the morphological or syntactic features that define verbs. For instance, verbs take inflections, such as the various suffixes on *likes*, *liking*, and *liked*.

3. A formal definition of the noun *television* would note that it contains a suffix, *-ion*, found only on nouns, and that it could optionally be preceded by an article and adjective: *the new television*.

4. Form deals with the structure of a particular construction. The construction *The weather* is a noun phrase because it contains a noun, *weather*, as head, and everything else in the noun phrase, the article *the*, is dependent on the head. However, noun phrases can have many functions in a sentence. In this case, *The weather* is functioning as subject because it occurs before the predicator, *has been*, and if the sentence were converted into a yes/no question, the operator, *has*, would change places with the subject: *Has the weather been awful lately?* The function that a form has is very dependent on its relationship with other forms in a clause.

5. In *I have never taken such a good course*, the word order is SVO, the most common and frequent word order in English and therefore an unmarked word order. In contrast, the sentence *Never*

have I taken such a good course contains inversion of the negative adverb *never* and the auxiliary *have*. Because this is a less common word order in English, it is a marked order. The effect of the inversion in this context is to emphasize that the speaker found the course especially good.

6. (a) *glass* (head of noun phrase)
   (b) *rapidly* (adverb phrase)
   (c) *happy* (adjective phrase)
   (d) *wished* (verb phrase)
   (e) *in* (prepositional phrase)
   (f) *farmers* (noun phrase)

7. 1 b, 2 c, 3 d, 4 e, 5 a, 6 c, 7 d, 8 a, 9 e, 10 a

8. The placement of adjectives in English and Spanish is reflective of the linear nature of syntax: how constituents are ordered.

9. (a) one main clause
   (b) one subordinate clause (*Although it ... last night*) and one main clause (*we did not ... any flooding*)
   (c) one main clause (the entire sentence) and one subordinate clause (*who were in the accident*) embedded in the noun phrase *all the individuals*
   (d) one subordinate clause (*To achieve success*) and one main clause (*people must work hard*)
   (e) one main clause (the entire sentence) and one subordinate clause (*Working extra hours*) that functions as subject
   (f) one main clause (*We left the party early*) and one subordinate clause (*because we were tired*)

6 English words: Structure and meaning

1. (i)   Inflectional morphemes can only be suffixes; derivational morphemes can be either prefixes or suffixes.
   (ii) Inflectional morphemes never change the word class or meaning of a word; derivational morphemes often do change the meaning or word class of a word.

2. *non-* (bound, derivational), *conform* (free), *-ist* (bound, derivational)
   de- (bound, derivational), *context* (free), *-ual* (bound, derivational), *-ize* (bound, derivational), *-ed* (bound, inflectional)
   repeat (free), *-ing* (bound, inflectional)
   up (free), *on* (free)
   scare (free), *-y* (bound, derivational, here spelled as *-i*), *-est* (bound, inflectional)
   un- (bound, derivational), *test* (free), *-ed* (bound, inflectional)
   care (free), *-less* (bound, derivational), *-ly* (bound, derivational)

3. The word *fight* could be a noun or a verb. Both of these word classes are open because they readily admit new members. The form class of auxiliary verbs, however, is closed because English is unlikely to add a new verb to the class of auxiliaries.

4. Lexical decomposition involves defining words in terms of semantic features. With abstract words such as *love* and *hatred*, lexical decomposition does not work very well because it is difficult to determine exactly which features these words should have. It is much easier to find features for concrete words such as *woman*: +human +female +adult.

5. The nouns *bull* and *man* share the features +animate and +male. However, they are different kinds of animate organisms: a bull would have the feature +bovine, a man the feature +human.

6. It is difficult to find words that are exactly equivalent in meaning, and that can be substituted one for the other in any context without some change in meaning. For instance, the words *hate* and *abhor* both express extreme dislike of something or someone. However, while *I hate*

spinach and *I abhor spinach* both express this dislike, *abhor* seems somewhat odd in this con-text: one abhors violence, but not food.

7. 1 b, 2 c, 3 a, 4 b, 5 c, 6 a
8. 1 b, 2 a, 3 c, 4 e, 5 g, 6 h, 7 l, 8 f, 9 k, 10 j, 11 i, 12 m, 13 d

7 The sounds of English

1. In a phonetic alphabet, each symbol equals one and only one sound. If the English alphabet became purely phonetic, all speakers of English would simply spell words as they pronounced them, and the current situation – one grapheme often corresponding to many different pronunciations – would cease to exist. However, spelling variation would ultimately increase because pronunciation varies considerably among speakers of English. Thus, a speaker of American English would spell *bath* differently than a speaker of British English. Thus, we are ultimately better off with the current system, which standardizes (though with some exceptions) how all writers of English should spell words.

2. The words *fast* and *feast* are minimal pairs: words that differ by one phoneme in the same position. Because the substitution of /æ/ for /i/ in this context produces a different word, we know that these sounds contrast and are therefore phonemes.

3. a 3, b 3, c 6, d 7, e 3 (though the vowel is a diphthong), f 7, g 6, h 9, i 10, j 7

4. 1 c, 2 a, 3 b, 4 a, 5 c, 6 b

5. (a)   the initial unvoiced plosive is aspirated, and the vowel is lengthened before the final voiced consonant
   (b)   the initial unvoiced plosive is aspirated, and the vowel is lengthened before the final voiced consonant
   (c)   neither process applies in this word
   (d)   the vowel is lengthened before the final voiced consonant
   (e)   the vowel is lengthened before the second to last consonant, which is voiced
   (f)   the initial plosive is aspirated
   (g)   the initial unvoiced plosive is aspirated, and the vowel is lengthened before the final voiced consonant

6. (a)   re.ci.'ta. tion
   (b)   pre.'dom.i.nate
   (c)   cig.a.'rette
   (d)   'con.test (noun) or con.'test (verb)
   (e)   'bur.eau
   (f)   con.'tent.ment
   (g)   dis.'like
   (h)   un.con.'vin.cing

7. tonic syllables in unmarked tone units:
   (a)   The turtle walked SLOWly‖ into the ROOM‖
   (b)   Our teacher HELPED us‖ with our HOMEwork‖
   (c)   With little or no reSIStance‖ the child put his SHIRT on‖
   If (a) were prefaced by a question such as *Who walked slowly into the room?* the tonic syllable would shift to *turtle*:

   The TURtle walked slowly‖ into the ROOM‖

   If somebody commented *I heard the turtle ran into the room,* the tonic syllable would shift yet again:

   The turtle WALKED slowly‖ into the ROOM‖

References

Aarts, B. (1992). *Small Clauses in English: The Nonverbal Types*. Berlin and New York: Mouton de Gruyter.

Aarts, B. and L. Haegeman (2006). English word classes and phrases. In B. Aarts and A. McMahon (eds.), *The Handbook of English Linguistics* (pp. 117–45). Malden, MA: Blackwell Publishers.

Aitchison, J. (1991). *Language Change: Progress or Decay?* 2nd edn. New York: Cambridge University Press.

Altenberg, B. (1990). Predicting text segmentation into tone units. In J. Svartvik (ed.), *The London-Lund Corpus of Spoken English: Description and Research* (pp. 275–86). Lund: Lund University Press.

Andersen, G. (2001). *Pragmatic Markers and Sociolinguistic Variation*. Amsterdam: John Benjamins.

Ashby, M. and J. Maidment (2005). *Introducing Phonetic Science*. Cambridge: Cambridge University Press.

Austin, J. L. (1962). *How to do Things with Words*. Oxford: Clarendon.

Bailyn, J. F. (2003). Does Russian scrambling exist? In S. Karimi (ed.), *Word Order and Scrambling* (pp. 156–76). Malden, MA: Blackwell.

Baldi, P. (1990). Indo-European languages. In B. Comrie (ed.), *The World's Major Languages* (pp. 31–67). New York: Oxford.

Béjoint, H. (2000). *Modern Lexicography: An Introduction*. Oxford: Oxford University Press.

Bell, A. (1984). Language style as audience design. *Language in Society*, 13: 145–204.

Biber, D. (1988). *Variation Across Speech and Writing*. New York: Cambridge University Press.

Biber, D., S. Johansson, G. Leech, S. Conrad, and E. Finegan (1999). *Longman Grammar of Spoken and Written English*. Harlow, England: Pearson Education Limited.

Blake, N. (1992). The literary language. In N. Blake (ed.), *The English Language*, Vol. II: *1066–1476* (pp. 500–41). Cambridge: Cambridge University Press.

Bolinger, D. (1977). *Meaning and Form*. London: Longman.

Brown, P. and S. C. Levinson (1987). *Politeness: Some Universals in Language Usage*. Cambridge: Cambridge University Press.

Cameron, D. (1995). *Verbal Hygiene*. London: Routledge.

Carter, R. and S. Cornbleet (2001). *The Language of Speech and Writing*. London: Routledge.

Chambers, J. K. (2003). *Sociolinguistic Theory*, 2nd edn. Oxford and Malden, MA: Blackwell Publishers.

Chomsky, N. (1957). *Syntactic Structures*. The Hague: Mouton. (Reprinted in 2002 by Walter de Gruyter, Inc.)

(1959). A review of B. F. Skinner's verbal behavior. *Language*, 35: 26–58.

Clemetson, L. (2007). The racial politics of speaking well. *New York Times*. February 4. Section 4, pp. 1 and 4.

Comrie, B. (1989). *Language Typology and Language Universals*, 2nd edn. Chicago: University of Chicago Press.

(1990). Russian. In B. Comrie (ed.), *The World's Major Languages* (pp. 329–47). New York: Oxford.

Croft, W. (2000). *Explaining Language Change: An Evolutionary Approach*. Harlow, England: Longman.

Croft, W. and D. Cruse (2004). *Cognitive Linguistics*. Cambridge: Cambridge University Press.

Cruse, D. (1986). *Lexical Semantics*. Cambridge: Cambridge University Press.

(2004). *Meaning in Language: An Introduction to Semantics and Pragmatics*, 2nd edn. Oxford: Oxford University Press.

Crystal, D. (2000). *Language Death*. Cambridge: Cambridge University Press.

(2003). *English as a Global Language*, 2nd edn. Cambridge: Cambridge University Press.

Daneš, F. (ed.) (1974). *Papers on Functional Sentence Perspective*. Prague: Academia.

D'Arcy, A. (2007). *Like* and language ideology: Disentangling fact from fiction. *American Speech*, 28(4): 386–419.

A Dictionary of Prefixes, Suffixes, and Combining Forms (2002). Taken from *Webster's Third New International Dictionary*, Unabridged. Springfield, MA: Merriam Webster's. www.spellingbee.com/pre_suf_comb.pdf (accessed March 17, 2008).

Dijk, T. A. van (1988). *News as Discourse*. Hillsdale, NJ: Lawrence Erlbaum.

Dijk, T. A. van and W. Kintsch. (1983). *Strategies of Discourse Comprehension*. New York: Academic Press.

Dixon, R. M. W. (1997). *The Rise and Fall of Languages*. Cambridge: Cambridge University Press.

Dresher, B. E. and A. Lahiri (2005). Main stress left in Early Middle English. In M. Fortescue *et al.* (eds.), *Historical Linguistics: Selected Papers from the 16th International Conference on Historical Linguistics* (pp. 75–85). Amsterdam and Philadelphia: Benjamins.

Dyson, E. D. (2005). *Is Bill Cosby Right?: Or Has the Black Middle Class Lost Its Mind?* New York: Basic Civitas Books.

Edmonds, P. and G. Hirst (2002). Near-synonymy and lexical choice. *Computational Linguistics*, 28(2): 105–44.

Fellbaum, C. (1998). Introduction. In C. Fellbaum (ed.), *Wordnet: An Electronic Lexical Database*. Cambridge, MA: MIT Press.

Fillmore, C. (1996). The pragmatics of constructions. In D. Slobin *et al.* (eds.), *Social Interaction, Social Context, and Language: Essays in Honor of Susan Ervin-Tripp* (pp. 53–70). Mahwah, NJ: Lawrence Erlbaum.

Firbas, J. (1992). *Functional Sentence Perspective in Written and Spoken Communication*. Cambridge: Cambridge University Press.

Fish, Stanley (2005). Interview. *On the Media*. 22 July 2005. Transcript available at: onthemedia.org/transcripts/transcripts_072205_open.html (accessed June 22, 2008).

Fournier, J.-M. (2007). From a Latin syllable-driven stress system to a Romance versus Germanic morphology-driven system: in honour of Lionel Guierre. *Language Sciences*, 29: 218–36.

Francis, N. (1992). Language corpora B. C. In J. Svartvik (ed.), *Directions in Corpus Linguistics* (pp. 17–32). Berlin: Mouton de Gruyter.

Frawley, W. (1992). *Linguistic Semantics*. Hillsdale, NJ: Lawrence Erlbaum Associates.

Gilliver, P. (2000). Appendix II: OED personalia. In L. Mugglestone (ed.), *Lexicography and the OED: Pioneers in the Untrodden Forest* (pp. 232–52). Oxford: Oxford University Press.

Gimbutas, M. (1956). *The Prehistory of Europe. Part I: Mesolithic, Neolithic, and Copper Age Cultures in Russia and the Baltic Area*. American School of Prehistoric Research, Harvard University Bulletin No. 20. Cambridge, MA: Peabody Museum.

Gordon, R. G., Jr. (ed.) (2005). *Ethnologue: Languages of the World*, 15th edn. Dallas, TX: SIL International. (Electronic version: www.ethnologue.com, accessed June 22, 2008)

Greenberg, J. H. (2000). *Indo-European and its Closest Relatives: The Eurasiatic Language Family*. Vol. I: *Grammar*; Vol. II: *Lexicon*. Stanford: Stanford University Press.

Grice, H. P. (1989). *Studies in the Way of Words*. Cambridge, MA: Harvard University Press.

Hake, R. and J. Williams (1981). Style and its consequences: Do as I do, not as I say. *College English*, 43.5: 33–451.

Hall, J. H. (2004). The dictionary of American regional English. In E. Finegan and J. R. Rickford (eds.), *Language in the USA* (pp. 92–112). Cambridge: Cambridge University Press.

Halliday, M. A. K. (1994). *An Introduction to Functional Grammar*, 2nd edn. London: Edward Arnold.

Halliday, M. A. K. and R. Hasan (1976). *Cohesion in English*. London: Longman.

(1985). *Language, Context, and Text: Aspects of Language in a Social-Semiotic Perspective*. Victoria, Australia: Deakin University Press.

Halliday, M. A. K. and C. Matthiessen (2004). *An Introduction to Functional Grammar*, 3rd edn. London: Hodder Education.

Hammond, M. (1999). *The Phonology of English*. Oxford: Oxford University Press.

Handbook of the International Phonetic Association (1999). Cambridge: Cambridge University Press.

Hewlett, N. and J. M. Beck (2006). *An Introduction to the Science of Phonetics*. Oxford and New York: Routledge.

Hogg, R. (2003). *An Introduction to Old English*. Oxford: Oxford University Press.

Huddleston, R. and G. Pullum (2002). *The Cambridge Grammar of the English Language.* Cambridge: Cambridge University Press.

Hull, D. L. (1988). *Science as a Process: An Evolutionary Account of the Social and Conceptual Development of Science.* Chicago: University of Chicago Press.

Hymes, D. (1971). *On Communicative Competence.* Philadelphia: University of Pennsylvania Press.

Jones, S. (2002). *Antonymy: A Corpus-Based Perspective.* London: Routledge.

Kay, C. J. (2000). Historical semantics and historical lexicography: will the twain ever meet? In J. Coleman and C. Kay (eds.), *Lexicology, Semantics and Lexicography in English Historical Linguistics: Selected Papers from the Fourth G.L. Brook Symposium* (pp. 53–68). Amsterdam: Benjamins.

Kintsch, W. (1998). *Comprehension: A Paradigm for Cognition.* Cambridge: Cambridge University Press.

Kirkman, A. J. (1992). *Good Style: Writing for Science and Technology.* Oxford: Taylor and Francis.

Kornfilt, J. (1990). Turkish and the Turkic languages. In B. Comrie (ed.), *The World's Major Languages* (pp. 619–44). New York: Oxford.

Labov, W. (1972). The stratification of (r) in New York City department stores. In W. Labov (ed.), *Sociolinguistic Patterns* (pp. 43–70). Philadelphia: University of Pennsylvania Press.

(1973). The boundaries of words and their meanings. In C. J. Bailey and R. Shuy (eds.), *New Ways of Analyzing Variation in English* (pp. 340–73). Washington, DC: Georgetown University Press.

(1994). *Principles of Linguistic Change: Internal Factors.* Malden, MA: Blackwell.

Ladefoged, P. (2001). *A Course in Phonetics,* 4th edn. Fort Worth, TX: Harcourt.

(2005). *Vowels and Consonants,* 2nd edn. Oxford and Malden, MA: Blackwell.

Landau, S. (2001). *Dictionaries: The Art and Craft of Lexicography,* 2nd edn. Cambridge: Cambridge University Press.

Lee, D. (2001). Genres, registers, text types, domains, and styles: Clarifying the concepts and navigating a path through the BNC jungle. *Language Learning & Technology,* 5.3: 37–72.

Leech, G. (1981). *Semantics,* 2nd edn. Harmondsworth, England: Penguin.

(1983). *Principles of Pragmatics.* London: Longman.

Lyons, J. (1977). *Semantics,* Vol. I. Cambridge: Cambridge University Press.

Malmkjær, K. (2005). *Linguistics and the Language of Translation.* Edinburgh: Edinburgh University Press.

Matthews, P. H. (1981). *Syntax.* Cambridge: Cambridge University Press.

(1991). *Morphology.* Cambridge: Cambridge University Press.

McArthur, T. (ed.) (1992). *The Oxford Companion to the English Language.* Oxford and New York: Oxford University Press.

Meyer, C. F. (2003). The Lexis/Nexis database as historical corpus. Paper presented at the 24th annual conference of the International Computer Archive of Modern English, Guernsey, British Isles.

Milligan, S. (2007). Democratic contenders unite against Bush. *Boston Globe.* 27 April: A1.

Milroy, J. and M. Gordon (2003). *Sociolinguistics: Method and Interpretation.* Malden, MA: Blackwell Publishers.

Milroy, J. and L. Milroy (1997). Varieties and variation. In F. Coulmas (ed.), *The Handbook of Sociolinguistics* (pp. 47–64). Oxford and Malden, MA: Blackwell Publishers.

Moon, R. (2007). Sinclair, lexicography, and the Cobuild project: The application of theory. *International Journal of Corpus Linguistics,* 12: 159–81.

Murphy, M. (2003). *Semantic Relations and the Lexicon: Antonymy, Synonymy and Other Paradigms.* Cambridge: Cambridge University Press.

Murray, J. A. H. (ed.) (1971). *The Compact Edition of the Oxford English Dictionary.* London: Oxford University Press.

Nelson, G. (1996). The design of the corpus. In S. Greenbaum (ed.), *Comparing English Worldwide: the International Corpus of English* (pp. 27–35). Oxford: Oxford University Press.

(2002). International Corpus of English: Markup manual for spoken texts. www.ucl.ac.uk/english-usage/ice/spoken.pdf (accessed March 26, 2007)

Nunberg, G. (2004). *Going Nucular: Language, Politics, and Culture in Confrontational Times*. New York: Public Affairs Books.

Olson, S. (2003). *Mapping Human History: Genes, Race, and Our Common Origins*. Boston: Houghton Mifflin.

Paradis, C. and C. Willners (2006). Selecting antonyms for dictionary entries: Methodological aspects. In F. Heinat, E. Klingvall, and S. Manninen (eds.), *The Department of English: Working Papers in English Linguistics,* Vol. VI. www.englund.lu.se/images/stories/pdf-files/workingspapers/vol06/Paradis_Willners_06.pdf (accessed June 22, 2008).

Pelsmaekers, K. (1999). Directness and (im)politeness: the use of imperatives in business letters. In G. A. J. Tops, B. Devriendt, and S. Geukens (eds.), *Thinking English Grammar* (pp. 263–79). Leuven/Louvain, Belgium: Peeters Publishers.

Plag, I. (2003). *Word-Formation in English*. Cambridge: Cambridge University Press.

Quirk, R., S. Greenbaum, G. Leech, and J. Svartvik (1985). *A Comprehensive Grammar of the English Language*. London: Longman.

Renfrew, C. (1987). *Archaeology and Language*. London: Jonathan Cape.

(2000). At the edge of knowability: Towards a pre-history of languages. *Cambridge Archaeological Journal*, 10.1: 7–34.

Rickford, J. (2004). Spoken soul: The beloved, belittled language of Black America. In C. Fought (ed.), *Sociolinguistic Variation: Critical Reflections* (pp. 198–208). Oxford: Oxford University Press.

Sacks, H., E. A. Schegloff, and G. Jefferson. (1974). A simplest systematics for the organization of turn-taking for conversation. *Language*, **50**: 696–735.

Saussure, F. de. *Course in General Linguistics*. [1916] Repr. 1983 ed. C. Bally and A. Sechehaye, trans. R. Harris. La Salle, IL: Open Court.

Schegloff, E. A. (2002). Opening sequencing. In J. E. Katz and M. Aakhus (eds.), *Perpetual Contact: Mobile Communication, Private Talk, Public Performance* (pp. 326–85). Cambridge: Cambridge University Press.

Schiffrin D., D. Tannen, and H. E. Hamilton (2003). *The Handbook of Discourse Analysis*. Oxford and Malden, MA: Blackwell.

Schneider, E. (2003). The dynamics of New Englishes: From identity construction to dialect birth. *Language*, 12: 233–81.

Searle, J. (1969). *Speech Acts: An Essay in the Philosophy of Language*. Cambridge: Cambridge University Press.

(1979). *Expression and Meaning*. Cambridge: Cambridge University Press.

Simon, J. (1981). *Paradigm's Lost*. New York: Viking.

Sinclair, J. (1991). *Corpus, Concordance, Collocation*. Oxford: Oxford University Press.

Sparck Jones, K. (1986). *Synonymy and Semantic Classification*. Edinburgh: Edinburgh University Press.

Sperber, D. and D. Wilson (1995). *Relevance: Communication and Cognition*, 2nd edn. Oxford: Blackwell.

Stockwell, R. P. and D. Minkova (2001). *English Words: History and Structure*. Cambridge: Cambridge University Press.

Svensson, A. M. and J. Hering (2005). Germanic prosody and French loanwords. *Moderna Språk*, 99: 122–8.

Tannen, D. (2001). *You Just Don't Understand: Women and Men in Conversation*. New York: Quill.

Tao, H. (2003). Turn initiators in spoken English. In P. Leistyna and C. F. Meyer (eds.), *Corpus Analysis: Language Structure and Language Use* (pp. 187–207). Amsterdam: Rodopi.

Thomas, J. (1995). *Meaning in Interaction*. Harlow, Essex: Longman.

Thomason, S. G. and T. Kaufman (1988). *Language Contact, Creolization, and Genetic Linguistics*. Berkeley: University of California Press.

Titscher, S., M. Meyer, R. Wodak, and E. Vetter (2000). *Methods of Text and Discourse Analysis*. Thousand Oaks, CA: Sage.

Tomlin, R. (1986). *Basic Word Order: Functional Principles*. London: Croom Helm.

Trask, R. L. (1996). *Historical Linguistics*. Oxford: Oxford University Press.

Watkins, C. (2000). Indo-European and the Indo-Europeans. In *American Heritage Dictionary of the English Language*, 4th edn. Boston: Houghton Mifflin. (Electronic version: www.bartleby.com/61/8.html, accessed June 21, 2008).

Watts, R. J. (2003). *Politeness*. Cambridge: Cambridge University Press.

Whaley, L. (1997). *Introduction to Typology: The Unity and Diversity of Language*. Thousand Oaks, CA: Sage.

Wierzbicka, A. (1996). *Semantics: Primes and Universals*. Oxford: Oxford University Press.

(2006). *English: Meaning and Culture*. Oxford: Oxford University Press.

Wilson, D. and D. Sperber (2006). Relevance theory. In G. L. Ward and L. A. Horn (eds.), *The Handbook of Pragmatics*, 2nd edn. (pp. 607–32). Oxford: Blackwell.

Wright, L. (2000). Introduction. In L. Wright (ed.), *The Development of Standard English: 1300–1800* (pp. 1–8). Cambridge: Cambridge University Press.

Yavas, M. S. (2005). *Applied English Phonology*. Oxford and Medford, MA: Blackwell.

Zipf, G. K. (1932). *Selected Studies of the Principle of Relative Frequency in Language*. Cambridge, MA: Harvard.

Index